THE HORNES

THE HORNES

An American Family

Gail Lumet Buckley

ALFRED A. KNOPF   NEW YORK
1   9   8   6

Grateful acknowledgment is made to the following for permission
to reprint from previously published material:

CBS Robbins Catalog, Inc.: Excerpt from "Jump for Joy"
by Duke Ellington, Sid Keeler, and Paul Francis Webster. © 1941,
renewed 1969 Robbins Music Corporation. Rights assigned to
CBS Catalogue Partnership. All rights controlled and administered
by CBS Robbins Catalog, Inc. All rights reserved. International
copyright secured. Used by permission.

Harcourt Brace Jovanovich, Inc.: Excerpt from "In These Dissenting Times"
(originally titled "Fundamental Difference") from *Revolutionary Petunias
and Other Poems* by Alice Walker. Copyright © 1970 by Alice Walker.
Open market rights administered by David Higham, Ltd, London,
as agent for The Women's Press, London. Reprinted by
permission of the publishers.

Illustration credits appear on page 265.

Library of Congress Cataloging-in-Publication Data
Buckley, Gail Lumet, [date]
The Hornes: an American family.
1. Horn family.   2. Brooklyn (N.Y.)—Biography.
3. Afro-Americans—New York—Brooklyn—Biography.
4. Horne, Lena.   5. Afro-American entertainers—
New York—Brooklyn—Biography.   6. Women singers—
United States—Biography.   I. Title.
F129.B7B83   1986   974.7'2300496073'00922 [B]   85-45783
ISBN 0-394-51306-1

This book is dedicated to the memory of my brother, Teddy.

When the Lord delivered Zion from bondage,
it seemed like a dream.
Then was our mouth filled with laughter,
on our lips there were songs.

PSALM 126

Contents

Acknowledgments   xi

Introduction   3

PART ONE—THE OLD HORNES

1   The Calhouns   13

2   The Horns   34

3   The Hornes   56

4   The Horne Brothers   81

5   Helena Horne   110

6   Lena   148

PART TWO—THE NEW HORNES

7   Lena and Lennie   203

8   Gail   230

9   Epilogue   251

Acknowledgments

This book could not have been written without the knowledge, assistance, and encouragement of Sterling Brown, Catherine Graves Nash Harris, Harriet Nash Chisholm, Ethelyn Scottron Miller, Myrtle Accooe Chandler, Christopher Lee, Audrey Waller Thompson, Aida Bearden Winters, Adelaide Holbrook Walker, Llwellyn Johnston Delsarte, Louis Delsarte, Ruth Johnson Wilson, Adele Logan Alexander, Frank Montero, Marion Montero Johnston, Rozier Cohn Johnston, Patti Johnston Guy, Eleanor Blackshear Fryer, the Hon. Franklin H. Williams, Constance Curry, Philip Holloway, Michele Hart-Rico, John Hammond, Barney Josephson, Marion Coles, Betty Comden, Adolph Green, Hyacinth Curtis, Edouard E. Plummer, Josh Ellis, Carol Craig, Mary Belle Burch (Indiana State Library), Joseph Solomon (estate of Carl Van Vechten), David Schoonover (Beinecke Library, Yale University), Dovie T. Patrick (Robert W. Woodruff Library, Atlanta University), Beth M. Howse (Fisk University Library), Deborah Ryan and Natasha Russell (Schomburg Center for Research in Black Culture), Guy C. McElroy (Bethune Museum and Archives), Maggie Fogel, Duncan Schiedt, Sara Lukenson, Robin Platzer, Sherman Sneed, Johanna

Flynn, Jean Kennedy Smith, Preston Brown, Joan Juliet Buck, Belinda Bull, Dr. W. Montague Cobb, William Woodward III, Ruth Leffall, Kitty D'Alessio, Mildred Newman, Liliane Tuck, Dr. Jeanne Noble, Frances FitzGerald, Arthur M. Schlesinger, Jr., Michael Marsh, William N. Hubbard, Marian L. Schwarz, Frederick A. O. Schwarz, Jr., Boaty Boatwright, Georgio Sant'Angelo, Sidney Lumet, Robert Benton, Harry Sedgwick, Michael Janeway, Lt. Col. Jesse J. Johnson, William Miles, the Rev. George Kuhn, Mary Maguire, Carol Atkinson, Lynn Nesbit, Terry Adams, Robert Gottlieb, my children, my husband, and especially my mother.

THE HORNES

Introduction

"All the Hornes had charm and a superior air," said an old Brooklyn family friend, "though all except Lena," she added, "could have used a good orthodontist." Personal charm, good looks, and a sense of identity marked the Horne family manner. The family manner had existed long before Lena—she was by no means the first star. They were *all* stars.

The Hornes had always been *special*. They had what the Harlem Renaissance poet Sterling Brown called "the Horne *thing*." Even within the minuscule world of the old black bourgeoisie, a society of the mutually "special," or "chosen few," the Hornes had always stood out.

The post–Civil War black bourgeoisie was America's historic family secret. It was born in 1865, and rendered more or less obsolete after the civil rights victories of the 1960s—a hundred-year phenomenon. Before 1960 America was, in many ways, an apartheid country. People like the Hornes represented the upper class of America's "untouchable" caste—the small brown group within the large black mass.

The Hornes always had a very secure knowledge of what they believed in and what they were about—despite the buffetings of time and history, and despite their own occasional cynicism or despair. The Hornes knew their own strengths, if not their own weaknesses. And their set of beliefs neatly coincided with that of their white middle-class fellow countrymen: Judeo-Christian morality; nineteenth-century bourgeois values; and the "American Dream." The Hornes *could* have belonged to any entrenched (and assimilated) middle class—"lace curtain" Irish or *Our Crowd* Jewish —if it were not for race (and money).

For the Hornes and people like them, the American Dream was really New World social Darwinism—the survival of the *super*-fit. Any black who entered the race had to be stronger, faster, and smarter than the rest. Not simply stronger, faster, and smarter than other blacks—but also stronger, faster, and smarter than most whites. The Hornes were solidly secure in their sense of *self* and superiority. And being well aware of life's essential unfairness, they remained more or less unselfish achievers.

I am a Horne, too. I was born Gail Horne Jones in the winter of 1937. It was the year that my grandfather, Teddy Horne, saved a menu from the Joe Louis Training Camp Restaurant—where the filet mignon was seventy-five cents. He also saved a registered-mail envelope printed "Fly United to the Fight on New Douglas Mainliners—None Faster, Lower Fares." (The sporting crowd was ahead of everyone in air travel.) Teddy was Lena's father. I am Lena's daughter. My daughters are her granddaughters. Family faces are magic mirrors. Looking at people who belong to us, we see the past, present, and future. We make discoveries about ourselves and them. Forms, faces, skin, stature all form a circle of existence. If you spin us we become a glittering chain of life.

Like tiles of mosaic, pieces of family history lay in the bottom of my grandfather Teddy's travel-scarred old trunk. Before instant obsolescence, people saved everything. My grandparents and great-grandparents saved avidly—bills, receipts, newspaper clippings, documents, souvenirs, letters, and photographs. They saved as if they could not trust memory. What they saved told them who they were. Besides the usual souvenirs of births, deaths, celebrations, and surprises, there were history and pride in what they collected.

There were photographs from the 1860s. Newspaper clippings from 1875. A young woman's college diploma dated 1881. There was an 1884 personal letter from a future President of the United States. And the fading, spidery autograph of a black Reconstruction congressman. There were nine twenty-five-dollar shares in the Penny Savings Bank of Chattanooga,

Tennessee, dated 1893. And tax receipts, from the turn of the century to the 1950s, on a house in Brooklyn, New York. There was a "deathbed" letter dated 1899. A flowery 1904 document of Roman Catholic confirmation. A 1908 certificate of one thousand shares of capital stock in an Arizona mining company. And a 1910 Tammany election ballot. There was a 1912 bronze medallion of the Smart Set Athletic Club—the "sine qua non" of black social clubs, founded in Brooklyn in 1905. And a 1919 issue of the NAACP's *Crisis* magazine featuring a photograph of baby Lena Horne, youngest member. There was a passport, and picture postcards, from a 1929 grand tour of Europe. A receipt for a $1,500 cash deposit on a 1930 Packard Custom Eight sedan. And ticket stubs for prizefights: Dempsey and Gibbons, Louis and Braddock, Robinson and LaMotta. There were baseball rain checks from the 1932 Colored All-Stars to the 1947 Brooklyn Dodgers. There was a New York *Daily Mirror* front page of the Louis-Schmeling knockout—and a 1942 Westbrook Pegler column extolling the black fighting man. There were wartime newspaper clippings of young Lena Horne, Hollywood's first black star. And also a lock of brown-gold human hair, a dried leaf from the olive trees in the Garden of Gethsemane, and some poetry.

Along with all this unabashedly middle-class and sentimental black Americana—along with the records of mortgage payments, motor cars, summer vacations, burial plots, divorce, disaster, good fortune, and taxes —there were also family names and faces. Perhaps because of African blood (and the fear of death of a soul), the Hornes never threw away a photograph. There were so many faded sepia portraits, so many creamy picture postcards and glossy snapshots. These faces clearly labeled themselves VIPs in the black American world.

The Horne circle of names encompassed several Catherines, Nellies, Edwins, Franks, Edwinas, and Lenas. The Edwins were mostly lean and coppery. The Franks were stockier and paler of skin. The Edwinas were very white. The Catherines and Nellies were usually brownish. And the Lenas, once again, were cheekboned and coppery.

The old black bourgeoisie was comprised of three segments of black society in existence before the Civil War: free Northern blacks, free Southern blacks, and "favored" slaves. Most of America, above the Mason-Dixon Line, had already freed its slaves by 1800. Free *Southern* blacks were a rarer breed—native mostly to Charleston and New Orleans, the only Southern towns big enough to be called cities. "Favored" slaves included household

servants, coachmen, cabinetmakers, the masters' kin—just about anyone
who was not a field hand. After the Civil War these three segments of black
society became the extended black bourgeois family.

Sociologists say that seven elements were necessary for black success in
white America: a history of family literacy; free status during slavery; lineal
descent from slave masters; special status during slavery; money and property; a strong father; a strong mother. Middle-class values (as well as bourgeois pretensions) came naturally to the Hornes and other founding
members of the black bourgeoisie. Many of the first black families to settle
in old Brooklyn (not yet a part of New York City) were from "favored" slave
backgrounds. It is said that when asked to perform some menial chore,
black Brooklyn children were often heard to retort, "We're not field niggers!
We're house niggers!"

In pre-1960 America the black bourgeoisie saw themselves, like the
Caribbean "colored," as a sort of buffer zone between the races, as ambassadors of interracial communication and good will. More often than not,
however, they were regarded as ambassadors of whiteness in black America
—to such an extent did they represent white standards and values. But
within this no man's land solid achievements were possible, and many
satisfactions were derived from an agreeable way of life.

The black bourgeoisie created for themselves an almost "ideal" world,
outside the racial crossfire that was the daily lot of average blacks. Before
the 1960s no black in the South had any legal right that any white needed
to respect. If, by contrast, blacks in the North could safely vote, they were
still shut out of good jobs, housing, education, and most public accommodations. But the black bourgeoisie could almost forget that racism existed
—except that there was still, of course, their own, directed against darker
and poorer blacks. Whites they pretended to ignore, as they busily lived
mirror-image white lives—with everything from Greek-letter societies to
debutante balls. They sought compensation in "practiced," if not perfect,
whiteness. They made their own clubland. Before the 1950s the majority
would have attended the same few black universities (there were always the
Ivy League exceptions, of course). In the late 1950s Dr. Horace Mann Bond
wrote that the majority of black Ph.D.s, physicians, and college teachers
were derived from perhaps five hundred families that had been in existence
since 1860.

The political, educational, and economic opportunities open to post-
1960s middle-class blacks go far beyond anything even imagined by the old
bourgeoisie. Although members of the black bourgeoisie were vastly more

successful than their poorer and blacker brethren, they rarely had opportunities to make *real* money. They were teachers, doctors, educated clergy, and small businessmen. Attributes based on family heritage, education, and conventional behavior were more important than income or occupation. Who you were and where you came from—"roots"—meant more than money.

All blacks in America were determinedly de-Africanized, and none more so than those who formed the black bourgeoisie. After the Civil War the gap between the "favored" or already free and the newly freed field hand was wider than ever. Blacks who could afford to travel after the war made "connections"—and the black bourgeoisie became a closed "family" circle. They intermarried, interacted, and passed opportunities from father to son. They became a mutually supportive network throughout America.

In freedom, as in slavery, they sought to distance themselves from the field hand. The black bourgeoisie took great pride in its separateness from ordinary black culture. This applied even to religion. Members of the black bourgeoisie were Episcopalian, Congregational, Presbyterian, or Roman Catholic, rarely Baptist or Methodist. They did not believe in religious emotionalism. When they sang spirituals, they sang them decorously—as did, for example, the Fisk Jubilee Singers. They heartily disapproved of the "blues." Respectability was key to the black bourgeoisie—compensation, perhaps, for the fact that kinship to masters always came from the wrong side of the sheets.

The Hornes were by no means peerless. In fact, in the private pond of pre-1960 black "society," the Hornes considered themselves comparatively small fry. More noteworthy in terms of *achievement* were, to name just a few, the Hunts and Bonds of Georgia, the Langstons of Ohio, the Delaneys of North Carolina, and the Robesons of New Jersey. There were also the Abbotts, Joneses, and Sengstackes of Chicago, and the Churches, Spauldings, and Walkers of Memphis. Other super-achievers were the Beardens, Wrights, and Powells, all of pre-1960 Harlem. In the hierarchy of northeastern black American middle-class life the best places to come from were Philadelphia or Boston, which signified "old" *freedom* as well as old money. Already in the time of the Revolution there were such rich, free Philadelphia blacks as the sailmaker James Forten (grandfather of the Civil War diarist Miss Charlotte Forten). Philadelphia also produced the interrelated Alexander and Tanner families, among whose members were jurists, ambassadors, and the expatriate painter Henry O. Tanner. Boston was the home of two of black America's most successful newspaper families, the

Walkers and the Trotters. The city ranking third in terms of prestige was
Washington, D.C., where there were both power (federal jobs) and brains
(Howard University and Dunbar High School, whose teachers were all
Ph.D.s, and whose private motto was "Sometimes last, always best").
Among the "big fish" of Washington were the socially superior Wormleys,
Rectors, Pinketts, and Syphaxes.

Brooklyn, New York, where the Hornes settled at the end of the nineteenth century, probably ranked after Washington. Brooklyn was a "comfortable" place, if a bit parochial and snobbish. It was considered cliquish
and slightly old-fashioned. Brooklyn did not have old money like Philadelphia or Boston; nor was it competitive and intellectual like Washington.
Brooklyn's claim to fame was its pretty girls: a Brooklyn bride was a great
catch in the eastern black bourgeoisie. In contrast, Harlem, which first
became home to blacks in 1910, was considered *nouveau riche*. Harlem was
a nice place to visit, but you wouldn't want to live there. In this milieu, the
Hornes were considered *old* (as in not *"nouveau"*), *comfortable* (not super-
rich, but property owners), *intellectual* (with teaching degrees and a certain
appreciation for "the arts"), *political* (from suffragettes to civil rights) and
famously *good-looking*.

The Hornes of old Brooklyn were Edwin and Cora Horne and their four
sons (one of whom was my grandfather Teddy). Edwin Horne was a man of
matinee-idol handsomeness, a cross between John Drew and the young John
Barrymore. His wonderful good looks made all the ladies (black and white),
circa 1899, swoon. Edwin Horne—born in 1859, son of the only-in-
America union of an English adventurer and a Tennessee woodlands native
American—was to become a figure of some importance in black New York
City politics. He was co-founder of a new black political lobbying group, the
United Colored Democracy, made up mostly of disgruntled black Republicans. His party was directly responsible for the defection of 50,000 black
male voters in the 1910 election—and the resulting Democratic victory.
The UCD leaders were well rewarded by the party. The chairman of the
UCD became chief of Black Tammany. And Edwin's own sinecure bespoke
the highest political patronage. By day a bureaucrat, and by night a boule-
vardier, Edwin was a courtly, blue-eyed "colored" man who did not look
black. He was very much in his prime in Gay Nineties New York. He
certainly would not have permitted an irrational category such as *race* to
come between himself and a wonderful time at the opera, the theater, or a
fashionable restaurant.

Edwin's wife was born Cora Calhoun, of Atlanta, Georgia. Cora was a petite, attractive woman, if somewhat less spectacular-looking than her husband. After giving birth to her four sons, this slim, mercurial creature who had been pretty enough, and smart enough, to win Edwin became a "new woman" and a suffragette. Cora was a college graduate, and she *always* considered brains more important than beauty. Edwin might have his theater and opera, but Cora had *meetings*. If Edwin was a bon vivant, Cora was a do-gooder. And Cora was a black aristocrat. She was a Calhoun.

Cora was born free, just. Her father had been a slave for half of his life. He was, along with his sister and mother, a *most* favored slave in the household of Dr. Andrew Bonaparte Calhoun, of Newnan, Georgia, a nephew of the great (and infamous) John C. Calhoun, Vice President of the United States under both John Quincy Adams and Andrew Jackson and slavery's greatest apologist.

Among families whose forebears were slaves on the rough and ready Kentucky borders before the War of 1812, claiming connection to vice presidents of the United States was not uncommon. Vice Presidents John C. Breckinridge and Richard "Tecumseh" Johnson (both of Kentucky) were famous progenitors when their respective states still belonged to the wilderness and the red man. Indeed, no black family with historical pretensions could outdistance the Trotters of Boston (Thomas Jefferson), or the Cyphax family of Washington, D.C. (Martha Washington's nephew). But unlike these other famous men to whom slave families could claim ties, John C. Calhoun maintained that slavery was ordained by God. Therein lies the irony of the black Calhoun condition. Despite the Calhoun record on race and slavery the black Calhouns were almost as "lucky" under the dark star of slavery as they were in the sunlight of freedom.

PART ONE
THE OLD HORNES

CHAPTER · 1

THE CALHOUNS

The founding mother of the black Calhouns was an example of true grit. Sinai ("Sinia" or "Siny") Reynolds, born in Maryland circa 1777, was most likely a first-generation American. Her mother probably came from Senegal. Sinai was my great-great-great-great-grandmother.

The liberal final quarter of the eighteenth century—after the Revolution and before the cotton gin—was, in relative terms, not such a bad time to be black in America. More than one hundred thousand slaves had been freed as a direct result of the American Revolution and the ideals set forth in the Declaration of Independence. Late-eighteenth-century slave discipline was moderate, and instruction of slaves tolerably permitted. Sinai enjoyed the favored slave position of household cook, and she would have learned to read and write—precious gifts to pass on to her children.

Sinai's Maryland was a cradle of black history. It was home to black inventor Benjamin Banneker—a typical eighteenth-century genius—who built the first clock made entirely in America; surveyed Washington, D.C.; and discovered that plagues of locusts occur in twelve-year cycles. Maryland was also the birthplace of Frederick Douglass, Harriet Tubman, and Josiah

Henson (the *real* Uncle Tom, a runaway slave who told his story to Harriet Beecher Stowe). By 1790, when Sinai was a young woman, blacks constituted over 19 percent of the country's population.

The name of Sinai's original owner is unknown. But it is known that by 1810 she was living in North Carolina, the mother of an infant daughter, Nellie, and the "wife" of Henry Reynolds. (Although marriage among slaves was, strictly speaking, illegal, they could be unofficially "married" at the discretion of their masters.) Henry, Sinai, and Nellie all were the property of Silas Reynolds, with whom they appear to have moved from North Carolina to Georgia in the early years of the cotton boom. Sinai eventually bore six more children in the Reynolds household. Two of them, both born between 1810 and 1817, were taken away from her. One was sold to Mississippi. The other was freed and sent to colonize Liberia.

In the face of the Haitian Revolution and escalating slave revolts, the embers of eighteenth-century liberalism died down. Slavery rules tightened, and repression against free blacks multiplied. In Southern eyes, the only "good" black was an enslaved one. The American Colonization Society was founded in 1816 to "rid the country of a useless and pernicious element": free blacks. (John C. Calhoun was a prominent member.) In 1822 the society purchased territory on the Ivory Coast to be the future home of resettled free American blacks. Among slaveowners, freeing a slave and sending him to Liberia was seen as setting a good example. For Sinai and Henry the loss of their children is surely one of the reasons they strove so desperately for freedom.

In 1839 the grand jurors of the superior court of Coweta County, Georgia, presented their last accusation of the March term against one Silas Reynolds. The accusation charged that "a negro man by the name of Henry and a negro woman by the name of Sina are permitted to live apart from their owners uncontested by any person whatsoever contrary to the Statute." The jurors "earnestly" recommended that the couple be "placed under the immediate control and management of some white person." Clearly, Silas Reynolds had permitted Sinai and Henry to live alone and earn their own living, which they were probably doing through Sinai's talents as a cook (she was famous for her pies and cakes). Since Silas Reynolds apparently could not afford to keep them—and since the law would not allow Henry and Sinai to live together as a family—Silas sold Sinai (for $300) and her eight-year-old son, Felix (for $200), to William Nimmons, a Coweta County neighbor.

Sinai's oldest child, Nellie, had been sold ten years earlier to another Coweta County neighbor: Dr. Andrew Bonaparte Calhoun of Newnan, Georgia. (As it happens, William Nimmons and A. B. Calhoun both lived on Newnan's Greenfield Street.) The Calhoun slave tradition (like the Reynolds) was old Old South, coastal, and pre–cotton boom. The Calhouns were a large, close-knit band of Celts. They owned everything as a family —including slaves, who were rarely sold, but simply passed from brother to brother. The Calhouns were among America's earliest tycoons, with deep, vested interests in its agriculture and minerals. Besides owning a great deal of the state of South Carolina, the Calhouns had vast holdings in Georgia, including one of the South's very few gold mines.

Nellie, like her mother, Sinai, was a household cook. She had two Calhoun children: Moses, born in 1829, and Sinai Catherine, born in 1830. (In the Calhoun circle slave children and legitimate children were often given the same names. Moses was named for Moses Waddell, a Georgian, who was A. B. Calhoun's uncle. And Sinai Catherine was named for A. B.'s aunt Catherine Calhoun Waddell.) Moses Calhoun is my great-great-grandfather. Moses and Sinai Catherine (called "Siny") clearly had a white father or fathers. In fact, a white man named "Judge Ezzard" (a William Ezzard was mayor of Atlanta just before the Civil War) is listed as Siny's father, which is curious because most often a nominal black "husband" was listed.

The Georgia into which Nellie Calhoun's two children were born was still the wilderness. In 1828 land that only two years earlier had belonged to the Creek Indians became the scene of the great Georgia Gold Rush, and among the mines that flourished was the Dahlonega gold mine, whose principal owners included South Carolina and Georgia Calhouns. At the same time Georgia was on its way to becoming the world's number one cotton producer. Men came from all over the world to make overnight fortunes in cotton. Populations and plantations exploded. The city that would one day become Atlanta grew up on the outskirts of the Calhouns' gold mine. The city was originally called "Terminus," because it was the southern end of the Chattanooga-based Western and Atlantic Railroad.

Two of the young cavalry officers who helped General Winfield Scott drive the last of the Creeks into Indian Territory (Oklahoma) were A. B. Calhoun's cousins James and Ezekiel. James later became Atlanta's wartime mayor. Ezekiel, like A. B., was a doctor. By the mid-1830s there were Calhouns all around the future city of Atlanta—up at Calhoun, of course, some seventy miles to the northwest; and down at Newnan, about forty miles to the south. In 1845 "Terminus" was officially renamed "Atlanta," once again in honor of the Western and Atlantic Railroad.

Atlanta was no charming Old South city like Charleston or New Orleans. (The Calhouns who left the charms of Charleston for the Georgia wilderness tended to be of the younger generation.) Atlanta's origins were rough and ready. Its women were much more robust than the swooning belles of the traditional Old South. Atlanta social life began when a certain Mrs. Mulligan, wife of a circa-1840s railroad foreman, demanded a plank floor on her log cabin house. Although there were no vast plantations within Atlanta's borders, there were big farms of up to several hundred acres nearby, and each of these farms was worked by ten to twenty slaves. Atlanta was essentially a new town for the new rich. The well-to-do built imposing mansions on Peachtree or Washington Street, with huge landscaped gardens, and slave quarters, in the back.

By the mid-1850s Atlanta (nicknamed the "Gate City") was the seat of the newly named Fulton County. There was a new courthouse, a new city hall, a new theater, and a majestic new depot called (unpresciently) Union Station. By 1859 Atlanta's population had swelled to 10,000, and there were 17 insurance companies, 13 churches, 6 banks, a lottery office, and 17 "major commercial buildings." The 1860 Atlanta census would list 126 railroad workers, 90 merchants, 49 prostitutes, 41 doctors, and 41 lawyers. Blacks, both slave and free, made up a significant percentage of the city's population. (Most of Georgia's 3,000 free blacks lived in Atlanta.) But the city apparently held insufficient appeal for Sinai Reynolds, who, throughout the twenty years she was owned by William Nimmons, continued to ply her trade, selling ginger cakes and persimmon beer on a Newnan, Georgia, street corner. By 1859 Sinai and Henry Reynolds had earned enough money to purchase freedom for themselves and four of their children, and on the eve of the Civil War they moved north to Chicago. The 1860 Chicago census would list the Reynoldses as living on Griswold Street. The two Reynolds boys had both become barbers.

In 1860 Sinai's oldest daughter, Nellie, was still the A. B. Calhoun family cook. There is a photograph of Nellie, taken circa 1870, in which she appears a stout, sturdy woman with a solid chin and a direct gaze. She clearly had a square-jawed, possibly white, father. She looks to be a woman of great self-confidence and very few illusions.

Nellie's son, Moses, was probably the Calhoun family butler. Her daughter, Siny, was a nursemaid to the Calhoun children and became housekeeper upon the death of A. B. Calhoun's wife. Siny was a lovely young woman, with a gentle expression. In July of 1860 she gave birth, in the Calhoun house at Newnan, to a daughter whom she named Catherine. Siny's nominal husband was Preston Webb, who died in 1868.

By 1861 Atlanta had gone from gold and cotton boom town to war boom town. Atlanta was both the medical center and the main supply depot of the Confederacy. But in 1861 the *real* war still seemed very far away. Atlanta's war was still a matter of dress parades, charity balls, and "entertainments." Unfortunately, the spring of 1862, with Admiral Farragut's capture of New Orleans (with the help of brave black Union troops), brought an end to the idyl. There was a Yankee spy scare. Soldiers guarded the depot and patrolled the streets. No alcohol could be served to men in uniform—and no blacks could be out after dark.

In the summer of 1863, after the fall of Vicksburg and Lee's retreat from Gettysburg, Atlanta became the Confederacy's last lifeline to the sea. By the following spring, the battles of Missionary Ridge, Lookout Mountain, and Chickamauga had sealed Atlanta's fate. Sherman, with Tennessee now in his pocket, began his inexorable march south. The town of Calhoun, Georgia, up near the Tennessee border, found itself in the line of both Union advance and Confederate retreat. In the 1850s the A. B. Calhoun family (including household slaves) had moved from Newnan to a brand new Atlanta house. They would remain in town for the duration. The two Calhoun doctor cousins, Andrew and Ezekiel, were important to Atlanta's medical war effort.

The war was being fought for cotton and slavery. But now cotton was useless—and slaves more important than ever. The Emancipation Proclamation of January 1, 1863, made absolutely no difference in the lives of Georgia's black Calhouns (although Sinai and Henry Reynolds, up in Illinois, must have wept for them). Slave prices rose by one hundred percent in the spring of 1864 because slaves were desperately needed to build roads, bridges, and fortifications and to work plantations while their masters were away. By May 1864 slaves were being requisitioned, at a dollar a day to their masters, to fortify the city itself. Atlanta was in a state of siege.

The first Union shells finally fell on the city in July. The only fatality was a child. The ninth of August, when Sherman's "Big Guns" arrived, became the worst day of the siege: five thousand bombshells fell on Atlanta, and scarcely a city block stood undamaged.

By the third week of August, Atlanta was nearly in a state of anarchy.

There were fires everywhere, rumored to have been set by spies and sabo-
teurs. As Atlanta citizens, with the help of their slaves, began to bury their
silver and valuables, some Atlantans may have noted a new truculence and
insubordination on the part of their human chattels. After all, Sherman
was not *just* Sherman—he was *freedom.*

According to family legend, when Sherman burned Atlanta in the early
days of September 1864, Nellie was too ill to travel, so she was placed on a
mattress in a wagon and joined the terrified throng of southbound refugees
on the clogged road to Newnan and safety.

At the war's end my great-great-grandfather, Moses Calhoun, had already spent half his life in slavery. Now suddenly, at age thirty-six, he was
being given a chance to begin again. He had to make up for lost time. He
asked a beautiful young woman, fifteen years his junior, to become his wife.
She was Atlanta Mary Fernando, born in 1845—and thus baptized the
same year as the city of Atlanta. Her mother's name was Charlotte Fernando, her sister was called Lottie, and her father was unknown. They
might have been free Atlanta "colored." Atlanta herself looked white. She
was clearly a Louisiana Creole—French, Iberian, native American, possibly
some African. Atlanta and Moses were married early in 1865, in the midst
of the rubble, dead horses, and homeless refugees of both races that Sherman left in his wake. Many of Atlanta's white citizens were starting over
again with nothing. But the blacks had something they had never had
before: freedom.

The years immediately following the war were difficult for all blacks in
the South. Four million slaves had been emancipated in a somewhat laissez-
faire manner, without provision for food or shelter, and without compensation. Most ex-slaves wandered the war-torn Southern roads like nomads.
The government's response to four million refugees was the first government welfare agency: the Freedmen's Bureau, a federally distributed, semi-
private, charitable organization under the umbrella of the American Missionary Association. The bureau distributed food and clothing and organized hospitals, schools, and refugee camps. In 1865 the death rate for
newly freed slaves was 38 percent; three years later it was 2.03 percent.
But Emancipation might as well have been a fantasy. "Slab towns" sprang
up—shanties built of barrel stavings and rope. Some ex-slaves simply squat-
ted among the ruins; others returned to familiar slave cabins. These blacks
might call themselves "free," but they were soon to be re-enslaved in the
infamous "Black Codes." The defeated South had, in fact, decided to ignore
the Emancipation Proclamation. South Carolina Black Codes, for example,

required agricultural workers to make unbreakable lifetime contracts with their employers. The Ku Klux Klan, the terrorist arm of the Black Codes, was founded in 1865 in Tennessee.

Responding to complaints from ex-slaves—now black Republican voters —President Andrew Johnson sent General Carl Schurz on a fact-finding tour of the South. What Schurz found was that "the freedman is no longer considered the property of an individual master, he is considered the slave of society." And it was the Schurz Report that "reconstructed" the South. The old Confederacy was divided into five military districts. New elections were authorized in which all adult males, regardless of color, could vote. An alliance of blacks, Northern white Republicans ("carpetbaggers"), and Southern white Republicans ("scalawags") rewrote state constitutions throughout the South. In 1867 there were 370,000 registered black voters in the South, and 250,000 whites. Twenty-two blacks were elected to Congress, two of them as senators. And blacks were elected to local office in numbers that would not be seen again for a century. Most of these black Reconstruction politicians had more formal education than Abraham Lincoln. Ten of the twenty-two congressmen had attended college. Five were lawyers, and one—Representative Robert B. Elliott of South Carolina (whose parents were West Indian immigrants)—was an old Etonian. Radical Reconstruction shook the Southern system to its very foundation.

Moses Calhoun was able to *make it* precisely because, for a brief decade, the American Dream was color-blind. (The years 1867–1877 became known in black history as the "Mystic Years.") Black Codes were eliminated just as Moses and Atlanta were settling into extended family life. For the first time in the history of the South, blacks enjoyed all the legal rights of white American citizens. They could vote, go to school, live where they wished, work as they wished, and marry whom they pleased—regardless of color. To be sure, only a very few were actually able to *enjoy* all of those rights. Black poverty was still pervasive and acute. But Moses and Atlanta were very lucky. They had a roof over their heads and over the heads of their loved ones. They could read and write. And, most important, they lived in Atlanta. Blacks who lived in town were much better off than those who lived in the country.

In the next ten years Moses Calhoun and the city of Atlanta, a phoenix from the ashes, would rise simultaneously. Moses, his wife, Atlanta, his mother, Nellie, and his sister, Siny—along with her daughter and her husband, Preston Webb—all lived together on Atlanta's Fraser Street. And

Sinai Reynolds, my great-great-great-great-grandmother, who in 1859 purchased freedom for herself and part of her family

Nellie Reynolds, who was cook in the household of A. B. Calhoun

*Moses Calhoun,
a prominent member
of Atlanta's black
bourgeoisie*

*The house in Newnan, Georgia, from which both black and white Calhouns fled
in the Civil War*

the Calhoun family grew. Moses and Atlanta's first child, my great-grandmother Cora Catherine Calhoun, was born in November 1865, and their second daughter, Lena Leo, was born in February 1869. Two months after Lena's birth Moses purchased (for $431) the lot next door to his house —on the corner of Fraser and Clark streets—where he opened a grocery store. Six months later he bought another parcel of land (for $393) at the corner of Crew and Glenn streets. The source of Moses' capital remains unknown; it's possible that, like the rest of middle-class America, he simply borrowed it. After all, Reconstruction banks treated blacks and whites more or less the same.

As the younger Calhouns were flourishing, the older order was passing. In August 1869 Moses' mother, Nellie, went to Chicago to attend the deathbed of her mother, Sinai Reynolds. I have a photograph of Sinai in very old age, taken in Chicago sometime in the 1860s. She appears tiny and, despite her years, very alert. Her small black face is framed in a Victorian bonnet, fleece-lined and tartan-ribboned. She wears a heavy cloak (against Chicago winters) and long gauntlet gloves, perhaps to hide arthritic fingers. Her eyes loom large and sad behind steel spectacles, and her gaze is distant, as if her thoughts were elsewhere. This eighteenth-century American child of West Africa had seen a great deal in her journey from the waters of the Chesapeake, to the Chattahoochee cotton kingdom, to Great Lake Michigan and America's newest boom town. Besides her westward progress across America, Sinai managed another extraordinary feat. She had managed to capture the American Dream. The American Dream says that you can *have,* or *be,* whatever you want—clearly a fantastic proposition in more ways than one. But for people like Sinai—people with grit, guts, and determination (beloved American attributes)—the dream can come true. She had managed to gain freedom for herself and most of her family, and her children would become pillars of Chicago's small black bourgeoisie (the 1869 black population of Chicago was less than 3,000). Sinai was both a typical American and a unique one—an American original. Her daughter Nellie wrote to Moses from Chicago to tell him of his grandmother's death: ". . . Deceased August the 6th at twelve minutes to two o'clock in the morning and we all feel lonely now. She diede happy in the Lord. . . ." Nellie's spelling was imperfect, but she wrote in a lovely eighteenth-century script. Sinai died at the age of ninety-two. Nellie herself would die at eighty-seven.

∙ ∙ ∙

In January 1870 A. B. Calhoun deeded a house and lot in Newnan, Georgia, to his former slave Siny Webb. What Siny did with her Newnan property remains a mystery. In the July 1870 United States census, Siny, now a widow, was listed as still living with Moses and his family on Fraser Street. Her profession is given as hairdresser. Cora and Lena are entered, as is Siny's daughter, Catherine, and their grandmother, Nellie, who is listed as a laundress. Moses, head of the household and "Retail Grocer," had "Real Estate" valued at $830—and a "personal estate" of $700. Under "Color" on the census record Moses is listed "B" for black. All the other members of the household, however, including his mother and sister, were listed "M" for mulatto.

Moses had great energy and ambition. His grocery store was so success-ful that he soon opened a small restaurant, with a fruit stand, on Decatur Street. His sister, Siny, married Joseph Murray, an Atlanta drayman, and she and her daughter, Catherine, moved a few blocks away to their own house. But Moses continued to collect Catherine in his grocery wagon every morning as he took his own daughters, Cora and Lena, to school. The girls attended the new Storrs Elementary School, at Houston and Cortland streets, a shining example of Radical Reconstruction. Storrs was established in 1867 by the American Missionary Association for small members of the new black middle class—that is, the children of literate black parents. Children who attended the Storrs School were prepared for higher educa-tion. Between 1861 and 1869 the Missionary Association created more than 4,000 academic and industrial schools—for 25,000 black students and 9,000 (mostly white) teachers. In 1865 one in twenty blacks could read and write. (By 1900 one out of two was literate, largely thanks to dedicated Missionary teachers.)

The first generation of Missionary teachers were white New Englanders for whom abolition was a Holy Crusade, and they sought to instill in the young future "leaders" of the black race a sense of what was truly valuable: real learning, real culture, perfect honesty and integrity. (The second gen-eration of teachers would be black.) The Northern missionaries taught the Yankee virtues of thrift, industry, and Puritanism while they reinforced a respect for "gentility" and bourgeois values.

As former house slaves, the black Calhouns were accustomed to white scrutiny. House servants generally lived, ate, slept, and worshipped under the master's roof. House slaves had only one role model: the white planter class. They were taught to approximate the master's speech, manners, and deportment. On large plantations they were taught to be spies. Every sig-

Atlanta Calhoun, wife of Moses, named for the city of her birth

Sinai Catherine ("Siny") Calhoun Webb

Siny Webb's daughter, Catherine, cousin and childhood friend of Lena and Cora Calhoun's

nificant early-nineteenth-century American slave rebellion was betrayed by house slaves. The strict division of house and field hand was central to the white power structure. Even now, as free people, they were still divided from the cradle.

The First Congregational Church, to which Moses and his family belonged, had also been established by the American Missionary Association for the edification of the new black bourgeoisie. Poorer black Atlantans called it "First Church" or "Big Church." It was as unlike the old emotional plantation churches as possible. It was, in fact, transplanted New England. Life for Atlanta's black aristocracy centered on First Congregational Church, select Atlanta University, and a handful of exclusive social clubs. And Moses Calhoun—possessor of a fine old Georgia name, a beautiful family, and a thriving business—was certainly a black aristocrat. By the 1880s Moses, now retail grocer, restaurateur, and boardinghouse owner, had two cooks and three waiters in his employ. By the mid-1880s the Calhouns had moved twice—each time, one presumes, to a more substantial house. Cora and Lena Calhoun were belles of the black South.

Black middle-class life in the 1880s was an almost comical microcosm of white upper-class life. Some of the richest names in slaveholding white Georgia now graced poorer, but liberated, brown faces at Atlanta's First Congregational Church. There were Calhouns, Colquitts, Joneses, Westmorelands, and Waddells—not to mention Hamiltons and Lees. Black Atlanta social life emanated from "Big Church." The black middle class was born "striving," or upwardly mobile. However religious Moses and Atlanta might be, they were certainly strivers. They wanted nothing but the "best" for their beautiful daughters.

Cora and Lena seemingly spent their girlhoods in a whirligig of parties, picnics, and flirtatious soirees. A scrapbook from the time contains a printed invitation to attend a "Masquerade Party" given by the "Gate City Girls" (Misses Webb, Townsley, Calhoun, Epps, Jones, Pope, et al.) at "Mr. M. Calhoun's, No. 34 Decatur St., March 24, 1882." The guests were urged to wear "full masque," and Cora, daughter of the grocer–restaurant keeper host, was modestly listed on the "Committee of Refreshments." There is also an engraved invitation to a "Reception" given by the "Young Men" (Messrs. Wimbish, Weaver, Thomas, Rucker, Smith, Graves, et al.) at Golden Rod Hall, Whitehall Street, Friday, December 28, 1883, 8 o'clock. The snap of the parasol and the rustle of taffeta made up in attention to detail what they lacked in "luxe." This was an almost flawless mirror image of upper-middle-class white life in the 1880s.

Unlike their white namesakes, however, the black upper classes could
not afford to be full-time social butterflies. They worked very hard. The
young black middle class was a very self-conscious elite. They were, after
all, a "chosen" people—selected by abolitionist missionaries (the founders
of both First Congregational Church and Atlanta University) to be the new
"uplifters" of the black race. Cora, Lena, and their friends were being
trained as teachers—and to be a *teacher* in those days, in that black world,
was to believe that the future of the race was truly in your hands. The
stern white Yankees at Atlanta University stressed intellectuality, responsibility, and *seriousness*. The black *crème de la crème* was highly educated
and often talented. Cora and Lena's Graves cousins (the grandchildren of
Moses' sister, Siny) were well-known classical music prodigies. Cora and
Lena's young cousin Antoine Graves, Jr. (Siny's grandson), was a celebrated
violinist in the black world. He trained in Europe before the First World
War and gave concerts throughout black America. His sisters and daughter
were also talented musicians.

Despite First Congregational's reputation for piety and charity, the
membership, like any upwardly mobile group, unfortunately made class
distinctions. Not only did the congregation bear old slaveholding white
names, they also bore old slaveholding white habits. The "big house"
and the "cabins" did not intermingle socially. The "leaders" of the race
kept to themselves, and cabin class was expected to be duly impressed.
The gulf between brown and black was enormous. Given the modern
analogy of the choice between "half-empty" and "half-full," First Congregational parishioners would sooner say "half-white" than "half-black."
It was a question of status. The black middle class was a world within
itself, isolated from both the larger white and black worlds. There is no
denying, however, that they seemed happy and confident within their
enclave.

There are photographs of the Atlanta Calhouns taken in 1883. They are
a very attractive family. Moses is bewhiskered, waistcoated, and in his
prime. He has his mother Nellie's direct gaze. He seems a man who is
satisfied with himself and his world. He certainly does not look as if he had
spent half his life in slavery. He appears the complete man of property—
solid, confident, and secure. Atlanta Fernando Calhoun, aged thirty-eight,
is of indeterminate race. Her eyes are dark and enormous, her face a pale
oval. She wears a silk dress, laces, a cameo, and a long rope of beads. It is
easy to see the young beauty she must have been. Atlanta appears now
primly New South *nouveau riche*.

Antoine Graves, Jr., a musical prodigy who studied and performed in Europe before World War I

116 Howell Street in Atlanta, Georgia, the home of Cora and Lena's cousin Catherine Webb Graves (seated on the porch)

Cora Calhoun, age eighteen

Lena Calhoun, age sixteen

Cora Calhoun, aged eighteen, is a slim and pretty young Atlanta miss, elegant and proud. With a parasol and a bustle, she wears ruffles, lace, and an ostrich-trimmed bonnet. Behind her—the photographer's conceit—is a waterfall of ivy. In reality, Cora was a bit too small, too thin, and too much of a bluestocking for popular 1880s taste. Cora anticipated the Shavian woman—independent, idealistic, and *thin*. She was a college graduate—member of Atlanta University's class of 1881, its fourth graduating class.

Atlanta University was known to be among the most "elite" of Missionary schools, both scholastically and socially. It was known for its stiff academic regime, as well as the relative prosperity of its student body. Cora's classmates were hand-picked, like herself, for star quality. Many became lifelong friends. Some even became generational friends. (One of Cora's classmates, Adella Hunt, belonged to a family that had been free in Georgia before the War. Adella was the daughter of a mulatto-Creek mother and a well-to-do white planter. In typical bourgeois network fashion, Adella's brother sponsored the academic career of Cora's future son. Adella's younger children were close friends of Cora's future granddaughter, Lena. And Adella's granddaughter became my classmate at Radcliffe.) Cora and her classmates led busy lives centered on home, church, and club—with plenty of time out for parties as well as cultural pursuits. And as graduates of Atlanta University, they admitted no superiors—and very few equals.

These first black college students, with their ante-bellum manners and New England values, would be the founding mothers and fathers of the twentieth-century black bourgeoisie. Of all the bourgeois symbols beloved of the black bourgeoisie, the college degree was most important. Before Emancipation, knowledge was a dangerous thing. With freedom, it was the key not only to greater opportunities, but to inner satisfactions—in the form of compensation in their relations with whites, most of whose education was inferior to theirs.

In 1885 it was Lena Calhoun's turn for Missionary college. At sixteen, Cora's younger sister, Lena, was the acknowledged family beauty. Lena was statuesque, with a classical profile, languorous eye, and silky black tresses. She was the young image of the stage star Maxine Elliott, an opulent 1880s white beauty. The gilded age was expansive, and so were its favorite women. Lena went away to Fisk University, in Nashville, Tennessee—where it was, naturally, love at first sight for young William Edward Burghardt Du Bois.

W. E. B. Du Bois came from the free North—from the only black family in a small Massachusetts town. He was of Dutch, French, African,

The First Congregational Church (known as
"Big Church") was the hub of black bourgeois
Atlanta's spiritual and social life.

A formal invitation to a party at the
Calhouns'. Cora, Lena, and their cousin
Catherine Webb are listed on the "Committee
of Refreshments."

G. C. G.

You are respectfully invited to
attend a

MASQUERADE PARTY

given by the

Gate City Girls,

At Mr. M. Calhoun's, No. 34
Decatur St., March 24th, 1882.

COMMITTEE OF ARRANGEMENT.
Mrs. Henry, Gordon, Ford.
COMMITTEE OF INVITATION.
Misses Clarke, Morgan, Thomas.
COMMITTEE OF RECEPTION.
Misses Jones, Munroe, Jackson, Howard.
COMMITTEE OF REFRESHMENTS.
Misses Webb, Townsley, Calhoun, Epps, Pope.

Compliments of

Gate City Girls

N. B.—All guests must appear in full masque.

Will be pleased to have you attend

A Lawn Party,

Complimentary to

Miss Cecile L. Barefield,
of Augusta, Ga.

At the Residence of Mr. Crawford Monroe,
110 Pine Street.

Thursday Evening, August 28, 1884.

Accompany Miss Katie F. Webb.

A summer party in 1884 that the Calhoun sisters
surely attended. Catherine Webb's escort received
this invitation.

My great-grandmother's college diploma, a proud possession for any black American in the late nineteenth century

Atlanta University—founded by the American Missionary Association to educate future leaders of the black South—as it appeared in 1881, when Cora Calhoun was a student there

and native American ancestry; he always "thanked God" that he had no "Anglo-Saxon" blood. Du Bois had never been South before and had never known many black people outside of his own family. The summer before he left home, Du Bois heard spirituals for the first time—at the Great Barrington, Massachusetts, Congregational Church—when the Fisk Jubilee Singers gave a concert to raise funds for their school. Now slowly trying to raise the money for Harvard, Du Bois had accepted a Fisk scholarship. A smallish, bookish lad, he entered Fisk as a sophomore in his freshman year.

According to his autobiography, the college carriage was waiting when the Nashville, Chattanooga and St. Louis Railway deposited Du Bois at the depot. From there it was straight up to Jubilee Hall, the Fisk dining room. The students were standing and singing grace in chorus. There were flowers, silver, snowy white linen . . . and the "rosy apricot" vision of Lena across the table:

> I was thrilled to be for the first time among so many of my own color or rather of such various and extraordinary colors. . . . Never before had I seen young men so self-assured and who gave themselves such airs, and colored men at that; and above all for the first time I saw beautiful girls . . . of one of these girls I have often said, no human being could possibly have been so beautiful as she seemed to my young eyes in that far-off September night of 1885. She was the great aunt of Lena Horne and fair as Lena Horne is, Lena Calhoun was far more beautiful.

Lena Calhoun enjoyed young "Willie" Du Bois' attention, but some of her classmates thought him a stuffed shirt. And he had an annoyingly superior attitude. He sometimes told the teachers that they were not pushing their students enough. In small classes taught by dedicated teachers Du Bois studied Greek, chemistry, physics, rhetoric, German, philosophy, and ethics. He would go from Fisk to Harvard to the University of Berlin. Du Bois called his fellow Missionary college students the "Talented Tenth"— the 10 percent who were meant to help raise up the other 90. His Massachusetts manners, however, did not restrain him from mocking what he called their "affectations and high flown" airs. Even Lena did not escape his critical eye. There were no exceptions noted when he listed his female classmates as appearing to be interested only in boys, chewing gum, and spring bonnets.

W. E. B. Du Bois remained hopelessly smitten with Lena. He described her future husband with a touch of jealousy:

Frank Smith of the class ahead of me was a yellow dandy, faultlessly dressed and a squire of dames. He later married Lena Calhoun with whom I was hopelessly in love; but Smith was over 25 years of age and ready for a wife.

Lena Calhoun and Frank Smith were married on Christmas Day, 1888, in Chattanooga, Tennessee, at the home of her sister, Cora—now Mrs. Edwin Horn. (Edwin would not add the *e* for almost another decade.)

∎ ∎ ∎

Reconstruction was essentially dead. By 1887 every Southern state had enacted "Jim Crow" legislation, the goal of which was the complete and total separation of the races, from cradle to grave—an unthinkable idea under slavery. When the Civil Rights Act of 1875 was declared unconstitutional (in 1883), white Georgia Democrats began breathing fire and Bourbonism on black Republicans. The South might have lost the war, but it had won the peace—by way of the Supreme Court.

Atlanta itself was daily becoming more and more impossible for energetic and ambitious blacks, especially Republican ones. By 1886 Moses Calhoun had already moved his family across the Chattahoochee River to slightly more liberal Birmingham, Alabama. Moses would still be a prospering merchant, but he would certainly be less optimistic. He had seen the birth of the New South, and now he was seeing its death. Moses' "lunch house" and also his "residence" were listed in the Birmingham City Directory—where there was a small "c" after his name, for "colored."

The old oligarchy had survived and was obdurate. The law of the land was the rope.

C H A P T E R · 2

THE HORNS

Edwin Horn (without an *e*) was born in Tennessee in 1859, the year of John Brown's raid on Harpers Ferry. But he grew up in placid, picket-fence Evansville, Indiana, on the beautiful Ohio River. Evansville was a place of dappled sunshine and Hoosier common sense, where children called their parents "Ma" and "Pa."

I have a photograph of Edwin's father. Founding father Horn was a long-boned, blue-eyed, white British adventurer who found himself captain of a Tennessee River trading boat in the years before the Civil War. His eyes glare fiercely into the camera. His gaze is dead-on and impassive. He looks a rootless, restless man. The stony eyes and the high-domed forehead make him look gloomy, as well as dangerous. He wears a dark coat and white frontier shirt—cravats were not worn west of the Alleghenies, not by *real* men anyway. Father Horn is seated, looking both controlled and wary. The only thing missing from the picture is a Winchester across his knees.

Edwin's mother was a native American. I have no photograph of her. But I am told that she was a tall woman, with black hair to her waist, who took in laundry—young Edwin's first memories were of white and red petticoats, billowing like sails in the sun—and kept a pet snake. The snake drank milk, slept behind the stove, and frightened away mice. Family legend has always made Edwin's mother a Blackfoot, but she was more likely Creek or Cherokee. Whatever her ancestry, Edwin's mother apparently did not lose touch with her spiritual heritage. In summer storms, she made her half-English children stand out in open fields—as electricity danced around their heads—so they would have no fear of nature.

Edwin had two brothers and a sister. The children all had proper English names—no "Tecumseh" Hornes. One of Edwin's brothers became the first mixed-race sheriff of an Indiana county. The other brother—captain of a trading boat, like his father—was dynamited off the river and killed, a victim of racial and border perils. Edwin's sister, Alice, seems to have lived a comparatively uneventful life.

Indiana was born a free state in 1816. The Battle of Tippecanoe and William Henry Harrison's defeat of the Shawnees in 1811 marked the end of the bloody "settlers versus natives" wars. The rest of Indiana's nineteenth-century history was relatively tranquil. Except for the fact that Morgan's Raiders used the state as a short cut to Ohio, Indiana had a battle-free Civil War. The state's Civil War governor, Oliver Morton, was a famous radical Republican abolitionist. Indiana was not a bad place to be a black American when Edwin Horn was growing up there.

In 1875, at age sixteen, Edwin was a schoolteacher in the Evansville Colored School, where he had once been a pupil. In the Midwest, sixteen-year-olds were already adults; and Edwin's father had given his children a leg up on education. What they did not get in school they got at home—including poetry, music, and languages. Father Horn, reprobate though he might be, educated his American children as if they were still in Victoria's England.

Edwin was clearly a young man with a future. He decided—or was chosen—early to become a spokesman for a race that he had adopted by virtue of Tennessee's mulatto category. The Horns had opted that their children be "colored" instead of "Indian." It was a wise decision. Between the frying pan of black life and the fire of red, blacks got a slightly better deal.

Edwin took his first giant step in January of 1875, when his dedication speech at the opening of a new colored school caused such a stir that it was reprinted in the Evansville *Journal,* the white daily.

The founder of the Horn family in America, c. 1860

To be the full equal of the white man, there are two particular things we need—education and wealth. . . .

Look to it, fathers and mothers; regard it as you do the obligation you owe your Maker, to see that your children are educated. . . .

If they be educated and virtuous, the greatness of our people is assured; if they be ignorant, depraved—for they will be so if not nurtured by the benign spirit of education—the book may well be closed now, for it will be of no use to read further; our history is already recorded and is familiar to the world.

Two months later, when Congress enacted the Civil Rights Bill of 1875, Edwin was once again called on by the Evansville *Journal:*

GOOD ADVICE TO COLORED MEN: BY ONE OF THEIR RACE
TO THE COLORED MEN OF EVANSVILLE AND VICINITY

Not long since I had the honor of submitting to you an article setting forth the educational facilities of our city. Since that time a new law has been passed by Congress, known as the Civil Rights bill. But before we can enjoy our rights and immunities there are certain duties that we must perform.

1. It is our duty to gain an education and be virtuous.

2. We must be self-denying, economical, frugal. By these virtues we shall gain public confidence and esteem. A certain degree of intelligence is necessary to make a man a good citizen of a free State. . . .

3. This new law gives us only equal rights . . . it only equalizes us in the sight of the law, and enables us to enjoy certain privileges which were denied us by a vicious, unthinking and ignorant class of people. If you go to places of amusement, hotels or barber shops, and attempt to *force* yourself into an element where you do not belong simply from impertinence and insolence, you will be treated as other ruffians who are likely to cause a disturbance.

4. The primary object of the bill is to *protect* you in the enjoyment of your rights as American citizens, and not to encourage you or protect you in the assumption of any rights or immunities not enjoyed by all the citizens alike. . . . The better part of the citizens, white and black, will mutually labor to avoid a collision of any description. . . . Any indiscretion committed by a colored man in the assertion of his rights under the Civil Rights bill, will not only bring

injury upon its author, but also do a great harm to the colored race as a whole. Let me beg of you, for the sake of yourselves—your children—and your race, to be prudent and careful how you act in this important period in the history of our emancipated people.

> Yours Truly, Edwin F. Horn,
> March 14, 1875.

Edwin had reason to take a cautious tone: he had seen, or heard, enough of border violence. Believing the pen mightier than the sword (he was a true child of radical Reconstruction), his campaign for education was a serious one. He started a night school for blacks that was duly noted in the daily press, although it was short-lived. At the same time he continued his exceptional work as a teacher of black children. The Evansville *Journal* noted:

> Last Friday at the close of the written examination of the Second Intermediate Schools, it was discovered that the pupils of the colored school of that grade, taught by Edwin F. Horn, had the highest general average of the city.

"Those who *can*, do; those who *can't*, teach." Edwin was actually a "doer" who happened to teach. He was not just a sixteen-year-old Hoosier schoolmaster and colored spokesman, he was also a professional journalist: editor of the colored weekly *Our Age* and official "colored correspondent" for the Evansville *Journal*. In December of 1875 he reported, both in sorrow and in anger, to the *Journal*'s white readers on the overenthusiastic revival meetings currently popular among the black Baptists and Methodists. For the colored paper—many of whose readers were in the grip of the revivalism (brought on, no doubt, by the moral and financial bankruptcy of Grant administration America)—Edwin sought to preach the values of reasonable Episcopalianism. He quoted Emerson:

> "Souls are not saved in bundles. The spirit asks every man, how is it with thee?"

■　■　■

Eighteen seventy-six was Centennial Year. The people of France sent America the torch-bearing arm of the Statue of Liberty; the rest of her would come later. In Evansville, Indiana, "Mr. Ed. Horn" (as he was referred to in the local press) played the flute in the Centennial Concert.

In the art exhibit at America's largest celebration of peace, prosperity, and plenty—the Philadelphia Centennial—a black painter, Edward M. Bannister, was awarded a Centennial Medal for his Barbizon School landscape, *Under the Oaks.*

Eighteen seventy-six was also an election year. The Republican Party that had won the Civil War and freed the slaves was now ideologically as dead as Lincoln. The party had fallen to the tycoons. The Democrats believed they were ripe for a win. And Southern Democrats were on the march to destroy the black Republican vote.

In June 1876 a black Mississippi Republican wrote to United States Senator George S. Boutwell: "The Democrats told the colored voters, if they went to the polls in election day they would be killed. . . ." A South Carolina Democrat proclaimed, "We must render this a white man's government or convert the land into a Negro man's cemetery."

In November the winner of the popular vote was Samuel J. Tilden, Democrat, although Rutherford B. Hayes, Republican, won the electoral vote. The election was thrown to Congress—but the real decision was made in a room at the Wormley Hotel in Washington, D.C., where on February 26 and 27, 1877, Hayes emissaries promised to remove federal troops from the South in return for the support of five Democratic congressmen.

The Wormley Compromise marked the official end of radical Reconstruction. W. E. B. Du Bois later called the years 1876 through 1896 the "nadir" of black life in America. Blacks lost the vote, their civil rights, and all claims to constitutional protection under the law. They were nearly more victimized (and certainly less protected) than they had been under slavery. Curiously enough, the owner of the notorious Wormley Hotel was a wealthy black man, James Wormley, the son of free Virginians, who rose from the blacksmith and livery business to successful hotel keeping. The Wormley family would be socially important members of the black bourgeoisie for more than a hundred years.

Almost as if to symbolize the end of an era, Oliver Morton—Indiana's abolitionist governor—died in 1877. Edwin Horn was chosen to eulogize the great man, on behalf of Evansville's colored population, in the *Journal:*

MORTON DEAD

BY EDWIN F. HORN

MORTON IS DEAD! On the western world
Gloom gathers thick and fast;

The starry flag in darkness furled,
Now droops upon the mast.
Voices of millions wail with grief,
Deep sorrow bows each head—
For Freedom mourns her noblest chief,
Her glorious champion—dead. . . .

Edwin's literary idol, circa 1877, was Goethe, the poet who bridged the
centuries of reason and romanticism, the poet whose last words were "More
light!" There was a page of printed poetry in my grandfather's trunk, with
handwritten notes by Edwin. At the top of the page he wrote: "Give *children*
the best of poetry. There is born in every man a poet who dies young."
And on the verses called "A Psalm of Life," he wrote "Inspired by
Goethe":

Life is real! Life is earnest!
And the grave is not its goal;
Dust thou art, to dust returnest,
Was not spoken of the soul.

Even if 1877 was not a good year to be black in America, there were still
two or three highly publicized events that gave blacks reason to be proud,
and to hope. Among them was the graduation from West Point of Henry O.
Flipper, the first of only three blacks commissioned into the post–Civil War
army until the next century. On June 15, 1877, *The New York Times*
reported:

When Mr. Flipper, the colored cadet, stepped forward and received
the reward of four years of as hard work and unflinching courage as
any young man can be called upon to go through, the crowd of
spectators gave him a round of applause. He deserved it. Anyone
who knows how quietly and bravely this young man—the first of his
despised race to graduate at West Point—has borne the difficulty of
his position.

And Isaac Murphy, the black jockey, continued his reign as king of the turf
by winning the St. Leger stakes. Murphy became the first jockey to win
three Kentucky Derbies. (From 1875 to 1902 black jockeys won fourteen

Kentucky Derbies—hence the rage for small black alabaster jockey figures.)

By 1878 Edwin had begun to branch out. He was still teaching school and still "colored correspondent" for the Evansville *Journal*, but he had also become publisher of *Our Age* and was writing for yet another black weekly, *The Courier*. He was even more serious at nineteen than he had been three years before, and he was spectacularly handsome. It is hard to imagine that many young women could resist him. Of course, the young Victorians of the "colored" elite were even more Victorian than their namesakes, full of prim "virtue" and high sentiment. Their flirtations, as well as their social life, were closely chaperoned and resolutely high-minded. Activities centered on musicales or artistic and literary appreciation. Edwin himself chronicled one of these meetings:

LITERARY REUNION AT NASHVILLE

Last evening was held at Nashville, Tenn., the annual reunion of the Thomas Literary Club (colored), a society comprising the most intellectual colored people of the South. The following poem for the occasion was read before it, and is from the pen of a well-known young colored teacher of this city. . . .

The poem was called "The Literati"—a seventy-four-line ode, with references to Aspasia, Athens, Rome, and Lucullus. Leaving classical references behind, it becomes a paean to the members of the Thomas Literary Club:

> *Here sober matrons oft are seen,*
> *Chaste wits, and critics void of spleen;*
> *Physicians fraught with real science;*
> *Republicans and Democrats in alliance;*
> *Poets, incipient, fulfilling common duties;*
> *Honest lawyers, reasonable beauties;*
> *Elders who preach, sometimes without pay;*
> *Conscientious laymen, who often pray;*
> *Learned antiquarians, who, from college*
> *Reject the dust, and bring the knowledge.*
> *And hear it age, believe it youth,*
> *Every one seeking honest truth.*

Hail! Conversation, soothing power,
Sweet goddess of the social hour . . .

The poem was modestly signed "Edwin Fletcher."

This Nashville literary reunion is where Edwin found first love and very early sorrow. We can assume that Callie Hatcher was one of Nashville's sweetly "reasonable beauties." All that we know of her, however, is found in two newspaper clippings from 1878, side by side in Edwin's scrapbook:

MARRIED

HORN–HATCHER—Saturday, November 30th, at the residence of Mr. John L. Thomas, Mr. Edwin F. Horn of Evansville, Indiana to Miss Callie Hatcher of this city. Rev. B. Green, St. Paul Chapel, officiating. No cards. Evansville papers please copy.

DIED

HORN—On Saturday, December 14, at 7 o'clock AM at the residence of Mr. John L. Thomas, Mrs. Callie L. Hatcher, the wife of Edwin Horn. Funeral services at St. Paul Chapel by the pastor Rev. B. Green, on Sunday Dec. 15, 1878 at 3 o'clock PM. Friends invited without further notice. Evansville, Indiana papers please copy.

Newlywed and widower, Edwin composed a poem in the shape of a cross. The tone was sad but hopeful. For *Our Age* he wrote a long piece on Tennyson's "In Memoriam." And he plunged into work.

■ ■ ■

By 1880 Edwin was finally old enough for politics. At the age of twenty-one he was elected alternate delegate from the First District in Indiana to the Republican National Convention in Chicago. (One hundred years later I was a delegate to the 1980 Democratic Convention, pledged to Senator Edward M. Kennedy of Massachusetts; 1980 Democrats more or less resembled 1880 Republicans.) Edwin was a partisan of Senator James G. Blaine of Maine, leader of the liberal Republican wing known as the "Half-Breeds." The conservative Republicans called themselves "Stalwarts." Edwin's convention was deadlocked between Blaine and "Stalwart" Ulysses S. Grant, but James Garfield, a "Half-Breed" dark horse from Ohio, was chosen on the thirty-sixth ballot.

Edwin went back home to Indiana and fell in love again. He was ready to give happiness another try. Miss Nellie Douglass, a beautiful young woman from Chicago who had come to teach in the Evansville school, was a student of Latin and Greek and a skilled debater. She and Edwin must have felt like soul mates. Nellie was not only beautiful and gifted, she was something of a celebrity. Her father, H. Ford Douglass (the second s honored Frederick Douglass, who made favorable mention of H. Ford in his autobiography), was a famous western black abolitionist, one of the most fire-eating in the country. An "agent" in the great Ohio Underground Railroad, he also advocated black emigration from the United States (to Central America or Haiti). Ford Douglass put his name on the abolitionist map with an 1854 speech that made him famous:

> I can hate this government without being disloyal because it has stricken down my manhood, and treated me as a saleable commodity. I can join a foreign enemy and fight against it, without being a traitor, because it treats me as an ALIEN and a STRANGER. . . . When I remember that from Maine to Georgia, from the Atlantic waves to the Pacific shores, I am an alien and an outcast, unprotected by law, proscribed and persecuted by cruel prejudice, I am willing to forget the endearing name of home and country, and as an unwilling exile seek on other shores the freedom which has been denied me in the land of my birth.

Despite his emigrationism, Douglass was the first black man in Illinois to try to enlist in the Civil War. He eventually became captain of the Union Army's only black regiment of light artillery. (Black Union soldiers belonged to the U.S.C.T., United States Colored Troops.) Douglass died at Fort Leavenworth in 1865, of typhoid contracted at the battle of Vicksburg.

When Ford's daughter Nellie settled down to young married life with young Edwin Horn, the couple soon moved to Indianapolis—a step up in sophistication from Evansville. Edwin became principal of a colored school, and he founded, along with his friend Edward E. Cooper, the weekly *Colored World*—later the Indianapolis *World*, a successful and long-lived black paper.

On September 18, 1882, a baby girl was born to the young couple. Less than a year later the baby was dead. Edwin's poem was published in the *World*:

THE BABY

Full short his journey was; no dust
Of earth unto his sandals clave;
The weary weight that old men must
He bore not to the grave.
He seemed a cherub who had lost his way
And wandered hither; so his stay
With us was short, and 'twas most meet
That he should be no delver in earth's clod,
Nor need to pause and cleanse his feet
To stand before his God.

Nellie also wrote a poem, never published, that was much more personal:

IN MEMORY OF OUR DAUGHTER

To some hearts, the summer breeze,
Cooing softly through the trees,
Kissing roses till they grow,
Red and pink and white as snow,
Sings a song of joys fled,
Breathes the words "she's dead—dead."
'Twas in summer's golden prime,
In the gorgeous happy time,
When the flowers and leaves have birth
And all nature makes to mirth,
That to my baby's heart
Death sent his chilling dart.
That is why the summer breeze
Cooing softly through the trees,
Kissing roses till they grow,
Red and pink and white as snow,
Sings to me of joys fled,
Breathes the words "she's dead—dead."

In 1883 the Supreme Court declared the Civil Rights Act of 1875—the act that Edwin wrote of in the Evansville *Journal*—to be unconstitutional. And the National Convention of Colored People, held in September in

Louisville, Kentucky, refused to endorse the Arthur administration and called for a separate black American political party.

The following year Edwin was elected alternate delegate-at-large to the Republican National Convention in Chicago. Edwin was getting his political aspirations in hand. He had hitched them to the coattails of an Indiana favorite son: General Benjamin Harrison, grandson of ex-President William Henry "Tippecanoe" Harrison. Edwin's newspaper was vociferously pro-Harrison. And in May of 1884 Edwin received a letter from his mentor:

From the U.S. Senate, Washington, D.C. May 13, 1884

Personal

Edwin Horn, Esq.
Indianapolis, Ind.

My dear Sir. Just before the receipt of your letter of the 9th inst. I had written to you to express my regret that I had failed to have a talk with you while I was in Indianapolis. You have been placing me under fresh obligations since by your kind words in the World. I have never consented to regard myself as a Candidate for the Presidency, and so have attempted no organization either in our own State or elsewhere. I have had some wish that my relation to my party in Indiana might not be misrepresented or misunderstood . . . and my wish has gone no further. However I have highly appreciated the kind of expressions which have been freely tendered by you and others of your people. I have never directly or indirectly sought to influence or even to know the preference of any of the delegates you refer to—but am glad to know that they have a friendly estimate of me. I shall hope to see you at Chicago & to have an opportunity to talk fully with you.

Very Truly Yours,
Benj. Harrison

Benjamin Harrison would have to wait another four years to fulfill his "reluctant" ambitions. James G. Blaine of Maine became the Republican nominee in 1844, and Grover Cleveland, the Democrat, won the election.

By 1885 Edwin was well enough known in midwestern politics and journalism to have acquired a nickname (courtesy of the Cleveland *Gazette*): "Windy Horn." He was successful and happy—and Nellie was pregnant again. This time she went back to Chicago to have her baby, and in May 1885 another daughter was born. But Nellie was not strong; childbirth had seriously weakened her. Edwin decided to move his family south to a warmer climate. Leaving his wife and the baby in Chicago, he went to investigate the prospects of life and work in Jacksonville, Florida. The city had a proud heritage for Southern blacks; in the Civil War it was captured and held by black troops. But Edwin's stay there was brief: by October Nellie was dead. Permanent happiness was proving illusive once again.

MRS. NELLIE DOUGLAS HORN

This community was startled last Sunday morning by the announcement that flew from mouth to mouth that Mrs. Nellie Douglas Horn was dead. It was so sudden and so unexpected that it seemed almost incredible. Yet it was all too true. . . . For several weeks past she had been ill, her physician pronouncing her malady extreme nervous prostration. Friends hoped she would rally and soon be restored to former good health, but the hope was vain. . . .

Her acknowledged elocutionary gifts and her great ability as a writer were inherited from her brilliant father, Henry Ford Douglass, and her untimely death alone cut short a career as wonderful as his. The deceased was married to Mr. Edward F. Horn, the well-known editor, of Indianapolis, and the two became one in their literary as well as their home life. To her husband she bore two children, both girls, the latter now four months old, surviving.

The funeral services occurred Tuesday, at 1 p.m. at Bethesda Church, the Rev. Podd delivering a scholarly and touching eulogy, being assisted in the service by Rev. De Baptiste. The song service by a select choir was above criticism, and, indeed every detail of the sad ceremony faultless. At last loving hands and aching hearts sadly bore her away to her eternal rest in the silent city of the dead.

In 1980, in my grandfather's trunk, I found three different poems that Edwin wrote in memory of Nellie. I also discovered a small, folded square of paper on which was written the words "Miss Nellie Douglas Horn, May 18, 1885, daughter of Edwin F. and Nellie Douglas Horn." The paper was yellowed, the ink had faded to brown, and Edwin's beautiful nineteenth-century script looked spidery and quaint. When I unfolded the paper I found a soft brown-gold curl of human hair—the color of an autumn leaf. Human hair is amazing; the curl was so delicate and alive after nearly a century.

Edwin was now twenty-five years old, and twice a widower. (His second daughter either died soon after her mother or stayed in Chicago to be raised by her grandmother.) Indianapolis and Chicago were both too full of grief and memories. Edwin needed to start all over again. He left the Midwest and went south to Atlanta, where, in partnership with A. W. Barnett, he edited a mildly crusading weekly called the Atlanta *Defiance*. But Edwin would stay only a year. In 1887 he moved on to "progressive, Republican" Chattanooga, Tennessee—the state that had, in fact, enacted the first Jim Crow railway law. So Edwin rode to Chattanooga in the colored first-class carriage. His new paper was called the Chattanooga *Justice*. It would be a success.

Edwin Horn and Cora Calhoun could have met just about anywhere—Atlanta, Birmingham, or even Chicago. Cora's second cousins, the Reynoldses, had lived in Chicago since before the war. And in that small brown world of the black bourgeoisie everyone knew one another. They kept closer contact with one another than with black neighbors who occupied a lower rung on the social scale. Under slavery, travel had been forbidden. Now it was the way contacts and relationships were kept and established. Cora Calhoun was already a well-traveled young woman, and hospitality was a way of life familiar to her. There were few hotels, after all—certainly very few for "respectable" black people.

Wherever they met, slim, serene, and serious Cora must have looked to Edwin like an answered prayer. They were married on October 26, 1887. Their wedding picture shows a handsome young couple looking purposefully toward the future. Cora's eyes are clear, cool, and unafraid—but Edwin's seem etched with grief, as he gazes off into the distance. So much unhappiness. Now so much *possibility* for happiness. (He certainly would have repressed any vague uneasiness about Cora's health, although she sometimes seemed a fragile little thing.) But Cora certainly believed in hope. She did not have to be robust, only resolute. She would be determined to make Edwin happy—a sentiment that many women probably felt at the sight of his melancholy good looks. Cora had not yet failed at anything. Edwin had failed only at happiness. There was reason for joy, for optimism. The South's black bourgeoisie made them the couple of the year.

A BRILLIANT EVENT

The marriage of Mr. E. F. Horn of this city [Chattanooga] and Miss Cora Calhoun of Birmingham, Ala., was a brilliant event in the history of the magic city. The nuptials were performed at the home of the bride on last Wednesday morning and the party left the same day for Chattanooga, their new home and field of labor.

The presents were costly and handsome. The bride is a lady of great taste and refinement, having figured very largely as the belle of Atlanta society. She has visited many of the principal cities of the country, and enjoys a wide circle of admirers.

The groom came to this city about one year ago, since then he has made a great success in editing and publishing a weekly paper called JUSTICE. So well has the business of the paper been conducted that it has become the principal organ of more than 2,000 people of this city alone. Mr. Horn is also a teacher in the Gilmer Street school. . . .

The prospect of a new life fired Edwin with ambition. Besides his teaching and his journalism, he was also a budding capitalist. In partnership with A. F. Perry, M.D., and H. M. Wilson, he was an owner of Perry and Company—"The People's Drug Store"—a "modern," three-story building on the bustling corner of Ninth and B streets, where "electric cars pass the door." Most important to Edwin, however, was his editorship of the Chattanooga *Justice:*

. . . from its first issue till now, it has been recognized as the leading colored paper in the State. Temperate in tone, conservative in policy, it has gained for the colored people of this city a consideration for their wants, a recognition of their rights on the part of their white fellow citizens, that were never before accorded. Policemen are less eager than formerly to club colored offenders. Largely through the influence of *Justice* the colored people of Chattanooga can boast of having recently erected the best appointed school building South of Washington. . . .

The front page of the January 5, 1889, edition of *The Freeman*—a "national Colored Weekly Newspaper" published in Indianapolis, Indiana

$\mathcal{M}^r$ and $\mathcal{M}^{rs}$ M. Calhoun
request your presence at the marriage
of their daughter
Cora Catharine
to
Edwin F. Horn
Wednesday morning, October 26, 1887,
at eight o'clock, at their residence,
2404 3rd Ave.,
Birmingham, Alabama.

*Mementoes of the wedding of Edwin Horn and Cora Calhoun,
my great-grandparents*

Cora Horn, in mourning for her father, Moses Calhoun,
poses with her firstborn son, Errol, in 1889.

Edwin Horn—the "Adonis of the Negro press"—on the front page of
The Freeman, a national weekly newspaper for blacks, 1889

—featured a portrait of Edwin at the age of thirty when he was known as the "Adonis of the Negro press":

> . . . He declined the nomination for the Legislature and has held no office save that of Secretary of the Hamilton County Executive Committee, but his influence is great. He has the respect and confidence of every Republican, white or black, in the county, and his advice is asked in all their counsels. He has refused rather than sought office.

The Freeman concluded:

> . . . Should the incoming administration desire to honor the younger element of the Republican Party South, we in the Third Congressional District of Tennessee (which largely by intelligent efforts of him, and such as he, has recently been wrested from the Democrats) present to their consideration the name of Edwin F. Horn.

By 1889 Edwin and Cora were the parents of their first son, Errol Stanley Horn. There is a photograph of Cora and baby Errol, in christening robes. Cora wears mourning for her father, Moses, who had recently died, and small steel-rimmed spectacles. The bluestocking girl had become a serious young mother. Edwin was by now looking beyond Tennessee—for a chance to make a national name. He almost made it. Four years earlier he had been an alternate delegate from Indiana for Benjamin Harrison. In 1888, in Tennessee, he lost out as a delegate but mustered the state's black vote for Harrison through speeches and through his newspaper. Now he looked for a political reward in one of the black patronage plums.

Judging from reports in the contemporary press, if Tennessee and Indiana (both white and black) had anything to say about it, Edwin F. Horn was going to be the next recorder of deeds of the District of Columbia. (Frederick Douglass had been the first black recorder of deeds, and since the Civil War the Republican Party had used the job to reward black Southern Republicans.)

True to the ways of politics, however, Edwin was passed over. Benjamin Harrison selected a man of greater age and reputation, a safe Republican choice: ex-Senator Blanche K. Bruce of Mississippi.

Edwin's year of near political glory ended on a trip to Washington, where at a convention of the National Editorial Association of Negroes he finally shook the hand of his hero, Frederick Douglass.

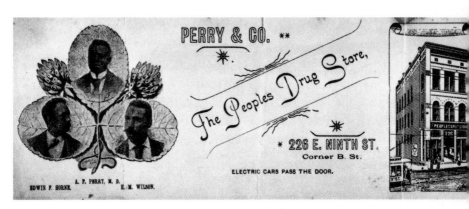

A newspaper advertisement for the Chattanooga drug store in which Edwin Horn was a partner

*Edwin (left) and friends, photographed in a middle-class
black neighborhood in Chattanooga, c. 1888*

Edwin (standing) with his business partner H. M. Wilson

■ ■ ■

The 1890 census reported that 57 percent of the black population worked in agriculture, fishing, or mining; 31 percent worked in domestic and personal service; 6 percent in manufacturing; 5 percent in trade and transportation; and 1 percent in the professions.

Between 1882 and 1894 more than 1,700 blacks were lynched in the South. Northern migration intensified. (The census of 1890 showed that the black population of Chicago had doubled in ten years—from 7,400 in 1880 to 14,800 in 1890.) Jim Crow was now king of the South. Schools, churches, hospitals, orphanages, funeral homes, morgues, asylums, cemeteries, parks, playgrounds, and public transportation were all strictly segregated. Mobile, Alabama, required all blacks to be off the streets by 10 p.m., and Birmingham law forbade blacks and whites to play checkers together. "Grandfather clauses" and poll taxes kept blacks away from the ballot. South Carolina politician "Pitchfork" Ben Tillman expressed the Southern attitude toward black voters:

> We have done our level best; we have scratched our heads to find
> out how we could eliminate the last one of them. We stuffed ballot
> boxes. We shot them. We are not ashamed of it.

The years 1890 to 1896 would be Cora and Edwin's final years in the South. Despite the death of political hopes, and the intense hostility of the political climate, Edwin's paper prospered (and his partnership in "The People's Drug Store" continued lucrative). In January 1893 he purchased ten twenty-five-dollar shares in the Penny Savings Bank of Chattanooga. Six months later my grandfather—Edwin Fletcher Horn, Jr., the second son—was born, and called Teddy.

The nineteenth century was dying—and with it, the hopes of the black South. In 1895 Frederick Douglass, the living symbol of black American history, died. The mystical promise of Reconstruction expired with him. In the same year Booker T. Washington, archenemy of the black bourgeois establishment, made his famous "Atlanta Compromise" speech at the Cotton States Exposition. This speech established the tone of black leadership for the next twenty years. Washington urged Southern blacks to give up all hope of political or social equality, and he advocated education only for the purpose of earning a living. He was not entirely cynical; he hoped, in exchange, for an end to lynchings and murder. Yet the first decade of the new century saw an appalling resurgence of violence—more than one thousand lynchings. But Washington and the Tuskegee Institute flourished, George Washington Carver and all. Theodore Roosevelt and William Howard Taft both consulted Booker T. Washington on all black political appointments. In 1896, with *Plessy* vs. *Ferguson,* the Supreme Court entrenched segregation—and the ideals of the "Atlanta Compromise." Edwin and Cora decided that it was time to emigrate North. They would move to New York.

C H A P T E R · 3

THE HORNES

New York's blacks originally lived in Greenwich Village, moving uptown as the Village became "gentrified." In 1896 New York City's entire black population (some 200,000) lived west of Seventh Avenue, between Sixteenth and Sixty-fifth streets. This area was called the "Tenderloin," and it was a racial powder keg. In the late 1890s much of the black population had been uprooted by the construction of Pennsylvania Station. Now blacks, Irish, and newer-arriving immigrants were fighting for the West Sixties. (Blacks won. The West Sixties came to be known as "San Juan Hill"—after the battle that Teddy Roosevelt won with the help of black cavalry.) This was Cora and Edwin's first Northern home.

The heart of the Tenderloin was Eighth Avenue in the Twenties, near the Grand Opera House, where "Cole and Johnson's Colored Speciality Company" and "Black Patti's Troubadors" appeared. The Little Savoy was a West Twenties cabaret where Edwin might have seen James P. Johnson, Willie "the Lion" Smith, "Jelly Roll" Morton, or Scott Joplin himself.

The West Fifties, where Cora and Edwin settled briefly, were known as "Black Bohemia"—the best part of the Tenderloin. West Fifty-third

Street's Marshall Hotel was the center of black literary and artistic life; sophisticated white couples, such as Diamond Jim Brady and Lillian Russell or Florenz Ziegfeld and Anna Held, liked to dine there. The Marshall was across the street from Jim Europe's Clef Club—a musician's club, labor exchange, and concert hall. Jim Europe's Clef Club Orchestra invented the "big band" sound (later copied by white conductor Paul Whiteman), and his orchestra ("James Reese Europe's Society Orchestra") toured with Vernon and Irene Castle and recorded all of their dance hits—turkey trot, fox trot, etc.—most of which he composed. And Jim Europe's Clef Club orchestra gave Carnegie Hall its first jazz concert.

The West Fifties were home, more or less, to poet James Weldon Johnson, novelist Charles Chestnutt, performer Bert Williams, and "cakewalk" king Paul Laurence Dunbar. The "cakewalk" was the first ragtime dance mania. The best "steppers" won a cake ("that takes the cake"). Dunbar was actually a talented poet, but he made his money on Broadway with one cakewalk hit after another. Ragtime belonged as much to urban liberated blacks as spirituals belonged to slaves.

Despite the proximity of bright lights and "culture" to their new West Fifties home, Cora and Edwin were eager to move. They had two small sons, Errol and Teddy, and the Tenderloin was a raw, dangerous place. The Horns hoped to find their dream house in Brooklyn, where there were fewer than 20,000 blacks.

By the time Edwin and Cora arrived, Brooklyn had only recently transformed itself from farmland into a brownstoned borough of high 1880s solidity. Brooklyn, circa 1897, was like an agreeable, good-sized town. There were broad skies, wide avenues, luxuriant parks, and acres of rolling cemeteries. The Horns found their new dream house on Chauncey Street, around the corner from bustling Bushwick Avenue. Bushwick Avenue was the epitome of modern Brooklyn and thoroughly pleased with itself. Within walking distance, on Nostrand Avenue, between Macon and Halsey streets, stood the new Girls High School, a magnificent example of 1880s pomposity. It was an ornate brownstone and brick behemoth, taking up a full square block. Behind the school was a small park with patterned flower beds and sheltering elms. Directly across the avenue stood an enormous mock-Moorish apartment building, also of brownstone and brick, with an inner courtyard.

In the street behind the apartment building stood 189 Chauncey Street, first in a row of four brownstones. Each house had a low wrought-iron gate, high front steps, and a sizable back garden. The Horn garden had a cherry

tree. The row houses stood on the "right" side of Chauncey Street. The
"wrong" side consisted of two-story wooden tenements, mostly inhabited by
poor Irish. The brownstones were bordered on one side by a large livery
stable (later a garage) owned by a family of Swedes with fiercely barking
dogs. On the other side, next to 189, was a white wooden farmhouse,
belonging to a relatively prosperous Irish family, that had a flower-filled
front garden and chickens in the back. A neighborhood youth center stood
at the corner of the street, next to the farmhouse. It was a small brownstone
building with a classic façade and the words "Boys Welcome Hall" carved
above the pillars.

In Cora's opinion the row house neighbors and the Irish farmers were
acceptable, but the Swedes were too grimy and the tenement Irish too rough
to be her children's playmates. The Horn boys found their real circle of
friends among the rest of Brooklyn's black bourgeoisie. (In the 1980s Girls
High School, the mock-Moorish apartment house, Boys Welcome Hall, and
all four brownstones were still intact. Late-Victorian architecture was designed to endure. Brooklyn's rural roots were hardy, too—both the livery
stable and the farmhouse survived. Only the "wrong" side of Chauncey
Street had changed. The firetrap wooden tenements had been replaced by
a cement and brick apartment project.)

Edwin taught for three years in New York City public schools. But
when a white teacher with less seniority was promoted over him, Edwin
sued the city—and won. The job, however, was not restored. In 1897
Edwin, who had then only recently changed his party affiliation and become
a Democrat, accepted a job as secretary general of the United Colored
Democracy, a voters' lobbying group that sought to draw blacks away from
the Republican Party. (The founder of the United Colored Democracy was
T. Thomas Fortune, a leading black journalist who in 1896 had become
publisher of the New York *Age,* one of the most influential black papers in
the country.) It was at this time that Edwin began to spell his name
"Horne," with an *e.* Perhaps he felt that the move North, as well as the
new party allegiance, merited some outward symbol of change.

Because of his lawsuit Edwin found himself in a problematical position
with the Board of Education. Thanks to his new political connections,
however, he would not go jobless. Edwin did excellent service in steering
blacks away from the Republicans, and Tammany always came to the aid of
its men. Black Tammany belonged to Ferdinand Q. Morton (of Exeter and
Harvard), a UCD co-founder and municipal office holder—one of the first

New York blacks to be so rewarded by the party. Edwin, with his friends Morton and Fortune, became an active and well-rewarded Tammany man.

On August 11, 1899, Edwin was appointed an assistant inspector in the Combustible Division (proto–bomb squad) of the New York Fire Department in Brooklyn. This was a monumental job for a black man at the time, bespeaking considerable political patronage. Edwin had no background or experience in fire inspecting, but Tammany's ways were sometimes mysterious. Edwin had been a big fish in the South and Midwest—but New York City was the ocean. He realized that teaching and writing did not pay black men in the big city—and Tammany did.

Cora was changing, too. She remained a Republican, however, though as yet voteless. Intellectual and free-spirited, she was becoming a "new woman": a founding membership in the National Association of Colored Women was a first step. But feminism still took second place to motherhood and the travails of childbirth. Cora's third son, Frank Smith Horne (named for his Aunt Lena's husband), was born in August 1899—the same week that Edwin entered the Fire Department—and Cora wrote a "deathbed" letter:

My Edwin:

The enclosed letter was written some days ago. Today I feel
that the hour of my trial is near. There is not anything to add.
Remember all I've asked. Be patient and long suffering with
our children. Remember I do not want Ma or Alice to have our
children. It is not a prejudice but the knowledge that it would unfit
them for this life or the world to come. I have tried to be nice to
them and have borne much but they cannot change their natures.

Again—my darling—let me love you and bless you and tell you
how happy—how very happy—I have been with you. My earliest
prayer is that we may have many long, happy years to-gether. I
love you. Remember this always, I love you and bless you.

Your loving wife, Cora.

"Ma" and "Alice," Edwin's mother and sister, were living in the South, and Cora clearly did not want her children raised as Southerners. But the question of guardianship remained moot, for Cora recovered, and little Frank Smith Horne thrived.

The baby's uncle and namesake was by now a prosperous doctor in

Nashville, and the beautiful Lena, grown to stately matronhood, was a high
school principal. They had two surviving children: Edwina, named for her
Uncle Edwin, and Frank Smith, Jr. With the new century the Smiths
moved to Chicago.

In 1900 Booker T. Washington published *Up from Slavery* and founded
the National Negro Business League. In the same year Cora and Lena's
friend W. E. B. (a.k.a. "Willie") Du Bois attended the London Conference
of African and New World Intellectuals and wrote that the "problem of the
20th century is the problem of the color line. . . ." The lone black congressman (from North Carolina) introduced an anti-lynching bill, which died in
committee—even though a bill to prevent the lynching of foreign nationals
had already been introduced that same year. One hundred and five blacks
were lynched, and in August New York City had a race riot. Also that year
James Weldon Johnson composed what came to be known as the Negro
National Anthem, "Lift Ev'ry Voice and Sing":

> *. . . Sing a song full of the faith that the dark past has taught us,*
> *Sing a song full of the hope that the present has brought us. . . .*
> *Let us march on till victory is won.*

Four years later—on May 1, 1904—Cora received the sacrament of
confirmation, from Archbishop Farley, at St. Benedict the Moor's Roman
Catholic Church in the Tenderloin. Cora's Creole mother had seen her
children baptized Catholics, but black Sunday worship in Atlanta had been
decidedly Congregational. St. Benedict the Moor was the parish of New
York City's black Catholics. It had moved up to the Tenderloin from Greenwich Village in 1896, the year that Cora and Edwin arrived in New York.
St. Benedict's was North America's first "civil rights" Catholic church,
calling attention to black issues and racial prejudice. Cora's reasons
for confirmation remain unrecorded, but it is clear that the occasion was
important to her. The priest who instructed her was an Irishman,
Father John Burke. A year later Cora named her fourth son John Burke
Horne.

In 1904 George C. Poag, of Milwaukee, won two bronze medals in track
and field at the St. Louis Olympics—he was the first black American to
enter the Games. Black America was thrilled, and in 1905 the Brooklyn
bourgeoisie founded the Smart Set Athletic Club, with the Hornes among
the original members. (A year earlier in Philadelphia, the first black Greek-
letter fraternity was organized to bring together "an aristocracy of talent.")

*Lena Calhoun Smith (right) with her husband, Dr. Frank Smith, their daughter,
Edwina, and son, Frank, Jr., in Nashville, Tennessee, c. 1900 (More than forty
years later cousin Edwina moved to California with my mother and me.)*

The Smart Set was to grow into one of the most important organizations in
the whole bourgeois network, uniting all generations, but in Edwin and
Cora's day the club was small and not terribly "social." It concentrated on
wholesome family-oriented get-togethers—and it definitely stressed sports.
The Olympic fallout had been intense. The older boys, Errol and Teddy,
developed and indulged a passionate interest in two late-nineteenth-century
sports inventions: the bicycle and basketball.

The three oldest Horne brothers were closest. There was more than a
decade between Teddy and young John Burke, who was called simply
"Burke." Teddy was considered the "handsomest," with his coppery skin
and sleek grace. Errol was thought the most "charming." Frank, who em-
ulated the great George Poag and became a runner, was considered the
"smartest" Horne brother. On June 30, 1907, Errol and Teddy both graduated from St. Vincent Ferrer High School. The only brown faces in a
sea of Irish freckles, they looked like young rajahs. Teddy Horne had
already discovered the power of wealth. He had a secret job after school—
as a page at the Astor Hotel—and was able to pay his brothers to do his
chores.

Teddy Horne wore "the Horne thing" like a snappy fedora. He could
charm the birds off any tree, and his sense of self was second to none.
Excepting his father and his two closest brothers, he considered no
man even his equal. Teddy was the only Horne black sheep, but being
a bad penny was not entirely his fault. He was partly a "victim" of his
times.

Teddy was a rip-roaring young man in the "Roaring" 1920s. In terms of
"generation gap" and social upheaval, the 1920s were comparable to the
1960s, but with less redeeming social value. Post–Great War young people
(known as "flaming youth") faced down Victorian fathers and mothers—
and, like their 1960s counterparts, were thought to be corrupted by illegal
substances (alcohol, not drugs), barbaric music (jazz, not rock and roll),
and sexual liberation. Teddy Horne, unlike his brothers, always rejected
the family "mantles" of service and achievement and thumbed his nose at
gentility. He believed that fun was more important than middle-class morality, and that money was *much* more important than a good name. Unfortunately, he became seriously committed to the pursuit of "the good life"
shortly after marriage and the birth of his only child. Both wife and child
suffered the results of his selfishness. But Teddy was so deliciously charming, so generous with his somewhat ill-gotten gains, that most people forgave his flaws. Such did Teddy's expansive pursuit of "pleasure" gain

mythic proportions in the eyes of old Brooklyn that he was generally known as "the fabulous Teddy Horne."

∎ ∎ ∎

Teddy's wife, Edna Louise Scottron, was also Brooklyn-born. The Scottrons were among the rare old black Brooklynites with a social edge on the Hornes. They were not particularly known for their charm or good looks; the Scottron edge of superiority was more tangible. They were richer. They were more Republican. They were more Episcopalian. And they had lived longer in what was called Stuyvesant Heights—they were among the first fifty black families to settle in that part of Long Island.

Edna's grandfather, Samuel Scottron, was a pillar of the black community—a successful merchant, a member of the Brooklyn Board of Education, and one of the borough's prominent "colored Republicans." He worshipped at both St. Philip's (in Manhattan) and St. Augustine's (in Brooklyn), two bastions of elite black Episcopalianism. He was also a thirty-third-degree Mason, belonging to a temple founded in pre-Revolutionary Boston.

The Scottrons were Yankee to their marrow—in Horne eyes, perhaps, an explanation in itself for their charmlessness. Samuel and his forebears came from Springfield, Massachusetts. His antecedents were probably West Indian–born Gold Coast Africans and the poorest of the British emigrants—indentured servants, seamen, small farmers, and artisans. They were also native Americans, probably from the Pequot tribe of the Algonquian family, original inhabitants of eastern Massachusetts.

Samuel Scottron was not only born free in New England, he was an ex-Union soldier from a storied black Massachusetts regiment. With peace, he migrated to New York and became a salesman for an import-export glass company, traveling between New York and Canada. On one of those trips he met his native American bride, Anna Maria Willet, born in Peekskill, New York, in 1844. The Willets, like the Scottrons, were members of an Algonquian family tribe. The young couple, with so much in common, settled down to married life in New York City, where Samuel managed not only to travel for the glass business, but to go to night school as well. Night school was free at Cooper Union (feisty old radical Peter Cooper's contribution to public education). Samuel graduated in May of 1875, with a degree of Superior Ability in Algebra. At a time when many Civil War veterans were begging in the city's streets, Samuel put his hand to inventing.

*My grandfather, Teddy Horne,
at age four, in 1898,
on his way to Public
School 54 in Manhattan*

Errol and Teddy Horne

Anna Maria Willet Scottron,
one of my two Native American
great-great-grandmothers

Louise Ashton Scottron,
my great-grandmother, who was
raised by her French-speaking
African grandmother

By 1888—when Samuel and Anna Maria bought their tall, narrow brownstone on the corner of Brooklyn's Stuyvesant Avenue and Monroe Street—Samuel was the owner of several registered patents. The one that made him rich was a "leather hand strap device" for trolley car passengers. Samuel also owned a prosperous Brooklyn furniture store that specialized in more of his own patented devices ("adjustible cornices, window cornices, pole tips, curtain rods and supporting brackets"). The Scottrons had three daughters and three sons, of whom Cyrus, the youngest, was Edna's father.

Samuel Scottron died in 1905, leaving his two sons Oscar and Cyrus comfortably settled in Brooklyn, with politically plum *Republican* jobs. Oscar worked in the Customs House; he also collected first editions. Cyrus was the first black railway postal clerk in New York, and little Edna learned to read from her father's railroad timetables. Cy had married a Brooklyn schoolteacher named Louise Ashton. The orphaned Louise and her sister had been brought up by their Haitian- or African-born, French-speaking grandmother, who had emigrated to America from France in the 1850s.

In 1908 young Edna Scottron, third-generation Brooklynite, was a member—together with her best friend, Kitty Holbrook, and the rest of black Brooklyn's "best" girls—of the "Sinceritas" Club. Kitty's brother, Frank Holbrook, and Edna's cousin, Charles Scottron, were two of Teddy Horne's best friends. Frank Holbrook kept a diary, from September 1909 to February 1910, that gives a cheerily explicit picture of that long-ago middle-class existence.

In September 1909 Frank Holbrook was eighteen years old and an apprentice draftsman in a downtown Brooklyn firm. The Holbrooks lived on Van Buren Street, halfway between the Hornes and the Scottrons. Frank was a protégé of Lewis Latimer, a Horne family friend and "Edison pioneer." Latimer executed the drawings for Alexander Graham Bell's telephone and assisted in the preparation of its patent applications. He was one of America's early electricians, and patented a method of making carbon incandescent lamp filaments. He was the only black "Edison pioneer." Some of the richest black men in Brooklyn were early Consolidated Edison maintenance men who bought stock in the company.

Frank was seriously job-hunting. He answered "2 want-ads in the N.Y. *Herald*," and vowed to "spend at least one-half hour each night on math." He was helped by Lewis Latimer: "Get a 'special' from Mr. Latimer to bring my drawings to meet a man."

Between September and Christmas of 1909 Frank also led an active social life. He attended a Booker T. Washington lecture ("good"). He watched the naval parade on Riverside Drive (America's Great White Fleet, battleships painted white, had circumnavigated the globe from 1907 to 1909) and pronounced it exhausting. The second day of the naval parade was the occasion of Frank's, and probably Teddy Horne's, first experience of overt racial prejudice:

> 9/30/09: Left office 1 PM met Ted [Horne] & Bobby at Bridge. Subway to 65th Street. Terrific jam all way along Fifth Ave. Stand on boxes to see parade. Parade fine. Leave and try to get something to eat. Refused for first time.

He also followed the Wright brothers: "Another postponement of aeroplane flight on account of rain." He went to the Electricity Show at Madison Square Garden ("fine"). And he went to hear Madame Schumann-Heink ("fine voice"). He also enjoyed other less baleful "firsts":

> 10/8/09: First Columbus Day holiday. Same as ever. Measure 6 feet 1 and ½ inches.

> 12/12/09: Go to chop suey joint for first time.

And Frank—as well as the Horne brothers—enjoyed the wholesome pleasures of the Brooklyn "crowd":

> —Elsie Downing's party. Had fine time. About 40 people there.
> —Ted, Fred & self see fine vaudeville show Fulton Theatre. Pool.
> —Met Robt. L. made arrangement to go to moving picture show next day.
> —To Hornes, P.M. Edna S. [Scottron] and Edna R. Fine time at Hornes.
> —Whole bunch stopped in Von Essen's for soda.
> —Boxed in back yard. [In 1908 Jack Johnson had knocked out Tommy Burns to become the first black heavyweight champion.]
> —Ted and Errol [Horne] play 7½ for toothpicks.
> —Crowd over. Club meeting. Crowd buys buns.
> —Eat ice cream.
> —Smart Set party. Bunch of girls here. Pretty good time. Take Ethel Harding home.
> —Upsilon Sigma party. Hardings go with us. Meet Errol Horne.

*Frank Holbrook, whose diary
is a wonderful record of
black middle-class life
in Brooklyn, c. 1909*

*Charlie Scottron,
my grandmother's cousin and a
friend of the Horne brothers*

Kitty Holbrook and Edna Scottron (my grandmother) as they appear in a scrapbook on a page devoted to members of the "Sinceritas" Club

Frank Holbrook, Charlie Scottron, Kitty Holbrook (seated, right), and a friend on a visit to Coney Island, c. 1912

Fine time. Stand on corner Fulton and Reid til half frozen. Hardings stay all night. Ted drops by. Hot cocoa. Bed 3:30 A.M.
—Go through Hudson Tunnel for basketball game in Jersey City.
—Dance at Hall. Tableaux good. "Acc" [Eugene Accooe] busted up minuet by falling pantaloons. Rest of dance fine. Fine time. 3 AM.

Frank Holbrook's "crowd" included the Horne brothers and the Scottron cousins—who were also Accooes and Wallers. The Wallers were special Scottron cousins in Cora Horne's eyes. Cora's best friend was Mrs. Cyril Waller, whose son married Florence Scottron. Mrs. Waller came from a black New York family with pre-Revolutionary roots. Dr. Cyril Waller was one of seven brothers, five of whom lived as white. The Wallers were very "upper" members of the black bourgeoisie. Of the five "white" Waller brothers, one was a university professor, one an Episcopal priest, and another a vice-president of Kodak. Another Waller spent his winters in Harlem as black and his summers in upstate New York as white. When Florence Scottron Waller's daughter went to visit them, the child was made to stay indoors all day: she was a little too brown.

■ ■ ■

Edwin dipped his feet in ocean-sized politics for the first time in 1910. He ran for the City Council on the Tammany ticket, and lost. It was the time of the "Black Peril" scare in New York. Blacks were barred from midtown restaurants and theaters, and black actors were forbidden to perform on Broadway. (Only Bert Williams, the superstar of the *Ziegfeld Follies*, escaped the ban. A pale mulatto from the Danish West Indies with an engineering degree, Williams in fact had to "black up" to meet the stereotype.) In 1910 Edwin's party could now stir up genuine black anti-Republicanism. Thanks to the United Colored Democracy, nearly 50,000 blacks bolted the party of Lincoln and Douglass, and a Democrat, John A. Dix, was elected governor of New York. The United Colored Democracy produced pamphlets and leaflets for the black voter. Edwin wrote many of them—such as "What Do We Want?":

Some Negroes would vote for the Republican party even if the party put them back into slavery. . . . [We want] colored policemen, colored firemen, garbage removed from our streets before noon, crooks driven out of the tenements, work for our boys, protection for our girls . . . civil rights as citizens in theatres and restaurants . . . a colored regiment in the National Guard.

Edwin's group won at least two of their demands. In 1911 Harlem got its first black police officer, the celebrated Samuel Battles. And "Harlem's Own" 369th National Guard Regiment was born.

Middle-class blacks were entering a stage of new militancy. Two years before the 1910 election there had been a race riot in Springfield, Illinois, in which—among others—an eighty-four-year-old black man was lynched. Oswald Garrison Villard (grandson of abolitionist William Lloyd Garrison) spoke out against the riot in his newspaper, the New York *Post.* Villard called for a "Committee for the Advancement of the Human Race." Some well-known black, but mostly white, reformers answered the call, and the National Association for the Advancement of Colored People was born. W. E. B. Du Bois, the only black officer, became editor of the official NAACP magazine, *Crisis.*

> The National Association for the Advancement of Colored People . . . represented a cooperative effort on the part of the so-called "militant" Negroes, who were opposed to the program of Booker T. Washington, and distinguished white leaders of public opinion who were opposed to the segregation and disfranchisement of the Negro. . . . Negroes who became identified with the National Association for the Advancement of Colored People were known as "radical." . . .
> —E. Franklin Frazier, *Black Bourgeoisie*

Cora and Edwin were early NAACP members.

The years 1912 to 1916 were among black America's darkest—mostly because of Woodrow Wilson, the first Southern Democrat to become President since Zachary Taylor. Wilson sent Washington, D.C., back to pre–Civil War days. His administration saw the greatest onslaught of anti-black legislation ever presented in Congress—including the exclusion of blacks from Army and Navy commissions, the segregation of black and white federal workers, and the exclusion of all black immigration. Wilson himself, by executive order, segregated all eating and restroom facilities for federal employees. He next abolished all "black" jobs. (The recorder of deeds and the ministries to Haiti and Santo Domingo became "white" jobs.) In 1913

Oswald Garrison Villard asked Wilson to appoint a National Race Commission to examine the fact that more than one thousand blacks had been lynched since 1900, but Wilson refused. Wilson had also refused, while president of Princeton, to consider the admission of Princeton-born Paul Robeson to the university. Cora Horne helped Paul apply for the scholarship he won to Rutgers.

Throughout this dark first quarter of the new century, Brooklyn's black bourgeoisie remained in relatively idyllic isolation. The men might suffer a little, but they were used to it, and their bourgeois wives and children were mostly protected from the stormy weather of American racism. Smart Set summer meetings in Flushing brought out the crowd—with Hornes, Scottrons, and Holbrooks very much in evidence. And the entire Northeast flocked to Brooklyn's merry winter parties.

The "splendid" isolation of the black bourgeoisie was actually captured on film. Oscar Michaux Productions was founded in New York City in 1914. Michaux was the first, and possibly only, black producer of black feature films. While Hollywood was turning out such classics as *Rastus in Zululand* and *Coontown Suffragettes* (not to mention *Tony the Greaser* and *The Chink at Golden Gulch*), Michaux produced well-made dramas for black audiences—always featuring light-skinned actors and "bourgeois" plots. Thomas Edison had filmed real black people in 1898: soldiers in the Philippines, happy mothers and children, and fabulous "cakewalkers." But commercial Hollywood had no interest in reality.

In the spring of 1915 D. W. Griffith's *The Birth of a Nation* was released. The movie was based on *The Clansman*, a novel about the life of Nathan B. Forrest, former slave-trader and Confederate Army general, who founded the Ku Klux Klan. (Forrest became notorious for the 1864 massacre of black Union troops holding Fort Pillow, Tennessee, *after* they had surrendered.) The movie portrayed Reconstruction as a racist nightmare. The author of the novel, Thomas Dixon, a good friend of President Wilson, wrote:

My object is to teach the north, the young north, what it has never known—the awful suffering of the white man during the dreadful reconstruction period. I believe that Almighty God anointed the white men of the south by their suffering during that time . . . to demonstrate to the world that the white man must and shall be supreme.

The film was praised and damned; even the governor of Alabama called it a "nightmare." The NAACP launched a nationwide campaign to stop the film's release, fearing it would be an incitement to riot. The National Board of Review was impressed enough to withhold its seal of approval until cuts were made and a "disclaimer" added:

> This is an historical representation of the Civil War and Reconstruction Period, and is not meant to reflect on any race or people of today.

In New York City a distinguished interracial group—including Du Bois, Rabbi Stephen Wise, and Oswald Garrison Villard—staged a sit-in at the mayor's office to protest the film. By 1918 the NAACP was successful in banning the film in several states.

■ ■ ■

Cora continued to come into her own in her new Northern home. Throughout 1913—while her sons played and partied—Cora was busy organizing and directing a YWCA Red Cross unit, and she was later appointed to the mayor's "Victory Committee" for her efforts. By 1918 she was a woman of many missions—the most important, the vote. The boys had grown up. Errol and Teddy were starting families of their own. Frank had just graduated from Boys High School, and Burke was about to enter it. They did not need a hovering mother, not that she ever really hovered—Cora had been bored with child-raising by the birth of her fourth son. Now she was free to follow her star, or so she thought.

Errol had been first to go. The 1915 sinking of the *Lusitania* made America war-mad. Errol enlisted in the Texas-based, all-black 10th Cavalry —the heroes of San Juan Hill. He was strong, athletic, and in love with the great outdoors; the army seemed a perfect career. He had his first taste of adventure in March 1916, when Pancho Villa, hero of the 1910 Mexican Revolution, invaded the American town of Columbus, New Mexico, and killed seventeen people. An all-black punitive force, under the leadership of "Black Jack" Pershing, was sent to capture the villain, but they chased Villa through Mexico for nearly a year without even a glimpse of him.

Back in Texas, young Sergeant Horne found a bride. There is a photograph of Errol in uniform, soon after the Mexican adventure, with his very pretty wife, Lotte, who looks as if she herself might be Mexican. Lotte is a

Gibson girl, from her middy shirtwaist to the fat ribbon on her long braid
of hair. Her walrus-mustached father looks like a real black cowboy—even
like Pancho Villa himself—in his gigantic sombrero. When Errol brought
Lotte home to Brooklyn, they were the couple of the hour, with her sweet
face, his handsome uniform, and their newly wedded bliss. Errol and Lotte
—as well as the war—made young Brooklyn marriage-minded.

Teddy Horne and Edna Scottron were an ideal couple on paper. It
should have been the happy ending of another Brooklyn fairy tale. But they
were both third-generation ne'er-do-wells. She was spoiled and badly educated—and he was fickle. Teddy could never bear any sort of shackle. He
had enjoyed a carefree bachelor life: fun, innocent gambling, parties, and
basketball—with a small clerical job provided by Tammany largesse. Young
women were often part of the game plan—but rarely the same young
woman twice. Teddy Horne spread his youth and radiant charm throughout
the bourgeois network. Although he loved money, Teddy always hated
work. As a second-generation Tammany man, he had ways of finding out
about easy money. And Edna was a black "princess." She read movie magazines. She was a fantasist. A freckled, green-eyed minx, Edna had known
Teddy Horne all her life. As soon as she was old enough to decide such
things she was bound and determined to land him. He was, after all, the
best-looking boy in the crowd, and she was one of its reigning belles. This
was certainly reason enough for a wedding. The wedding must have been
wonderful—all those "Sinceritas" Club bridesmaids—but the marriage was
awful. Edna and Teddy moved in with Cora and Edwin. Edna had no doubt
imagined a rose-covered cottage—or at least her own brownstone row
house. But there she was, on Cora's top floor, having to endure her mother-
in-law's disapproving glance whenever she descended the stairs. Fortunately, Cora was rarely at home.

It was a decidedly compartmentalized household. The dining room and
kitchen, opening onto the garden, were on the ground floor. Here Edwin
would sit—in the kitchen or garden—to smoke his pipe, read his paper,
and listen to his phonograph records of Bert Williams and Caruso. Burke,
in and out of the house with club or athletic activities, did his homework in
the kitchen, while Frank—City College poet, track man, and scoutmaster
—was seldom at home. The first floor up was Cora's. The parlor was her
sitting room, and the library her bedroom. Edwin, Burke, and Frank had
rooms on the next floor, and the newlyweds moved into Teddy and Errol's
old quarters at the top.

When Cora was at home she could be found resting on her chaise

Sergeant Errol Horne, c. 1915

Edwin and Cora Horne's twenty-fifth wedding anniversary portrait, 1912

Cora (seated, center) with members of her YWCA Red Cross unit, c. 1914

longue, sipping tea, nibbling zwieback, and reading a novel or a pamphlet. Cora's energy was nervous and mercurial—she wished to spend little of it cooking or housekeeping. Edwin prepared meals for Burke and himself, and a woman came in once a week to do the laundry. Cora usually ate alone in her sitting room.

Something had happened to Edwin and Cora's marriage in the very early teens. Edwin was rumored to have had a love affair with a liberated white lady editor of *Vogue* magazine. He was publicly black, but privately he was pretty much whatever suited his convenience. He went everywhere that blacks did and did not go. He was handsome and distinguished-looking and cultivated an air of sophisticated detachment. At heart, however, he was still the sentimental Victorian—believing, with Goethe, that a line of verse, some good music, and a beautiful picture made every day richer.

At any rate, Edna's new home featured a mother-in-law who coolly enunciated, "Good morning, Mr. Horne," if she happened to encounter her husband as she emerged from her first floor bedroom and he descended from his on the second floor. "Good morning, Mrs. Horne," would be Edwin's politely mournful reply. Young Burke was entrusted with delivering family messages of the more lengthy sort.

In early 1917, while Edna was pregnant, Teddy—with the help of Black Tammany—got a proper paterfamilias job. He became the first black member of the Claims Division of the Industrial Commission of the New York State Department of Labor. (One of the commissioners was Frances Perkins, later first woman Cabinet member under Franklin D. Roosevelt.) Teddy, high-collared and dark-suited, was photographed with his colleagues, looking very pleased with himself. He labeled the pictures "Horne and his staff."

Edna and Teddy's daughter, Lena Mary Calhoun Horne, was born on June 30, 1917, at a small Jewish lying-in hospital. It was the summer of the NAACP Silent Protest Parade against lynching. In early July an East St. Louis race riot saw nearly forty blacks killed, hundreds burned out of their homes, and the NAACP defending ten blacks for murder. The parade took place on July 28. It was one of the most awesome events in black history. Ten thousand black men, women, and children marched down Fifth Avenue in total silence—the women and children wearing white, the men with black arm bands. The march was orchestrated and coordinated by the NAACP, but all the middle-class clubs and mainstream organizations participated. Baby Lena was less than a month old; her parents' marriage was still intact. Cora would not have missed that march for anything.

Edna Scottron Horne with her newborn daughter, Lena, my mother, in 1917

Teddy Horne (second from left) with members of his staff at the New York State Department of Labor, 1917

In 1918 young Lieutenant Errol Horne went to France. Like all black troops, he was attached to a French unit—the Wilson government would not permit American blacks and whites to fight under the same flag. But blacks were 11 percent of the American Expeditionary Forces. Four black regiments received the regimental Croix de Guerre from the French. They fought at Château-Thierry, Belleau Wood, Vosges, Metz, and Maison-en-Champagne. The first American soldiers cited for valor were two blacks from New York's 369th, the first Allied troops to reach the Rhine. But a secret American army communiqué advised the French "not to commend too highly black troops," and the American War Department insisted that black American soldiers not be depicted in the heroic frieze of France's Panthéon de la Guerre. Young Lieutenant Horne did not survive the war. He did not die in battle, but from that other 1918 enemy, influenza. After 1918 Cora wore only black, white, or gray.

One of the NAACP's "youngest members"—baby Lena Horne—as she appeared in the October 1919 issue of the association's Branch Bulletin

THE HORNE BROTHERS

Baby Lena Horne was already an NAACP cover girl at the age of two and a half. She starred in the October 1919 issue of the NAACP *Branch Bulletin:*

> This is a picture of one of the youngest members of the NAACP. Her name is Lena Calhoun Horne and she lives in Brooklyn, N.Y. She paid the office a visit last month and seemed delighted with everything she saw, particularly the National Secretary and the telephones.

The national secretary was then James Weldon Johnson, the poet and author of 1912's revolutionary black novel *The Autobiography of an Ex-Colored Man.* The NAACP spoke out against lynching, mob violence, and black second-class citizenship. *Crisis,* edited by W. E. B. Du Bois, lay next to the Bible in most middle-class black homes; in 1919 it sold 100,000 copies a month. At that time New York had recently instituted America's first public accommodations civil rights law since 1875. But most black Americans remembered the summer of 1919 as Red Summer—red for blood. Between June and December 1919, seventy-six blacks were lynched and twenty-five race riots broke out. The Chicago riot lasted nearly five days.

No wonder baby Lena Horne looks serious as well as stolid in her NAACP photograph. She wears a white dress and high-topped boots and holds a rose in her sturdy little fist. She also wears a frown. She had reasons for being glum—even beyond the state of the world. Her father was about to go West. And her mother was about to go on the stage. They would soon be divorced.

Teddy Horne decamped from wife, child, and Chauncey Street in the summer of 1920. He told his bosses at the State Labor Commission that he had to go West for his health. Tuberculosis, a terrifying commonplace of the 1920s, was feared. (What he told Edna we will never know.) Teddy was actually never in better health. It was just that three years of family life had been enough. The Labor Commission office was on East Twenty-eighth Street, in Manhattan, and it was not easy to get home to Brooklyn early every evening for dinner with the little woman, who mostly sulked and complained anyway. From playing "7½" with toothpicks in 1910 to big games with big boys in 1919 was easy as pie with the Tammany connection. Teddy's new best friend was Bub Hewlett, Dutch Schultz's right-hand protection man in Harlem. Hewlett's middle-class family had no idea that he was in the rackets, but Brooklyn began whispering, in 1919 and 1920, that Teddy Horne was "up to something" in numbers and gambling. They also whispered that he "knew something" about the Black Sox baseball scandal, and that he had made a "killing." Teddy Horne may or may not have been in on the fix, but Brooklyn always believed that he was.

In late August 1920 Teddy took a Pullman from New York to Chicago. Three days later, in an upper berth of the Chicago, Milwaukee and St. Paul Railroad, he was on his way West. Just about the first thing he did in Seattle was have his picture taken, posing in a handsome new Stetson, with what appears to be a pearl or diamond stickpin in his tie. He must have felt very safe and far away.

Teddy Horne prospered in Seattle—at least, he spent money. And he met Irene, his second wife, a slightly older Seattle lady, of independent means. She was a divorcée and a far cry from Brooklyn's bourgeois feather-heads. She was also a shrewd woman, apparently never possessive or jealous. Teddy bought her some furs at G. E. Ahlquist Company ("Seattle's

*Teddy Horne and his
soon-to-be second wife,
Irene, in Seattle, 1921*

Expert Furrier—Specializing in Alaska Seal"), and they were photographed together in the spring of 1921: Irene wears a large fashionable hat, and Teddy holds a straw boater.

Little Lena, like her parents, was born to live, marry, and spend her life, if not in Brooklyn, at least in the crowd. But in the early 1920s Teddy and Edna were doing the unthinkable. Theirs was probably among the earlier black middle-class divorces. By the late 1920s black values had changed, of course, along with everyone else's, but divorce continued to be rare. Lena was always the only child of divorce among her Brooklyn friends (as later she would be the only divorcée). She always felt that she was an object of pity among the Brooklyn crowd—indeed, Lena's Brooklyn nickname would be "Salvation Sal." And she felt "crippled" by her parent's divorce, as if her condition were some sort of infirmity. But Teddy and Edna would see it another way. They belonged to the Jazz Age. (The year of Lena's birth, 1917, was the year that Scott Joplin died, the year that *The New York Times* first used the word "jazz.") Cora considered Edna and Teddy to be selfish "moderns." As far as she was concerned, little Lena was well rid of them both.

Lena now became Cora's last child—and her only daughter. Since Cora would not give up her newfound freedom to stay at home, little Lena became a fixture at Cora's meetings. And Lena's future was mapped out. She would be a teacher and a feminist. She learned early not to behave as a child:

"Don't sulk."

"Don't cry."

"Stand straight."

"Speak clearly."

"Sit still in public."

She learned to listen carefully when grown-ups were speaking—in case Cora questioned her later. Cora was still small, thin, and mercurial, but now her hair was streaked with gray, her mouth was thinner, and she removed her steel spectacles only at bedtime. She had always been vain about her feet, however, and still wore beautiful shoes.

In 1921 Cora, as a member of the Brooklyn Board of Directors of the Big Brother and Big Sister Federation, met President Harding in Washington. A group photograph taken at the meeting appeared in the Saturday Graphic section of the New York *Evening Post*. (Warren Harding, when questioned about his rumored black ancestry, said, "How do I know? Maybe one of my ancestors jumped the fence.") Cora now groomed Lena in the serious role of mini-activist. "When I take you to meetings, I want you to listen," said Cora. "When you speak, articulate clearly—don't use slang." Lena didn't know what "slang" meant. "Don't say 'ain't,' " said Cora. "Don't hunch your shoulders. Always look at the person you're talking to." Lena learned the rules and tried to obey them.

Parents of Cora's generation were not emotional with their children; the tone was Olympian aloofness. Cora never raised her voice to Lena, nor would she have dreamed of striking her. On the other hand, she never hugged or kissed. It was Edwin's laughter and cozy hugs that gave Lena some sense of family. Lena feared Cora's cool displeasure, but Edwin was never displeased with his granddaughter. Burke was fun, too—he and Edwin played games with Lena. Every night after prayers, in the little room off Cora's where she slept, Lena kissed a small picture of Edna and a larger one of Teddy. Lena knew she had parents, even though she no longer really remembered them, because presents would occasionally arrive from them. Edna sent dolls, and a sky-blue wool chinchilla coat (with brass buttons) that Lena adored. Teddy's presents were even more spectacular: a player piano, a real bunny fur coat, and a large red-haired "Effanbee" doll who "cried" when turned upside down. Lena adored the doll's bright blue eyes and tiny, perfect teeth. (Forty years later, a little the worse for wear but with "cry" intact, the doll was passed on to a grandchild.)

One momentous early evening when she was four or five, Lena realized that she could read. She was lying on the floor of Cora's sitting room looking at "Little Orphan Annie" when she spelled out the word "asylum." She did not know what it meant. "That's fine, Lena, tell me another word," came Cora's cool, floaty voice from the other room. Lena could tell she was pleased. And soon Lena was asked to read aloud short passages from books and memorize little poems. The first book that Lena remembers seeing Cora read was *The Forsyte Saga*. But all of Lena's favorite books would be about orphans.

Lena went to kindergarten at the Ethical Culture School, a private school in an old brownstone on South Oxford Street near Fort Greene Park. Cora had established an Ethical Culture scholarship in her name, with Lena as the recipient. (One of Lena's Ethical Culture schoolmates was Betty Comden, of Broadway's future Comden and Green.) School was mostly a matter of naps, plays, crayons, and cutouts. In a photograph of Lena's class in which the children appear to be wearing paper Epiphany crowns, Lena's is the only brown face. Except for kindergarten, and excursions to Cora's meetings, Lena's life essentially revolved around Edwin and Burke. Edwin got up first every morning, to light the furnace and make the

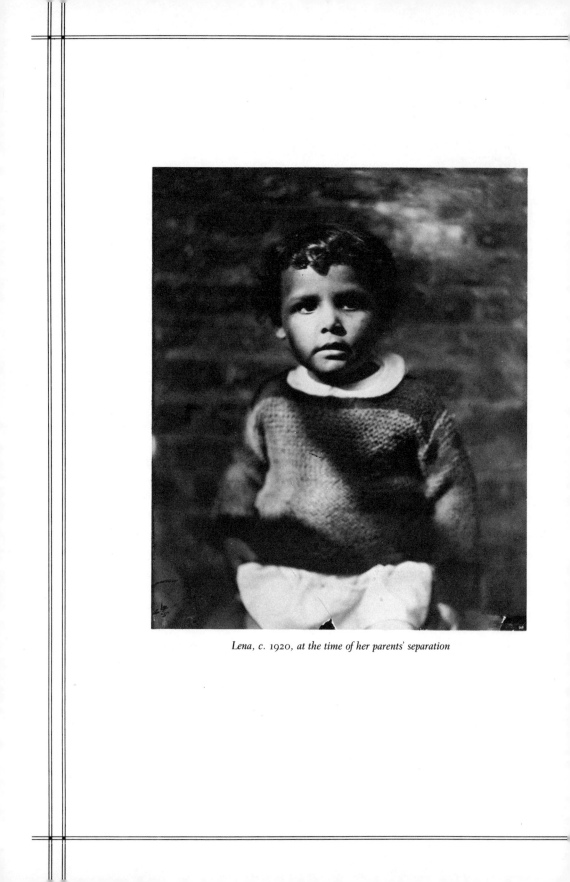

Lena, c. 1920, at the time of her parents' separation

A photograph from the New York <u>Evening Post</u> shows Cora (her head circled) and other members of the Big Brother and Big Sister Federation meeting President Warren G. Harding in Washington, 1921.

My great-great-aunt, Lena Calhoun Smith, holds her baby granddaughter, Isobel. Next to them in the back seat is cousin Edwina. The photograph, made in Nashville in 1921, is by Frank Smith, Jr. My grandmother Cora took my mother to visit the Smiths around this time.

oatmeal. Then Burke would take Lena to school and pick her up afterward. Lena was given a hot lunch at school. And every day, on the Chauncey Street kitchen table, there would be an apple and a Hershey bar—to be eaten, in good weather, under the cherry tree. Burke would make sure that Lena had a key on a string around her neck, and then he'd be off. In bad weather Lena read or played with her dolls. Her favorite game was dress-up, which she was permitted to play with Cora's old dresses from the 1880s and '90s, with strange sleeves, collars, and bustles. But most of all, Lena loved to play in Cora's bedroom. There were so many things to play with: the drawers in the Chinese chest, and the ivory dresser set, with boxes in all shapes and sizes. One afternoon Cora was in the parlor and Lena was in the bedroom playing with the ivory boxes. "What are you doing, Lena?" came Cora's voice from the other room. "I'm in the bedroom," said Lena. "When I ask you a question, Lena, don't volunteer information I already know—answer the question. What are you doing?" asked Cora once again. "I'm playing with the boxes," said Lena.

Sometimes she played with the grimy Swedish garage children, but she never crossed the street to play with the tenement Irish. Cora thought they did not "speak well." Lena generally passed her afternoons alone, reading or daydreaming; when Cora came home late in the day from her meetings, she always asked Lena what she had read. Lena never saw Cora in the kitchen. Edwin made the meals for Lena and Burke, but on Saturdays Edwin and Lena would walk to the delicatessen on Reid Avenue and bring home cold cuts, pickles, and sauerkraut. In the summer when the vegetable man's cart appeared, they would always buy fresh okra for Cora (a taste of her Georgia childhood). On Sunday mornings Lena and Burke went to mass at St. Peter Claver Church. Cora rarely attended mass now. She had thrown herself as wholeheartedly into Ethical Culture as she had once thrown herself into the Church. Still Cora received weekly reports from Lena on the state of her reading, her nails (Lena bit them), her clean clothes, and her Catholic prayers.

Once Cora and Lena were on the trolley, and Lena was pleading to have her hair bobbed—she had long hair that she wore either in pigtails or in Mary Pickford curls, which Cora wet and coiled around a toothbrush. Lena hated those curls, but Cora put bobbed hair in the same category as divorce. Lena decided to try to embarrass her grandmother into the bob by making a fuss, by *attracting attention* on the trolley car. "Please, please, Grandmother," Lena ardently whined, tugging at Cora's arm, "please let me get my hair bobbed." Lena knew that *attracting attention* was a major sin, but she also knew that Cora would never reprimand her in public. Cora simply stared stonily ahead. When they got home, however, Lena was sent to her room to say many Hail Marys.

Despite her unusual parents, little Lena was still very much a small cog in the inner workings of her larger social order. Brooklyn black society in the early 1920s was still familial and sedate. At Christmas, for example, the eastern black establishment all met at the Comus Ball, sponsored by what was probably the most exclusive club in the whole network. Being a Brooklyn club, the Comus was "exclusive" about family and color. (One of the big chiefs of the Comus was a bellhop at a downtown Brooklyn hotel— but his family came from Charleston, and, most important, he looked white.) The Comus Ball was held every year at the Brooklyn Academy of Music, and the elite of Boston, Philadelphia, Washington, and Harlem arrived in force. The big annual summer party was given by yet another Charlestonite Brooklyn club, the Coterie.

Every age and sex had a club: Jack and Jills, Junior Debs, Gay Northeasterners, Girl Friends, Maimars, Links, Rinky Dinks, Nonchalants, and the What Good Are We Club (a group of richer men, mostly doctors, who gave "wild" parties). By the mid-1920s the puritanical post-Reconstruction middle class had been replaced by modern black Americans. Along with equally prospering white counterparts, the black middle class discovered cocktails, polite adultery, automobiles, and summer resorts (Oak Bluffs on Martha's Vineyard, and Sag Harbor on Long Island). Some of the richer Brooklyn families went to Florida in the winter. And some boys went away to the few unsegregated schools—Exeter, Williston Academy, or the Quaker schools. For middle-class girls there was a YWCA camp called Fernwood, where the 1920s camp counselors included Yolande Du Bois (daughter of W.E.B.) and Harriet Pickens (daughter of William Pickens of the NAACP), who would become the first black WAVE.

Travel, of course, was the great middle-class activity. Cora took Lena to Chicago to visit her namesake, great-aunt Lena Calhoun Smith. Aunt Lena lived in a big stone house, had a funny little dog, and drove an electric car. Lena played with Aunt Lena's granddaughter Isobel, who was the daughter of Edwina Smith and her first husband, Andrew Johnson of Tennessee. Edwina was another black sheep divorcée, but in 1925 she married Dr. Malcolm King of Milwaukee and was welcomed back into the fold. Dr. King adopted Isobel. (But people always said that Edwina was really in love with her cousin, Teddy Horne.)

Brooklyn's black society in the 1920s consisted of a few dozen families who all lived near one another outside the black neighborhoods and had mostly always known one another. There were Johnstons on Halsey Street, Pollards (Frederick Douglass "Fritz" Pollard was a Walter Camp all-American the same year as Paul Robeson, and the first black professional football player) and Bournes on McDonough Street, Monteros on Macon Street, and Johnsons on President Street. There were Petersons, Pickens, Hoffmans (he was a stock-rich former Consolidated Ed maintenance man who gave a fabulous annual party with an orchestra and entertainment), Lawrences, Pogues, and Mickeys. By now the Hornes, Scottrons, Holbrooks, Wibbikins, Trotmans, and Wallers were considered the older set. Everybody (except for the few Catholics or Methodists) went to St. Augustine's Protestant Episcopal Church, whose rector, the Reverend George Frazier Miller (from Charleston) was a pillar of the black religious establishment.

Among the more interesting newcomers was William Pickens, field secretary of the NAACP. Pickens, who became a close Horne family friend, overcame skin color to join the inner circles of black society sheerly on merit. Pickens's skin was very black. He had no knowledge of his ancestry beyond his maternal grandmother (a former slave, crippled by beatings). And his parents were Arkansas sharecroppers—but they lived near Little Rock, and a good black school. Bill Pickens got up every morning at 4 a.m. to work a half day before school. And every day, after school, he went back to work. He graduated first in his class and won a scholarship to all-black Talladega College, and Talladega's white president helped Pickens win a four-year scholarship to Yale. In New Haven he received regular fifty-dollar checks from an unknown New York benefactor. He graduated with Phi Beta Kappa honors and a flood of national congratulations, becoming the most celebrated black college graduate since Flipper of West Point. He was offered a European-American lecture tour. On the advice of Paul Laurence Dunbar, he opted for academics. He became dean of Morgan State College and was invited to the NAACP's 1916 annual Amenia Conference, where he became a new NAACP force. The Amenia Conference, held at the upstate New York farm of wealthy white NAACP officer Joel Spingarn, was a study in elitism. The blacks all slept in tents. Only James Weldon Johnson was permitted to sleep in the main house. Pickens was field secretary for twenty-five years. The older Pickens children, Harriet and Bill, were close friends of the younger Horne brothers. And the youngest Pickens daughter would marry the youngest Holbrook son—a union of old and new Brooklyn.

In school, the children of middle-class families did not play with black children whom they did not know, though this was not strictly observed among the boys. The YMCA was in what was becoming an all-black neighborhood, and the boys were allowed to interact in sports. But the girls kept to themselves. One of Lena's best friends was Llewellyn Johnston. The Johnstons (Charlestonites) were rich, even by Brooklyn standards. They were second-generation owners of a family field-glasses company, with concessions at all the stadiums and race tracks. Llewellyn's brother was named Cohn Johnston, after his Jewish grandfather (who was Abraham Lincoln's tailor). Frank Horne was Cohn's scoutmaster at the YMCA. When Cohn first saw Frank, he thought that Frank was white, and indeed, Frank, with his gray eyes, did not look black. Frank was also scoutmaster to Frank Montero (whose sister would marry Cohn Johnston). The Monteros were from Virginia and claimed distant kinship to Nat Turner. Mrs. Montero grew up in Amherst, Virginia, where her grandfather blamed any of his children's misdeeds on his cousinship to Ol' Prophet Nat. Mrs. Montero was an assistant high school principal and one of Cora's younger friends, just as her son Frank Montero was a pal of Burke's. Marion Montero (Frank's sister) remembered when Burke brought Lena to the Montero house for the first time. Lena was six or seven, and Burke said, "Now dance, Lena!" Marion thought Lena was a wonderful dancer, but also thought she was too thin, and too somber by far. To Frank Montero, Lena was a skinny little kid who was all teeth and legs.

Lena's other best friend was Ruth Johnson, who lived on President Street, a broad, tree-lined, substantial Brooklyn avenue, a street of deep front gardens and leafy shade near Prospect Park. It was Ruth's mother who named Lena "Salvation Sal." During the Depression Mrs. Johnson worked in McCreery's as a "white" saleslady. Many middle-class blacks passed for white as a matter of convenience; some even made it a life-style. Cohn Johnston's cousin—known as "the Harvard Man"—regularly appeared at weddings and funerals; otherwise it was "Don't call me, I'll call you." When Cohn and Marion (who both looked white) went to Florida in the winter, *she* traveled in the white car and *he* traveled in the black car. "It's a curse to look white and be black," said Marion Montero. This did not mean that they wanted to be white. "How can you kiss a white baby?" Margie Wormley (of the Washington hotel Wormleys) asked Marion, her future sister-in-law. But black as a color was a handicap to be overcome in black society only by virtue of great ability, rarely by virtue of great wealth. ("Why, if I had ever called a colored person black when I was a girl, they would have been deeply offended," said Marion Montero Johnston in 1982.)

The elder Hornes continued to be seen as perfect examples of the old ideal; they were "family" people, not flashy. They were educated and accomplished, although Edwin by now seemed a rather distant figure, hiding behind his paper and his pipe. He came alive only with Lena. Lena, in turn, found Edwin beautiful. He reminded her of "Little Eva's" father in her illustrated copy of *Uncle Tom's Cabin:* those sad blue eyes, that silvery hair.

All the boys were wary of Cora; they called her the "Tiny Terror." Paul Robeson never forgot the sight of Cora in the 1920s haranguing hooky-playing boys on Harlem street corners. Frank Montero (who became an assistant director of the initial Kennedy Peace Corps) felt that Cora was one of the few women of her age and class with a "social conscience."

Errol Horne was still talked about in the 1920s as one of the legendary young men who died in the war, and Frank Horne, poet-athlete, was a hero to the younger boys. When Frank graduated from City College, Uncle Frank Smith helped his namesake enter Central Illinois School of Ophthalmology, where Frank Horne passed as white. Burke Horne remained in the bosom of Brooklyn—overwhelmed by his older brothers, but Lena's great friend.

Teddy Horne was another matter. He scorned all middle-class value and opinions, especially Brooklyn's. But what he lacked in social conscience he made up for in charisma. ("Teddy Horne was so handsome, so gorgeous, you could swoon," said Marion Montero.)

By the summer of 1923 Teddy felt "healthy" (or safe) enough to leave Seattle. He celebrated that July Fourth in Shelby, Montana—with hundred-dollar ringside seats at the Dempsey-Gibbons fight. A week later he was at "Boyle's Thirty Acres" in New Jersey for more boxing. Teddy Horne and the automobile had found each other. On the twenty-fourth he was at Yankee Stadium for the lightweight championship, and two days later he was at the Polo Grounds for more boxing: Criqui versus Dundee. (One presumes that he saved some time for little Lena.) In mid-August he left New York for Chicago to visit his Smith cousins and some "business" acquaintances. If speak-easy cards are any indication, the black "Roaring Twenties" were good fun for Teddy. In October 1924 "Mr. Teddy Horne"

A studio portrait of Teddy Horne, Seattle, 1921

Two of the speak-easy cards that Teddy collected in his travels

was issued a "certificate of membership" in the "Fifty Club" (city unknown) —expiration "never." He also belonged to "the Exclusive Social Literary Club" (Detroit), "the Citizen's Progressive Club" (Pittsburgh) and "the Pullman Athletic Club" (Chicago).

The year 1924 was a momentous one in little Lena's life. One day a woman with bright blue eyes appeared in the front yard at Chauncey Street. Cora was not at home; the vote had changed her life, and she was totally involved in the 1924 election. Lena was alone, playing dress-up. The blue-eyed woman (who looked white) announced that her name was Augusta Byrd, that she was Lena's cousin, and that Lena's mother, Edna, was ill and wanted to see her.

Edna had run away from Brooklyn, motherhood, and marriage only shortly after Teddy absconded to Seattle. She had run first to Harlem— where black Brooklyn had "fun"—and joined the Lafayette Stock Company. The Lafayette, whose sidewalk held Harlem's "Tree of Hope," was a touring company formed in 1914 to promote black theater. Its repertory consisted of all-black productions of Broadway hits and standard revivals. Most of the great black actors of the 1920s—Charles Gilpin, Rose McClendon, Jules Bledsoe, and Paul Robeson—appeared at the Lafayette. Edna had leading parts in *The Count of Monte Cristo, Dr. Jekyll and Mr. Hyde,* and *Madame X.* Mostly, however, she was the star of her own melodramas.

In the eyes of Brooklyn—certainly those of Cora Horne—a divorcée on the stage was barely a step away from prostitution. Edna, on the other hand, believed herself to be courageous and independent. But she had been isolated for so long in her middle-class enclave that her grasp of reality was tenuous at best. In the bourgeois black world of Brooklyn, Edna Scottron Horne *was* somebody. (E. Franklin Frazier called black society "status without substance.") In the great big black-and-white world outside, she must have looked like a natural victim. Edna had thrown herself into a world she had never been brought up to face.

Lena had actually visited Edna twice in the four years since her mother had left. The first time Edna took Lena on stage, as the child in *Madame X.* Lena's role was to lie quietly in a crib, but she was in an agony of stage fright. (She would suffer that same emotion every time she appeared in public for the rest of her performing life.) The second time Lena sat backstage with the other theater kids and watched stock company favorite *Way Down East* from behind the false fireplace set. And once Edna had come to another Chauncey Street brownstone and sent the neighbor to Lena in the back yard to say, "Your mother is here, she wants to see you." And Lena had run over to find the beautiful lady who hugged her, and cried, and said, "Don't tell your grandmother."

This time Lena's cousin Augusta Byrd (actually she was a Scottron or Waller cousin who lived in Chelsea as white) took Lena to Harlem in a taxi. And there in a Harlem apartment was Edna, alternately crying, coughing, and kissing Lena. As she held Lena's hands tightly, Edna said that she was ill, that she had to go South for her health and was taking Lena with her. It was necessary for Lena to get away from Chauncey Street, she said, because Teddy was going to *kidnap* her. Lena was absolutely dumbfounded. She started crying, too, but she wasn't sure whether she was more afraid of her father's kidnap plot or of Edna's high hysterics. At the same time she was thrilled to be with her mother, even for a moment. Her mother was so beautiful, and she kissed and hugged Lena, which no one on Chauncey Street ever did. (Of course, Teddy had no plans to "kidnap" his daughter. He was delighted with the Chauncey Street arrangement and sent regular support money. Edna was the "kidnapper.") What was real, in the whole situation, was that Edna was truly ill (probably borderline tubercular) as well as emotionally overwrought. In her melodrama, Edna had decided that Cora was the villain. And she was determined that Cora would not *have* Lena, forgetting in the drama of the moment that one of the things she herself had run away from was the responsibility of motherhood. But now Edna told Lena, "I'm the only one who loves you."

So Lena and Edna went to Miami on the train, taking the regular train to Washington, then the Jim Crow car to Miami. Lena had traveled to Chicago to see Great-aunt Lena Smith, but she had never been on a Jim Crow train. Lena was worried about not being able to get in touch with her grandmother—but she had a mother at last. In Miami they went to a little frame house, with a latticed porch, near the railroad tracks. The house belonged to Edna's best friend, Lucille Noble, another Lafayette actress. Lucille had dyed red hair and often passed for white. Lena and Edna shared a small bedroom. The top of the dresser was filled with Edna's collection of French perfume in cut crystal bottles—which Lena was never, never to touch. Lucille, whom Lena called "Aunt Lucille," had the other bedroom. There was a kitchen, where Lena was nightly fed camomile to ward off malaria. And there was a living room that Lena was not permitted to enter; it was reserved for Edna and Lucille's grown-up friends. The grown-ups were usually other touring black repertory and tent show actors. Lena was very lonely. She missed Brooklyn, and she found her mother odd. Unlike Cora, whose manner toward Lena was always the same, Edna was either

Lena at her "Aunt Lucille's" house in Miami, c. 1927

My grandmother Edna on stage in <u>Madame X</u>, c. 1921

Lena (center) with two of her Southern schoolmates, c. 1927

extravagantly affectionate or violently angry. Lena was beaten for the first time in her life—for leaving her sweater in school. School itself was a one-room affair, a far cry from Ethical Culture. Lena was put ahead of her grade, but the other children all hated her. They made fun of her accent, her skin color, and her clothes. And she did not know how to play any of their games. She was beaten again, this time for not wearing her shoes. She was not allowed to go barefoot as the other children did, and her Miami-bought shoes hurt her feet because blacks weren't allowed to try on what they bought. Lena was deeply unhappy. Her only friend was Lucille's big chow dog, named Chin. Lena had always wanted a dog, but Cora didn't believe in pets. Now she had a pet—but she missed Cora. Lena thought her mother was the most beautiful creature in the world, but she was more frightened of her than she had ever been of her icy grandmother.

Just when Lena was getting used to her lonely Miami life, Edna suddenly decided that they were going to Jacksonville. In Jacksonville, Edna and Lena stayed with some theater friends of Edna's. One night after supper, early in the visit, Edna, Lena, and their hosts set off in the car for the Silas Green Tent Show (a famous black traveling show). Lena didn't know what a "tent show" was, but she liked car rides. On the road out of town, however, their car was suddenly flagged down by a black man who said, "Get away from here! There's going to be a lynching!" Once again Lena didn't know what grown-ups were talking about, but she knew they were frightened. She could feel the extraordinary tension as they sped toward home—the grown-ups talking, and exchanging glances, above her head. Lena was frightened, too. She had already begun to have terrible nightmares, and this night's would be one of the worst. A few weeks later Edna told Lena that she would be going back to Brooklyn to visit her grandmother for a while. Lena wept with happiness.

For the next three years Lena was shunted back and forth between Cora and Edna, between Brooklyn and wherever Edna happened to be. She also went back and forth between Brooklyn's Public School 70 and any number of Southern one-room schoolhouses. She learned a great deal in those three years. She learned, for example, that Cora was very different from most Southern grandmothers, who seemed to work very hard at home and spent a great deal of time in the kitchen. She also learned to change her accent and personality, depending where, and with whom, she was. And she learned especially to cherish her Brooklyn friends in preparation for Southern loneliness. Her "visits" with Edna more and more became visits with Edna's friends. Edna was always leaving and arriving. On one occasion

Lena was left with a middle-class doctor's family in Ohio, where she shared the top floor with a maiden aunt who allowed her to read late in bed. This was kind; Lena was too afraid of nightmares to fall asleep easily.

Once, in Macon, Georgia, Lena was left with two old women: a great-grandmother over ninety who dipped snuff, and her daughter, a woman Cora's age. With them were the younger woman's two small grandchildren, one a little girl of Lena's age called Thelma. Lena was happy there. The old great-grandmother told the children Bible stories every night—and Lena's nightmares stopped. Lena got rickets, but the great-grandmother wrapped Lena's legs in brown paper and vinegar until the pain went away. And Lena scored a small coup in her Macon school. When a teacher came in to announce the death of Florence Mills, Lena was the only child in the class who had heard of her. Florence Mills, like Paul Robeson, was an international black star of the 1920s—her career was meteoric. Lena wanted to *be* Florence Mills when she grew up.

One day Lena was playing outside of the little house in Macon when a man whose face seemed vaguely familiar, but whom she did not know, appeared and said, "I'm your Uncle Frank, Lena, and I've come to take you to Fort Valley." In 1927 Frank Horne was dean of students, and assistant to the president, at Fort Valley Junior Industrial College, about thirty miles outside of Macon. The college was in no way of the caliber of Atlanta University or Fisk, both created specifically to educate a black "elite." Fort Valley epitomized the ethos of Booker T. Washington. Boys learned basic reading and writing skills, some high school math, and farming. Girls were taught reading and writing plus cooking and handicrafts.

Lena loved Fort Valley. She lived in the girls' dormitory with Frank's fiancée, Frankye Bunn, a Philadelphia flapper who taught English. Lena idolized Frankye, who was slim and chic, with long auburn hair she wore in a chignon. Her clothes, in Lena's eyes, were fabulous. Her figure was perfect for the "boyish" silhouette. Lena herself was as skinny as ever, but eating all the time.

Lena went to the little school across the road from the college where, as usual, the children mocked her Northern accent and asked her why she and her uncle were so light-skinned. They called her "little yellow bastard," and she played in the sun so her skin would darken. Although Lena lived in the dorm, Frankye forbade her to talk with the other girls, who were all teenagers. Lena, of course, ignored the rules and spent as much time with her dorm mates as possible. She was fascinated by their talk of boys, clothes, and cosmetics. On Saturday afternoons the girls got together for hair straightening parties, in preparation for the evening, when boys were permitted to visit. Lena wanted desperately to be one of the group and begged the girls to straighten her hair. When they did, Frankye was furious. She was "never" to do that again, said Frankye. Lena did manage to wheedle a *bob,* with a *dip* over one eye, out of the controversy (good-bye Mary Pickford curls). She continued, as usual, to change accents and personalities depending on whether she was with Frank and Frankye, the teenagers in the dorm, or the kids in the one-room schoolhouse across the road.

■   ■   ■

If Teddy Horne was considered the black sheep of the family, then Frank Horne was the whitest of white. He had the family charm, plus a certain gentleness and sweetness that endeared him to everyone. He also loved beautiful women, although he was probably as naïve on the subject as his brother Ted was shrewd. By the late 1920s Frank was already a celebrated junior member of the Harlem Renaissance.

> . . . Sterling Brown has described the Negro Renaissance as being concerned with "(1) a discovery of Africa as a source of race pride, (2) a use of Negro heroes and heroic episodes from American history, (3) propaganda or protest, (4) a treatment of the Negro masses (frequently of the folk, less often of the workers) with more understanding and less apology, (5) franker and deeper self-revelation. . . ."
> —Frazier, *Black Bourgeoisie*

Frank's poetry came under the heading, perhaps, of "franker and deeper self-revelation." His first published collection, written in 1920 (a turbulent Horne family year), was titled *Letters Found Near a Suicide.* He was anthologized in Alain Locke's famous 1925 *New Negro,* which defined the Harlem Renaissance as a movement. In the same year he won an honorable mention for short story in the Urban League's Opportunity Awards. (Among the judges were Fannie Hurst, Eugene O'Neill, Alexander Woollcott, and Robert Benchley.) The prize winners were Countee Cullen and Langston Hughes.

Frank's own best poetry was about his Brooklyn boyhood and youth: Smart Set athletic meets at Flushing, the Holbrooks, all that lost world of innocence and games (he seldom wrote about "the Negro"). Frank's best lifelong friend was James Holbrook, younger brother of Frank and Kitty.

TO JAMES

Do you remember
how you won
that last race . . . ?
how you flung your body
at the start . . .
how your spikes
ripped the cinders
in the stretch . . .
how you catapulted
through the tape . . .
do you remember . . . ?
Don't you think
I lurched with you
out of those starting holes . . . ?
Don't you think
my sinews tightened
at those first
few strides . . .
and when you flew into the stretch
was not all my thrill
of a thousand races
in your blood . . . ?
At your final drive
through the finish line
did not my shout
tell of the triumphant ecstasy
of victory . . . ?

(from *Letters Found Near a Suicide*)

Poet Sterling Brown says that black students of the 1960s rediscovered Frank, and that of all the Renaissance poetry they were most curious about Frank's *Suicide* poems.

After graduating from the Illinois ophthalmology school in 1923 Frank had set up shop as an eye doctor in Harlem. In his spare time he wrote reviews for the Urban League's *Opportunity* magazine. The differences between the Urban League and the NAACP went beyond the religious denominations of their major benefactors: Jewish for the NAACP, and Episcopalian for the Urban League. The NAACP magazine *Crisis* was un-diluted W. E. B. Du Bois—always important, but often heavy going. The Urban League's *Opportunity* (edited by Charles Johnson) offered fiction, criticism, plays, poetry, and "entertainment." In 1925 Frank inadvertently became the center of an NAACP–Urban League quarrel with a withering *Opportunity* review of NAACP leader Walter White's second novel. It was so scathing that the NAACP demanded an apology from the Urban League. *Opportunity* backed down with a rebuttal to Frank's review by Walter White's protégée Nella Larsen Imes.

(Walter White, who would succeed Du Bois as the dominant figure in the NAACP, was one of the most remarkable people in America. He was a blond, blue-eyed, white man who chose to be black. White's mother was one-sixteenth black, and his father one-quarter. He was born in Atlanta and by Georgia standards was black. But White's "protective" coloring made him the perfect double agent. Working in the Atlanta NAACP office, he filed an eyewitness report of the Mary Turner lynching in Valdosta, Georgia, that made him famous throughout America. Mary Turner, eight months pregnant, was hung upside down from a tree while still alive, doused with gasoline, and set afire. Her abdomen was slit with a hunting knife, and the baby crushed underfoot. After Valdosta, Walter White was no longer safe in Georgia. He went to New York to join the NAACP's Harlem office and for three decades presented the NAACP's voice to the world.)

Frank was the Horne family's resident Harlem intellectual. While the rest of America was Babbitt country—with the Ku Klux Klan on the march and rabid puritanism the rule—Harlem became the hub of the 1920s inter-national cult of the "Negro," from cubist France to the Broadway stage. The very air of Harlem was electric with excitement. New York's "night-club" mayor Jimmy Walker, the right man at the right time, put Harlem on the official city VIP tourist list. Harlem was not only black America's intel-lectual mecca, it was also Prohibition America's Paris. Limousines were lined up for miles on Seventh Avenue every night of the week.

Frank, with his medical career flourishing, still found the time to write and act with W. E. B. Du Bois' Krigwa Players—Harlem's answer to the Provincetown Playhouse; Harlem intellectuals shunned the Lafayette as not meaningful to the "New Negro." In 1926 they would also despise the commercial successes of Broadway's *Lulu Belle,* a drama of Harlem low life with blacked-up white stars, and Carl Van Vechten's novel *Nigger Heaven,* a pastiche of "exotic primitivism"—both of which sent white tourists flocking uptown. Du Bois believed that black theater, like black art, should be "About us . . . By us . . . Near us. . . ." Frank was a founding member of Krigwa and acted a small part in a *Crisis* magazine prize winner.

Harlem's better-off intellectuals lived in the brand-new Paul Laurence Dunbar Apartments, built by John D. Rockefeller, at the request of the Urban League. Among the tenants were Du Bois, Countee Cullen, A. Philip Randolph, Fletcher Henderson (the big band star), and E. Simms Campbell (the *Esquire* illustrator). Rockefeller was considered a "friend" of blacks—as were H. L. Mencken, Dorothy Parker, Sinclair Lewis, Hart Crane, Muriel Draper, Van Wyck Brooks, Heywood Broun, Eugene O'Neill, Horace Liveright, Alfred Knopf, and Alfred Stieglitz. (You could almost count them on two hands.) Harlem's middle class was photographed by James Van Der Zee. And Harlem's youth changed clothes twice a day for flirtatious strolls along Seventh Avenue.

It must have been difficult for Frank to tear himself away from Harlem and go South, but he needed the money that white philanthropic societies paid "Missionary" teachers. (The white Missionary teachers of the nineteenth century had been replaced by educated blacks.) In 1928 Frank and Frankye were married and moved into their own house on campus, in which Lena's room—full of books—doubled as Frank's study. On weekends Frank and Frankye were nonstop entertainers, with jars of pure corn liquor ("white lightning") dug up from cool garden burial plots. Frank and Frankye's set was considered "fast." They tended to be highly educated young northerners, overqualified for their jobs. (If the white American myth was log cabin to White House, the black American myth was Ph.D. to Pullman porter.) They also considered themselves to be "modern." Lena would lie in her bedroom, with the door ajar, listening to talk of politics, poetry, and people—conversations that, to her, seemed the epitome of sparkling sophistication.

One spring day in 1928, out of the blue Teddy Horne arrived in Fort Valley, driving a long black car, a Pierce-Arrow or LaSalle. He had come South to recuperate from an accident. The car, which he kept in a garage in town, became the cynosure of white Fort Valley attention. To his daughter the fabled Teddy Horne was like a stunning apparition. Lena thought he looked like Fredric March, the handsomest movie star of all.

After flirting with Chicago and Detroit, Teddy had settled down in Pittsburgh with his second wife, Irene. They purchased a small hotel, which Irene ran, on Wylie Avenue—the heart of the black district. Teddy was at leisure to concentrate on local politics and easy money. He liked Pittsburgh—the bustling "smoky" city where the three rivers meet. The city had a large black population that consisted mostly of steel mill workers. Pittsburgh was also home of one of the most important black newspapers in the country, the Pittsburgh *Courier*. And it had the two best black baseball teams in America, the Homestead Grays and the Crawford Giants.

Teddy's "sporting" instincts remained primary. In 1926 he got his first legitimate job since Tammany with the Pennsylvania Athletic Commission. A license was issued to Edwin F. Horne of 1308 Wylie Avenue, Pittsburgh, as a referee for the year of 1927. Teddy and Irene's new best friends were the William A. Greenlees. "Gus" Greenlee, a black World War I veteran, owner of Wylie Avenue's Crawford Grille, was known as "Big Red" to those who were not his intimates. He was one of the biggest numbers kings in the East. Teddy prospered in Pittsburgh, thanks largely to his friend Greenlee.

Lena was stunned by Teddy. She had never met anyone like him, and he was so different from Uncle Frank. Although he openly sneered at college and college life, he gave as much advice as Cora, most of which Lena thought funny. "Trust no bush that quivers," he would say. Or, "Ask for no mercy, and give less." But Teddy did consider himself a mathematician, and he drilled Lena to the verge of tears in arithmetic.

Teddy's 1928 visit became a festive rallying point. Grandfather Edwin came down at Easter, with his old Brooklyn pals James Holbrook and "Bye" Waters. There are photographs of that happy Georgia Easter, Lena, holding her Easter hat, posing with "Bye." There are also proud, faint pictures of the interior and exterior of Frank and Frankye's pretty new house. And, naturally, a picture of Teddy's car, with the Hornes and "Southern friends" gathered around it. On the way home from Fort Valley, Teddy stopped off in Louisville for Derby Day at Churchill Downs. Later that summer he went home to Brooklyn for the first time in nearly a decade—and both his panache and his enormous car proved impressive to family and friends.

Lena spent the summer of 1928 in Fort Valley, shuttling between Frank and Frankye's house and the house of the woman who taught girls' handicrafts at the college. But eventually, like a bad penny, a letter from Edna turned up. "At last we'll be together with a roof over our heads, a home of our own," she wrote. Edna and her friend Lucille had rented a house in Atlanta to be their headquarters between trips to Miami. Edna had found a rich "foreign" admirer in Miami who had offered her the money to house Lena—as long as it was outside of Florida. Edna's new friend was a white

The Horne house in Fort Valley, Georgia, where Lena went to live in 1927

Teddy and Edwin Horne in Georgia, 1928

Edwin and his daughter-in-law Frankye Horne, Georgia, 1928

Brooklynites Jim Holbrook (left) and "Bye" Waters (seated) celebrating Easter with Southern friends in Fort Valley, Georgia, 1928. Frankye Horne is third from right.

Cuban army officer, and when she was with him, Edna, who spoke Spanish, passed as "white." So Lena left Fort Valley for a pleasant red brick house on Atlanta's West Hunter, a stolidly middle-class tree-lined black neighborhood. The house had a front garden, a back yard, a sun porch, two bedrooms, a nice warm kitchen, and a piano in the parlor. Lena went to dancing school and to Booker T. Washington Junior High School, and she enjoyed the agreeable Atlanta bourgeois life—where no one mocked her accent or skin color. She played with the three Blackshear sisters next door and joined their "club." Teddy had begun lavishing an intermittent but substantial allowance upon Lena, and whenever it arrived she shared treats with the Blackshears. "Aunt" Lucille would take the club mates early in the morning to the black swimming pool—they went early in order to avoid the "other crowd" of black children. On June 30 Lena was given a surprise eleventh birthday party. At the party Lena did her famous "Snake-Hips" dance (named after Cotton Club star Earl "Snake Hips" Tucker). The club's dancing won a prize at the Auburn Avenue Royal Theater's "Kiddie Review." Eventually, of course, Edna and Lucille returned to Florida and left Lena with a woman called "Aunt" May. For Christmas Edna sent Lena a copy of *Little Women*, which Lena read over and over. It joined her list of favorites: *Sara Crewe: A Little Princess*, *Daddy Long-Legs*, and *A Girl of the Limberlost*. Her favorite heroines were still orphans. Alone with "Aunt" May, Lena would come home from school to do the dusting, chores, and homework. Wednesday and Saturday nights were reserved for baths—and beatings. Lena would be beaten, more or less severely, depending on her behavior that week. Edna came to visit several times, but Lena never complained. Finally someone informed Edna of "Aunt" May's mistreatment. "Why didn't you tell me?" Edna was very angry with Lena. Lena felt that Edna was *embarrassed* about the neighbors' knowing something she did not. "Why do I have to hear this from other people?" Early in 1929 Lena was sent back to Brooklyn.

Brooklyn was the only place where Lena Horne was sure of who she was: she was a Horne of Chauncey Street. She did not have to change her accent to suit her companions, and her skin color was quite correct. In Brooklyn she had her best friends, Ruth and Llewellyn; she also had the Peter Pan Club, and a school where she was not made fun of. She was welcomed home by young Uncle Burke and his gang: Harriet and Bill Pickens, the Monteros, Cohn Johnston (Llewellyn's big brother). She also reclaimed her grandfather. Edwin and Lena went everywhere together: to the Aquarium and the Bronx Zoo, to the Met to see *Aida*, to the Civic Repertory

Lena posing in her new fur coat,
a gift from her father,
Brooklyn, 1929

Lena wearing one of Cora's
dresses in the back garden
at 189 *Chauncey Street,*
Brooklyn, 1929

Lena (kneeling, far right)
with "Junior Deb" clubmates,
Brooklyn, c. 1929

to see Eva Le Gallienne in *Peter Pan,* to the movies to see Garbo, and to
lunch at the Automat. In September Lena started Girls High School and
Teddy sent her a real fur coat. She posed for her photograph, looking every
inch a flapper. The only clouds on Lena's Brooklyn horizon were her
pitched battles with Cora on the subject of Edna. Lena always defended
her mother, while Cora denounced her as a "weak, foolish woman." "The
worst thing you could possibly be, Lena," Cora would say, "is just like your
mother!"

In the autumn Cora embarked (courtesy of Teddy) on her long-planned
grand tour, in the company of her good friend Mrs. Minta Trotman, a co-
activist in the NAACP. Cora and Mrs. Trotman sailed to Europe on a
smallish French liner called the *De Grasse* (the same ship on which, twenty-
one years later, I also sailed to Europe for the first time).

S. S. De Grasse
September 30, 1929

Mother's Burke:

Wish you were here to eat all this delicious food I cannot eat. This
is the "eatingest" place on earth. Breakfast and four other eating
times. I do wish I could hand you these ducklings, baby pigeons,
chops and all the gorgeous fruit, and of course you have two bottles
of wine with every meal. *I have my breakfast in bed.* Please take time
to ring Mrs. Rollock up and tell her that the Cabin Steward brings
my delicious breakfast and would tuck me in bed if I let him. I
obeyed Ted's instructions and we own the boat. [Note: Ted's "instructions" were to grease the palm of every hand in sight.] The
headwaiter personally conducts us to our table; the head Steward
comes down to see that all goes well. The waiter hovers near paying
perfect service and O, such food! *I have not been ill one moment.*
What do you think of that? Not the slightest symptoms. Mrs. Trotman was "nauseated" the second day and *"droopy"* for two or three
days but is O.K. now. Your young mother has been a real
sailor. . . . The people are good sports. I'm sending you a passen-
ger list. Stay on your job. This is the life! Give up old Harlem and
take these sorts of "jaunts." You can do it very reasonably. There
are exhibition boxing bouts in the Gym. Concerts in the Grand
Salon every evening, movies every afternoon; horse races in between; dances; deck tennis matches; all sorts of things. I've been

two evenings to the lovely concerts but am resting and resting.
Usually take long nap in the afternoon before it is time to dress for
dinner. The Deck Steward is all attention, looks after my robe,
serves hot tea, cake, bouillon and all with such a flourish because
all have been *"Seen"* from the big ones down to the *least* (tips).

Take care of your Daddy. Be my dear, good Burke. Run by to
see Lena every day. I forgot to leave money for her music but hope
you paid it as Dad will surely return it to you. I worried about it.
Let me know. . . . Remember what I told you about your father.
Be thoughtful and kind to him. Mother loves you. Get teeth fixed
at once. I arranged with Willis [dentist]. Is hot water tank cut off?
Have not been ill a moment.

While Cora was away, Lena stayed with Cora's good friend the indefat-
igable Mrs. Laura Rollock—of the Urban League, the NAACP, and amateur dramatics (*The Junior Follies*)—in whose house Lena had her own
room and her own radio, and where she was allowed to have club meetings
(by now she had graduated from the Peter Pans to the Junior Debs), which
Cora had always discouraged. Throughout the next several months Cora
corresponded frequently with the members of her family. In January 1930
she sent a card from Vienna:

Had a nice letter from Lena yesterday. She had done her Xmas
shopping and was very happy over the coming Xmas. She is a dear
little girl. . . . Did you have a nice Xmas? Do tell me all about it. I
told you I had been forced to dig up all the "harness" and "doll" up
every evening. You know the general idea that *all* Americans are
rolling in money. Everyone is lovely . . . we have a grand chambre
as the French say—it would make a 3 room apartment in N.Y.
beautifully furnished. Best Love. Mother.

CHAPTER · 5

HELENA HORNE

Teddy Horne, unlike most of the civilized world, seems to have spent the Depression with no financial worries and nary a political thought. In March of 1930 he lent his parents $3,000 to pay the mortgage on their Brooklyn house. In June he bought "his" and "hers" automobiles from the Packard Motor Company of Pittsburgh.

In 1931 the Pittsburgh *Courier* campaigned: "Wanted! One Million Signers, a Nationwide Protest Against 'Amos and Andy.' " The NAACP successfully defeated Herbert Hoover's nomination of Judge John J. Parker for the Supreme Court (Parker was against suffrage for blacks) in what *The Christian Science Monitor* called "the first national demonstration of the Negro's power since Reconstruction." And Teddy Horne was still only serious about having a good time. He spent the summer of 1931 on the road. In early July he was ringside at Cleveland Stadium, with twenty-five-dollar seats, for a championship fight. Two weeks later he was in Philadelphia to see Kid Chocolate at the Phillies' ball park. In August he drove down to Atlantic City to sport on the beach with Gus "Big Red" Greenlee and "Baby Joe" Gans, along with assorted wives, girl friends, and cronies.

Gus Greenlee was entering the prime of his professional life. He had political control of Pittsburgh's black Third Ward, and he also controlled the local numbers racket. Now he was about to become a force in black baseball and boxing. The annual Christmas party at Gus's Crawford Grille was a highlight of Pittsburgh's sporting and political life. Gus had already built, with his own money, a stadium complex on Bedford Avenue, not far from black Pittsburgh. When blacks played at the Pirates' Forbes Field, they were not permitted to use the locker rooms. But Greenlee Field had everything: the playing field was of major league proportions and there were first-class facilities for the athletes. In 1931 Gus made a giant step. He took over the old Crawford Giants, and in late summer of 1931 he bought Leroy "Satchel" Paige's contract from the disbanding Cleveland Cubs for $250. He then proceeded to grab all the black baseball talent in sight. Within a year Gus Greenlee's Crawford Giants were known as the Yankees of black baseball and were overwhelming all of their Negro League opponents. Some of the Crawford Giants of 1932 are considered among baseball immortals: Satchel Paige, Judy Johnson, Josh Gibson, and Jimmie Crutchfield. Although the major leagues were still closed to black players, winter baseball was integrated. Blacks, whites, and Latins played together for fantastic salaries (and fanatic fans) in Cuba, Puerto Rico, the Dominican Republic, and Mexico.

The Crawford spring training camp was at Hot Springs, Arkansas. Teddy joined the Greenlees there in the spring of 1932. Hot Springs, with its Oaklawn Jockey Club, was home to a hearty black sporting subculture. Gus Greenlee (whose background was middle-class, but whose occupation kept him out of it) was now able to re-enter the bourgeoisie on his own terms. Just as great ability could finally overcome a black skin, so a very great deal of money could overcome a shady occupation.

Teddy's visit to Hot Springs was merely a stopover on a trip West to see Frank and Frankye (Frank was earning his master's degree at the University of Southern California) and to attend the 1932 Olympics at Los Angeles, where blacks Eddie Tolan and Edward Gordon won gold medals in track and field. He also visited cousin Frank Smith, Jr., who had fallen in love with the Golden West and now operated his own photography studio in Los Angeles.

Teddy returned to Pittsburgh in early September, just in time to receive Burke's wire:

MOTHER DIED UNEXPECTEDLY AT FIVE TODAY.

In the photograph, taken in the early 1920s, that accompanies her
obituary in the Brooklyn *Eagle,* Cora wears mourning for Errol. Her regard
is firm and resolute. Hers is the serious face of an intellectual and spiritual
seeker. Cora seemed always to be looking for answers. Her obituary listed
her as either an officer or member of the following organizations: the Urban
League, the Big Sisters, the Big Brother and Big Sister Organizations, the
National Association of Colored Women, the Brooklyn Urban League, the
Brooklyn Bureau of Charities, the Katy Ferguson–John Hegeman Houses
(Sunday schools), the New York Branch of Women's International League
of Peace, and the Foreign Policy Association of the International Council
of Women of the Darker Races (one of the first Third World groups,
founded by women—Cora among them—from America, Africa, Haiti, the
West Indies, and Ceylon, who first convened in Washington in 1922).

Cora's funeral arrangements also reflected a spiritual pilgrimage: the
Congregational Church of her proper Atlanta childhood, the Episcopal
Church of Brooklyn's black elite, and Bahai. (Cora, who had become a
Bahai disciple in the late 1920s, often took her granddaughter Lena to Bahai
meetings. The Bahai movement, founded in Persia in 1863 by Prince Hu-
sayn Ali, had only recently arrived in America, along with such other
Middle Eastern mystics as Gurdjieff and Gibran. Bahai stressed the essen-
tial unity of all revealed religions: men should worship God by serving others
—regardless of race, nationality, or religion.) Only the Catholic Church of
Cora's birth and middle age refused to accept her ecumenicalism.

The Pittsburgh *Courier* obituary stressed the celebrity of her son
(" 'Ted' Horne's Mother Buried in Brooklyn") and followed the list of Cora's
immediate survivors with the statement: "All were present at the interment."

And thereby hangs a tale. For, in fact, fifteen-year-old Lena was missing. Edna hated her mother-in-law so much that she would not permit Lena
to attend her grandmother's funeral. Of all of Edna's irrational cruelties,
this, for Lena, would always be the worst. But Lena was not Cora's granddaughter for nothing. She refused to obey her mother and ran out of Edna's
new Brooklyn apartment, sobbing hysterically, toward Carlton Avenue and
the funeral home—with Edna, equally hysterical, huffing and puffing behind. Lena managed to reach the door of the funeral home, where Edna,
gasping, caught up with her and proceeded to create a scene of scandalous
proportions. Edwin would never forgive her, and neither would Brooklyn.
This was Edna's "final straw" as far as most of the Scottrons, Wallers, and
Accooes were concerned.

In a letter to Teddy and Irene in December of 1932, widower Edwin wrote:

> I am much pleased . . . that you sent something to Lena. I sent
> her $5.00. Her mother wrote me another letter but I never open
> her letters. I cannot fail to remember her action to create a scandal
> and humiliate all of us on the day of the funeral. I shall never have
> anything to do with Lena's mother. She is a skunk. . . .

Edna's next-to-last "straw" had been her second husband.

After Charles Gilpin died, Rose McClendon (true to the spirit of the decade) organized the Negro Peoples' Theatre stock company at the Lafayette and began to experiment with serious social drama. At that point Edna took off for Havana, where in the early 1930s she met Miguel Rodriguez, a white Cuban army officer. Rodriguez was a partisan of the soon to be ousted dictator Machado, and he and Edna fled Havana just before the onslaught of the subsequent dictator, Batista. Miguel, whom Edna called "Mike," had no doubt cut a dashing figure in Cuba as a cigar-smoking, mustachioed officer in Machado's army. In America, however, he appeared rather pathetic, just another refugee, full of misplaced machismo and no English. Lena disliked her stepfather, both because he was the "wrong race" and because he could not be understood. Edna and Mike took an apartment near Chauncey Street so that Lena could live with them while she continued to go to Girls High School. Cora let Edna know in no uncertain terms how much she disapproved of Lena living in an interracial ménage, and Edna swore that Cora would never see her granddaughter again—even in death.

Despite, or because of, the crimes of her errant mother, Brooklyn seemed to take Lena especially under its wing. After school she spent more time at Ruth Johnson's or at Mrs. Rollock's than with her mother and Mike. Thanks to Laura Jean Rollock, Lena did not neglect her artistic pursuits. Even Edna had always seen that Lena took dancing lessons—she might be another Florence Mills, after all. Now there were dramatic and singing lessons as well. Lena sang "Indian Love Call" at every 1933 Junior Deb club tea party. She also studied at the Anna Jones Dancing School in Brooklyn, which in 1933 won a week's engagement at the Harlem Opera House. The students performed an Isadora Duncan dance, with scarves, to "Stormy Weather," Harold Arlen's hit song from that year's Cotton Club show.

*Frankye and Frank Horne in Los Angeles, 1932,
at the time of Teddy's visit to attend the
Olympic Games*

*Mr. and Mrs. Gus Greenlee—Teddy Horne's
"best friends"—at the Crawford Giants
training camp in Hot Springs, Arkansas,
in the spring of 1932*

Mrs. Horne, Civic
Leader, Succumb

Funeral Held for Woman Who Served
Numerous Movements in City and
Nation—Rites Private

Cora Calhoun Horne, prominent over a period of 27 years
the civic and social worlds of Brooklyn, died Thursday fr
natural causes at her home, 18⁄ Chauncey street. She was
Burial of the body was made in Evergreen Cemetery on Monda

Her funeral services, held at the ⁹
A. Q. Martin funeral home, 392 Carlton avenue, were conducted by A. C.
Holley of the Baha'i, a religious cult,
assisted by the Rev. Dr. H. H. Proc-
tor, of Nazarene Congregational
Church and the Rev. George Frazier
Miller of St. Augustine P. E. Church.
Only the immediate family and close
friends of the deceased were admitted to the rites. A vocal solo was
rendered by Miss Ida Brown of Philadelphia.

Mrs. Horne, a native of Washington, Ga., was educated in the public
schools of Atlanta and at Atlanta
University. She became the wife of
Edwin F. Horne of Birmingham, Ala.,
in 1887. Migrating to this city, she
began her public career in 1913. During the late World War she organized
and directed a Y. W. C. A. unit for
the American Red Cross, and in recognition for her work in this connection was appointed a member of
the then mayor's victory committee.

During the Presidential campaign
1924 Mrs. Horne was national organizer and secretary of the National
Republican Women's Auxiliary, eastern division. At her death she was
either an official or a member of the
following widely known organizations:

Urban League, Big Sisters, Big
Brother and Sister Organizations, National Association of Colored Women,
National Council of Women, Brooklyn Urban League, Brooklyn Bureau
of Charities, Katy Ferguson-John
Hegeman Houses, New York Branch
of the Women's International League
for Peace, Foreign Policy Association
and the International Council of
Women of the Darker Races.

The deceased is survived by her
husband, an inspector in the department of combustibles of the New
York Fire Department; a sister, Mrs.

Leader Dies

Mrs. Cora Horne.

Frank A. Smith of Chicago; th
sons, Edwin F., Jr., of Pittsbur
Dr. Frank S., dean of the Fort V
ley Normal School of Fort V
Ga., and John Burke, a gradu
pharmacist of this city. All w
present for the interment.

*Cora's obituary notice in a Brooklyn
newspaper, September 1932*

My grandmother Edna, c. 1935

Edna's second husband, Miguel Rodriguez, in Havana, 1932

Another, much more exciting, theatrical event was the Junior Theatre Guild of Brooklyn's annual charity show, in which Lena, as the favorite of the director (Mrs. Rollock), landed the starring role. Listed in the playbill as Lena C. Horne, she played the part of "Lolita Kingston, Herself" in *Marriage via Contract,* a romantic comedy about a Broadway producer and a famous singer. There were smaller parts, of course, for many of Lena's friends: Llewellyn Johnston, Ruth Johnson, Llewellyn Hudnell, Theresa Birnie, Louis Delsarte, Frankie Bourne, and Donald Fulcher. All of Brooklyn's young black society belonged to the Junior Theatre Guild, and rehearsals every Saturday were huge group get-togethers. Since the boys and girls went to separate schools, coed events were a great treat. But Lena had no time to flirt. She not only had the biggest part, she also had all the best songs: "Night and Day" (Act II) and "I've Got the World on a String" (Act III). A photograph of Lena in her finale costume—as a bride—appeared in the Brooklyn papers:

No, Boys, it's not a real wedding. You see, Lena C. Horne will play the role of the bride in "Marriage via Contract" when the Junior Theatre Guild appears Tuesday night at the Central Y.M.C.A. . . .

The Junior Theatre Guild show woke Brooklyn up to Lena's budding talents. She sang so sweetly, and looked so pretty in the finale, that people who had known her all her life stood up and shouted "Bravo."

■   ■   ■

In 1933 Angelo Herndon, a middle-class nineteen-year-old black from Cincinnati on a hunger march through the South (to protest white withholding of black relief), was convicted of incitement to insurrection and sentenced to twenty years on a chain gang. Teddy Horne's 1933, however, was as carefree as ever. He attended Gus Greenlee's first annual National Colored All-Star baseball game at Comiskey Park in Chicago, then stopped in at the World's Fair to see Sally Rand's fan dance. Next on the itinerary was New York's Polo Grounds and the opening game of the World Series. He dropped in on Brooklyn long enough to give Lena a new beaver-trimmed coat.

The Batista coup had ensured Mike's permanent exile from home, and with no good prospects for work, he and Edna decided to move to a smaller apartment in the Bronx. Lena was heartbroken by the move. She cheered herself up enough, however, to have one club meeting—and to send Teddy a picture of herself in her new coat taken at the Bronx Zoo. By now she

Fifteen-year-old Lena

A Brooklyn newspaper announces a 1933 charity show starring sixteen-year-old Lena Horne.

NO, BOYS, it's not a real wedding. You see, Lena C. Horne will play the role of the bride in "Marriage via Contract" when the Junior Theatre Guild appears Tuesday night at the Central Y. M. C. A. for the benefit of the Brooklyn Urban League's mothers' and babies' camp fund.

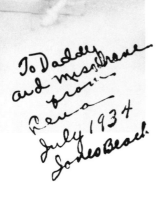

A photograph taken at Jones Beach in 1934 that Lena sent to Teddy and Irene. Lena had recently begun performing at the Cotton Club.

had left Girls High School and was enrolled in secretarial school. But Edna
had a secret plan: she wanted to put Lena on the stage. Brooklyn's amateur
theatrics had proved that Lena had some talent; maybe the Florence Mills
dream was not so crazy after all. Edna looked up her old Lafayette pal Elida
Webb, who was now dance captain at the Cotton Club. Elida thought Lena
was a bit young, but saw no reason why she shouldn't audition for the 1934
show, and although there were only two openings for it, one of them went
to an adorable girl called Winnie [Wini] Johnson and the other went to
Lena.

Sixteen-year-old Lena was tall, slim, and not quite fully developed. She
had lost weight since the Junior Theatre Guild show and possessed a wil-
lowy new grace. Her diet had been a simple combination of poverty and
unhappiness. She was still an adolescent, but her sparkling eyes, dimples,
and ravishing smile made her stand out in the crowd. Back in Brooklyn,
Edna was now deemed worse than ever. Cora Horne must be reeling, said
horrified Brooklynites. Lena became an object of scorn as well as pity.
Middle-class Brooklyn came to regard her as a social outcast, although
Ruth, Llewellyn, and a few diehard Junior Debs stood by her on her rare
visits home.

The Cotton Club was queen of Harlem's nighttime world—the most
famous and lucrative speak-easy of all. Beer built the Cotton Club: it was
started by big-time gangster Owney Madden, who manufactured Madden's
Number One beer. In 1927 Madden advised the Philadelphia nightclub
owner then holding Duke Ellington's contract to "be big" or "be dead." By
1928 Ellington was such a Cotton Club superstar that the club relaxed its
"whites only" policy. VIP blacks—including Teddy Horne—could sit at
some of the side booths, near the kitchen.

Cotton Club shows were instantly legendary: Ellington's "Jungle" orchestra; songs by Dorothy Fields and Jimmy McHugh; and three (8:30,
11:30, and 2 a.m.) elaborate shows every night featuring the greatest black
musical talent and the most beautiful "tall, tan, and terrific" show girls in
America. The Cotton Club sound was what jazz was all about in the late
1920s. It was the place to go—and everyone went, from Lady Mountbatten
to Garbo. Young George Raft, not yet a movie star, was hired to dance with
the mobsters' girl friends. The Cotton Club had everything New York
tourists seemed to want after dark: gangsters, jazz, booze, and beautiful
black women.

The nightclub was a large horseshoe-shaped room with tables on two
levels and booths all along the walls. It held six or seven hundred people a

show. Chinese or Mexican food was served at the first two shows, and fried chicken at 2 a.m. Show business people and celebrities always came to the last show, especially on Sundays. The management spared no expense on costumes (the barer the better) or sets. The club presented two new shows each year, in the spring and the fall—each a two-hour extravaganza. Dan Healy, the white choreographer, and Clarence Robinson, the black assistant who did all the work, believed in speed, dazzle, and flash. There were girl dancers, boy dancers, show girls, principals, and stars. The 1931 show featured Cab Calloway's "Minnie the Moocher" and "Kickin' the Gong Around," not to mention Aida Ward singing "Between the Devil and the Deep Blue Sea." The years 1932 and 1933 introduced two great Harold Arlen songs: "I've Got the World on a String" and "Stormy Weather," sung by Ethel Waters. In 1934 Arlen and his partner, Ted Koehler, went to Hollywood, and Lena's first Cotton Club show—despite Cab Calloway, and Adelaide Hall singing "Ill Wind" and "Primitive Prima Donna"—was not a smash hit.

Lena was important enough, because of Cora and Teddy, to have her nightclub debut noticed by the black press. Her smiling picture appeared in the *Amsterdam News:*

Schoolgirl Plus

Miss Lena Horne is a woiking goil but earning her bread does not interfere with the business of getting an education. She is a member of the new revue at the Cotton Club and attends Wadleigh Night High School. She has completed two years at Girls High, Brooklyn. Miss Horne is a Bronxite now. She has appeared with Mrs. Laura Jean Rollock's amateur groups and with Anna Jones' presentation at the Lafayette.

Lena was the youngest, and certainly among the most innocent and protected, of the Cotton Club dancing chorus. Edna hovered in the already crowded dressing room, or lurked backstage. Lena was chaperoned to a fare-thee-well. This was even an area where Mike was allowed to display some machismo. And Teddy Horne had put the word out in Harlem that his little girl was "protected."

Lena's "protection" was a result of the 1931–32 gang wars, in which Vincent "Mad Dog" Coll kidnapped Big Frenchy De Mange (Owney Madden's right-hand man) and Connie Immerman (of Connie's Inn), and forced

Madden to pay $50,000 in ransom. A year later Coll was ambushed in a telephone booth by Dutch Schultz (who owned the Bronx and wanted Harlem). Owney Madden got so tired of it all that he voluntarily committed himself to Sing Sing to clear up some tax problems, and to have a year's rest. In 1933 Madden retired, alive, to Hot Springs—counting his blessings, no doubt. Lena was "protected" by Dutch Schultz's mob, through Teddy's Harlem friend Bub Hewlett.

The Cotton Club's front man was Herman Stark, a typical cigar-chewing theater manager. Lew Leslie, who helped to make Florence Mills a star, was one of the producers. Stark and Leslie both liked Lena—and Lena thought that they, and everyone else, were pretty nice. As the youngest, she was the pet. Cab Calloway and all the boys in the band called her "Brooklyn." She also loved the salary: twenty-five dollars a week for three shows a night, seven days a week, and no extra pay for special shows or tours. Stenographers made only about sixteen dollars a week, and salesgirls five or ten. The one thing Lena didn't like was the fact that there was only one ladies' room, and it wasn't backstage. The chorus girls all shared a single dressing room, and Lena became everyone's kid sister. She was so starry-eyed that she was funny. Her best friends were two of the other younger girls, Winnie Johnson and Hycie Curtis. Among the older girls was the glamorous "Estrelita"—to Lena, part of the stratosphere. Quite a few of the girls had mink coats, one or two were famously "kept," but most of them still lived at home. The mob preferred "nice" girls—if a girl got herself talked about too much, she could be fired. Sunday night was not only celebrity night but also dress-up night, when the girls exchanged jewelry, bags, and long white gloves. Lena sat mesmerized, watching the older girls get dressed to go out. She, Winnie, and Hycie devoured Hycie's fashion magazines. Outside the dressing room, however, life was not much fun for Lena. She wasn't even allowed to go lindy-hopping at the Renaissance. "Ask my mother," she begged Winnie or Hycie. But Edna never gave permission.

One night, toward the end of the spring show run, Aida Ward got a sore throat. Herman Stark let Lena go on to sing and dance "As Long As I Live" with Avon Long. Aida Ward's costume was too big for Lena, but wardrobe managed to come up with a big picture hat and a heavy white crepe dress that fit like a dream. Lena looked so wonderful that she was photographed for the papers. Aida Ward, naturally, recovered in record time—and Lena was given no more featured assignments until the show did a week in a theater, with Claude Hopkins's orchestra. She was chosen then to sing and dance "Cocktails for Two" with Hopkins's boy singer. Edna regarded this as her chance to badger the Cotton Club management into giving Lena a featured spot in the fall show, with Jimmie Lunceford's band. Meanwhile Lena was beginning to be noticed. She had her picture taken at Jones Beach, wearing a white bathing suit and playing with a beach ball. She was labeled the "Long As I Live Girl." And Herman Stark began letting her sing for the songwriters. She was a conscientious ingenue whose mother wanted her to be a star, and Lena liked the idea, too. It seemed the best of all possible options.

■ ■ ■

Edwin had spent the winter of 1934 in Fort Valley, an unhappily retired widower. By July, he was back in Brooklyn, writing to Teddy and Irene:

> I was delighted to read your letter of last week. I am killing time to my satisfaction. As you know I am not much of a social or "society" individual. During my waking hours I read in parks, visit museums and art galleries and important musical concerts given in some of our many parks daily. I am a fan about music and about motion pictures. I mostly go in the mornings when the price is 25 or 30 cts. I am in my room at 7 almost every night. Frankye and Burke do the night runs of the city and are enjoying themselves. . . . By the way the Cotton Club will next Thursday be at the States-Loews Broadway Theatre and Miss Lena is one of the featured performers!

In August of 1934 Teddy Horne was at Chicago's Comiskey Park for the National Colored All-Star baseball game. In September he was in a field box at Yankee Stadium for the Colored World Series Classic. He also went to the Cotton Club to see his daughter. Teddy was an idol of Harlem's demimonde—so well regarded by the Cotton Club mob that he was permitted to sit in one of the VIP black booths to see Lena dance in the chorus. Lena's dressing room mates all agreed that Teddy was "gorgeous." Lena questioned all the Harlem regulars about her father; she wanted to find out everything she could about this glamorous stranger. And Teddy asked Jack Fuller, the owner of a popular Lenox Avenue restaurant, to "take care" of Lena.

Teddy also witnessed Lena's second "big" show biz break. In the fall of 1934 Broadway producer Laurence Schwab, who had noticed Lena in the Cotton Club line, convinced the Broadway mob (Legs Diamond's) to convince the Harlem mob to let Lena appear in his new show. *Dance with Your Gods* was a drama, with music, about voodoo. Lena was billed last in the program, as "a Quadroon girl." She danced a hypnotized bride solo in a "voodoo" ballet. Brooks Atkinson, of *The New York Times,* called his own review of the piece an "ungrateful task," but he admired Donald Oenslager's sets for Lena's voodoo ballet. Doubling between Broadway and Harlem, Lena skipped the first show at the Cotton Club every night and had to rush uptown on the subway to make the last two. She had no time for a Broadway curtain call.

Black themes were popular that season on Broadway. Teddy also went to the Civic Repertory to see Rex Ingram, Jack Carter, and Edna Thomas in the all-black *Stevedore.* Two other Broadway hits with black interest were the Gertrude Stein–Virgil Thomson opera *Four Saints in Three Acts,* and *They Shall Not Die,* a play about the Scottsboro Boys starring Claude Rains and Ruth Gordon. Blacks also made great tabloid copy when English steamship heiress Nancy Cunard, editor of *Negro* and author of *Black Man and White Ladyship,* arrived in New York and went to live in Harlem. Nancy was a dear friend of black poet Sterling Brown, who, like most of Nancy's black friends, agreed that she was sincerely left of center and straight on race, but that a lot of her behavior was strictly to *"épater les bourgeois."*

After *Dance with Your Gods* Edna went on badgering the Cotton Club management for a solo spot for Lena. They finally promised her one, for sure, in the first 1935 show, and meanwhile they gave her a five-dollar raise. This shut Edna up temporarily, but only strengthened her determination to get Lena out of the Cotton Club altogether. This was easier said than done, since the mob let people go only when they had no more use for them. While Mike was telling the management that Lena intended to quit —and getting his head shoved into a toilet for his efforts—Lena and Edna were spirited into a waiting taxi by a phalanx of chorus girls.

Luckily, they had a job to go to. And luckily, too, it was on the road. Edna had persuaded the well-known black producers Miller and Lisles to arrange an audition for Lena with Noble Sissle, who was looking for a girl singer. Although these were the years of great jazz and swing—Ellington, Lunceford, Chick Webb, and Fletcher Henderson—Noble Sissle (coauthor of *Shuffle Along* and former guitarist-singer with Jim Europe's Clef Club and 369th Regiment bands) played "sweet." Noble Sissle's orchestra was not only sweet, it was social—beloved of the black middle class, and a favorite of elderly white society who liked black musicians but not necessarily black music.

Lena—now "Helena"—with orchestra leader Noble Sissle, c. 1935

Lena (fourth from right) performing at the Cotton Club, 1934

Lena auditioned quite properly with "Dinner for One, Please, James,"
and was hired for the "Noble Sissle Society Orchestra" tour. Sissle bought
her a black tulle dress at Wanamaker's and outfitted her with a female
version of the band's uniform of red jackets and white trousers. Hers was a
red bellman's jacket, with white ascot, and white crepe culottes. Lena and
the boy singer, Billy Banks, who had a high sweet voice, sat in front of the
orchestra and bounced sedately to the music. Lena was also given an
Eleanor Powell tap dance routine for which she wore a sequin tail coat, top
hat, and black crepe trousers. But she was a somewhat shy and serious
soubrette, less confident than Edna that the horrors of road life were worth
it. Out of sheer boredom and misery, however, she began to enjoy what she
was doing on stage. It was the only interesting part of the day. Off-stage
life was mostly a matter of long bus rides and bickering with Edna. Lena
knew she could dance—at least she moved gracefully—and she really
wanted to learn to sing. Noble Sissle helped. He was a fiend about diction
and phrasing. Lena, thanks to Grandmother Cora, already had superb diction, and Sissle helped her to phrase it around a song (she sang mostly
ballads). His favorite singers were Adelaide Hall and Elisabeth Welch, both
of whom had sweet soprano voices, exquisite diction, elegance, and charm.
Sissle was interested in poise and polish, not passion. Sissle was so pleased
with Lena that gave her a new name: Helena Horne.

∎ ∎ ∎

In 1935 Lena's uncle Frank Horne went to Washington to join the New
Deal. Frank was named assistant director, Division of Negro Affairs, in the
National Youth Administration. His boss was Mary McLeod Bethune, the
first black department head of a federal agency. They both belonged to
FDR's so-called Black Cabinet. Mrs. Bethune, a large, dark, grandmotherly
woman—known affectionately as "Ma" Bethune—was famous for her magnificent indignations. She was the heroic founder of a school for the rural
poor, as well as the National Council of Negro Women. Cora Horne had
raised money for her in New York, and Mrs. Bethune's Washington friend
Eleanor Roosevelt helped make her famous. She was admired by blacks and
whites alike as the perfect symbol of resolute black matriarchy.

Frank moved to Washington in time to join the Gourmet Club, the new
social group of his fellow "Black Cabinet" member Al Smith. (Alfred Smith
was a Washington journalist and organizer of the first black press club.)
According to poet Sterling Brown, Al was the only gourmet—the rest were
just hungry. Some of the other members were C. Herbert Marshall, Jr. (a

Georgetown physician), Otto McClaren (public relations director of Howard University), and Dr. W. Montague Cobb. Monty Cobb was an Amherst graduate, with three degrees, who played the violin—he hated jazz; "you niggers ain't got no culture," he would say to his club mates. Frank Horne was considered a gentleman and a serious intellectual. Lacking the common touch politically, he let his hair down among his peers. The Gourmet Club met in Georgetown, then a black district. None of the members had much money, but they represented the Washington elite: professors from Howard, doctors, lawyers, and government workers.

While Lena was on the road with Sissle and Frank was in Washington with FDR, Teddy was still going to the fights. On June 25, 1935, he paid $11.50 for a rear mezzanine ticket to see a new black heavyweight named Joe Louis fight Italy's Primo Carnera at Yankee Stadium. The Louis-Carnera fight attracted 60,000 people, among them 15,000 blacks and 1,300 police. Police Commissioner Lewis J. Valentine indicated that the extraordinary police precautions (300 extra detectives, tear gas, and four patrol wagons) were because officials regarded "mixed heavyweight bouts with mixed emotions." It was not even a championship match. Joe Louis (born Joseph Louis Barrow in Alabama) was a beardless youth of twenty-one who had won the national amateur championship fifteen months before and had made his professional debut the previous Fourth of July. The New York *Herald Tribune* described the enormous black crowd:

> They came from Harlem just across the river, from Brooklyn, from Detroit, where Joe Louis lives; from Chicago, where he fought his way to sudden fame in less than a year; from Boston, Philadelphia, Washington and way stations, all desirous of seeing the most publicized and spectacular heavyweight of their race since Jack Johnson fought James J. Jeffries at Reno twenty-five years ago.

Among the crowd, which included the mayors of three cities, and the "customary gathering of bigwigs from the political arena, the judiciary, the stage and screen, the sporting field . . . ," were black celebrities: Ferdinand Q. Morton, civil service commissioner, head of Black Tammany, and Edwin's former colleague; Hubert Delaney, tax commissioner; Dr. C. B. Powell, Harlem's X-ray specialist and chairman of the board of the Victory Life Insurance Company; Harry Bragg, assistant state attorney general; William T. Andrews, assemblyman; Walter White, secretary of the NAACP; Dr. Louis T. Wright, New York police surgeon and only black fellow of the American College of Surgeons; the Reverend Adam Clayton Powell, Jr., assistant pastor, Abyssinian Baptist Church; Fritz Pollard, former All-American at Brown and a Horne neighbor; orchestra leaders Duke Ellington and Claude Hopkins; Police Lieutenant Samuel Battles (New York City's first black cop, circa 1911); George Gregory, captain of Columbia University's championship basketball team; Congressman William Mitchell of Chicago; Professors Ralph Bunche and Emmett (Sam) Dorsey of Howard University (who, together with E. Franklin Frazier, were putting Howard's sociology department on the map); editors Carl Murphy of the Baltimore *Afro-American,* Robert L. Vann of the Pittsburgh *Courier,* and Robert Abbott of the Chicago *Defender.* Teddy must have enjoyed the audience as much as the fight. Most of them were friends or acquaintances of the Horne family.

In August Teddy was back in Pittsburgh to see Gus Greenlee's presentation of heavyweight champion James Braddock in an exhibition match against Jack McCarthy (Teddy got Braddock's autograph on his program).

Edwin suffered a stroke in the summer of 1936. In September he visited Pittsburgh to recuperate. A month later, back in New York, he wrote to Irene:

> I hate Chauncey Street. I hate New York. The street is
> Africanized and the whites are the scum from torn-down
> tenements. . . . I am uncertain if I will ever get well. I think my
> span of life is nearly run. My old time friends of your mother and I
> are gone. . . .
>
> I told Burke to write you and Ted—to tell you not to spend any
> money on the house for my occupancy. *Sell* it. Trade it off. As an
> income from renting the class of negroes will not pay any rent.
> They never stay more than a month and then they steal everything
> I have there. I am certain Frank would not care to live there. Nor
> would Burke and New York does not appeal to Ted. It is not the
> city we once knew. The way to make money is practically shut
> down. But I am not interfering with your and the boys' plans. We
> might get into a better section of town or get out of New York. *I
> want no more of Chauncey Street.*

Lena, on the road with Sissle, was having fun in Washington and Baltimore. Late in 1936 Sissle's orchestra became the first black band to play at Boston's Ritz-Carlton Hotel. Lena's big ballad was "Blue Moon."

And she was attracting a large and vocal college fan club, mostly from Harvard, that returned night after night. Ed Winer, the manager of the Ritz-Carlton nightclub, called John Hammond, recording director for Irving Mills (the man who "owned" Ellington), to say, "John, I have a terrible band on the roof called Noble Sissle—but the girl singer is so beautiful it makes up for everything." Hammond knew Lena from the Cotton Club and thought that her voice was not spectacular. He was deaf to everyone but Billie Holiday, anyway. But Hammond remembered that Lena looked marvelous. He remembered the self-confidence that made her stand out among the other Cotton Club cuties, and he attributed it to what he knew was her good Brooklyn background. John Hammond was a rich white Yale dropout who saw Florence Mills in *From Dover to Dixie* in London when he was twelve years old, and committed himself thereafter to jazz. By the time he was in college he was one of the world's experts on the subject and had become the American correspondent for *Gramophone,* the English jazz magazine. He was also left of center and racially liberal—a board member of the NAACP. Hammond was proud of his friendships with black intellectuals and musicians. He knew Frank Horne quite well, and many of his other black friends were close to the Horne family. At this point John Hammond wished Lena well on the basis more of her family and friends than of her talent, but he did think that she was wonderfully pretty.

Lena, too, knew she was pretty in late 1936—but she never assumed that anyone would think her beautiful. Beautiful was Estrelita of the Cotton Club, or Garbo. Lena was a nineteen-year-old who had never had a boyfriend. Edna remained intractable on the subject. Lena was going to become a star, and for both their sakes there would be no sidetracks. But at Christmas Teddy flew in to Cleveland to see Lena with Sissle, and to take in the Cleveland *News'* Christmas Boxing Show (Joe Louis versus Johnny Risko). Ted's traveling companion was a handsome young man from Pittsburgh named Louis Jones, the youngest of four children of the Reverend William Augustus Jones of Louisville, Kentucky. The Jones siblings now all lived in Pittsburgh. The older Jones brothers, Paul and Spurgeon ("Buddy"), were both lawyer-politicians in Gus Greenlee's Pittsburgh ward who had rendered good service to the Democratic machine. Kid brother Louis, a graduate of West Virginia State College, had been rewarded with a job as registrar of the coroner's office. He was twenty-eight years old, politically well connected, polite, and eminently eligible. Lena liked the idea that he was a college man and was charmed by his good manners and sense of humor, but she wondered if he hadn't been spoiled by a succession of wealthy stepmothers. The mother of the Jones children had died young; the reverend had married, and buried, several rich widows. While Louis, as a carefree bachelor, enjoyed the aura of Teddy's sporting life—Louis himself belonged to a high-stakes bridge club—he was also an extremely respectable and conventional young man. And he was looking for a respectable and conventional wife.

Lena decided almost at once to marry this seemingly perfect young man: a husband was even better than a boyfriend. Edna now swore that she would never "forgive" Lena if she gave up her career, but Lena didn't care; she was prepared to be clasped to the bosom of respectable black Pittsburgh.

They were married in brother Paul Jones's living room, with only Ted, Irene, and the Jones family on hand. The Reverend Jones married them. Lena didn't tell her new father-in-law that she was a nominal Catholic—at that point, even a lifetime of sin was preferable to life on the road with Edna. Anyway, she really liked her father-in-law, who reminded her of Edwin, and she also liked her new brothers and her pretty sisters-in-law. She finally had a place to go for Thanksgiving and Christmas.

Lena quickly settled down to a life of newlywed domesticity. Until their first child was born, Louis and Lena lived on the top floor of Paul's house. Lena was mad about her husband. As a high school dropout addicted to the movies, she saw him as the rather unlikely combination of her three favorite stars: Noel Coward, Leslie Howard, and George Raft. Unfortunately, Louis was somewhat less sophisticated than Lena's idols. He had, for example, old-fashioned ideas about wifely duties. He believed in perfectly ironed shirts, piping hot biscuits, and demon needlework. Lena, whom neither Cora nor Edna had seen fit to prepare for homemaking, could sing, dance, and make intelligent conversation, but she could barely boil an egg. She was also a great reader—the only solace of a lonely child—and while Louis filed papers at the office all week, Lena was more often to be found reading a magazine than darning socks. Tears and recriminations would follow. Fortunately, Lena got pregnant early in the marriage and was permitted to go easy on the housework.

Lena soon learned that Louis' circle of friends was jolly, if limited. Bridge club spouses who didn't play were left to their own devices at weekend parties, and Lena made friends with a few other nonplaying deviants. But Teddy's rather more expansive social set welcomed the young couple as an attractive addition. And almost at once Louis and Lena found themselves living beyond their means.

In June of 1937 Teddy was ringside in Chicago to see Joe Louis defeat

James Braddock and become heavyweight champion of the world. A peaceful crowd, estimated at one hundred thousand, swarmed the streets of Harlem to celebrate the victory. Teddy's newest best friend was John Roxborough, Louis' manager. In August Teddy received a registered mail letter from the 20th Century Sporting Club, Inc.

Dear Ted:

Enclosed find four (4) tix as per your order. Hope they are OK. Everybody is fine. Joe says "Hello." He's in wonderful shape. Regards to the madame.

Sincerely,
John W. Roxborough

While Lena was pregnant her Junior Deb friends came to see her, and they were photographed for the Pittsburgh *Courier* wearing similar floral print dresses: "Brooklyn beauties visited Smoketown last week. Ruth Johnson, Llewellyn Hudnell, Llewellyn Johnston, Lena Horne-Jones—their hostess." (Lena was very avant-garde about hyphenating her name. She was not Cora's granddaughter for nothing.)

The few black mothers at the Pittsburgh hospital where I was born had their own special ward. "Buster" Cornelius, the family doctor of VIP black Pittsburgh, was cheerful and comforting, but he neglected to tell Lena the rules of the game. He would see her "every day," he said, but he could not treat her at the hospital. Buster assumed Lena knew that black doctors could not practice in the hospital. But Lena didn't know, and she was hysterical. On December 21, 1937, after many hours of agonizing labor, Lena was finally delivered of fat, healthy me. And soon afterward Lena, Louis, and baby Gail moved into their own little white stucco house in Herron Hill—with living room, dining room, and kitchen downstairs and two bedrooms upstairs. My parents were head over heels in debt—but I, a happy, healthy Christmas present, temporarily took their minds off money. My only problems were a slightly crossed eye and an allergy to spinach. I outgrew both.

■ ■ ■

When I was about four months old Lena got a phone call from Harold Gumm, her sometime New York agent, who offered her the costarring part, without a test, in an all-black quickie musical to be shot in Hollywood.

*Teddy Horne and friend at
Gus Greenlee's Pittsburgh
stadium, 1936*

*A Pittsburgh newspaper records the
arrival of three "Brooklyn beauties"
on a visit to their "Junior Deb"
friend "Lena Horne-Jones."
The hyphenated hostess
(far right) was pregnant
with me at the time.*

*FDR's "Black Cabinet," 1938. Frank Horne
is in the front row, fifth from left.
Next to him stands Mary McCleod Bethune.*

My father, Louis Jones, sees my
mother off to Hollywood to make her
first movie, The Duke Is Tops.

Lena waiting for her flight with
Pittsburgh sportsman "Woogie" Harris,
whose wife's fur coat she borrowed
for the trip

Louis, Teddy, and Lena at the airport

Ralph Cooper, suave and handsome, was to be the male lead. Cooper had starred in 1936's popular all-black gangster movie *Dark Manhattan* and was known as "the Black Bogart." He had once been tested at Fox to play one of Shirley Temple's avuncular black retainers but was rejected for being too "good-looking." The producers of the new film, *The Duke Is Tops*, were the Popkin Brothers, shoestring independents.

The shooting schedule was only ten days. Louis' sister, Marguerite, could stay with Gail. The money was fabulous. How could Lena refuse? How could Louis resist the financial benefits? It seemed like an answered prayer. When Louis, Ted, and all the Horne/Jones family friends then made the decision that Lena should go to Hollywood in style, Lena ended up spending a fortune she didn't have on a traveling outfit and new luggage. Mrs. "Woogie" Harris, whose husband was a cohort of Gus Greenlee, loaned Lena her Persian lamb coat. And naturally, Teddy insisted that flying was the only way to go. So Lena took TWA's Pittsburgh–Los Angeles flight, a backbreaking, weather-wracked, forty-eight-hour lifetime. The plane was grounded in Arizona and seemed to make about four hundred hideous, bumpy stops before reaching Los Angeles. Lena hated the entire trip and swore she would never fly again.

The bumpy trip was perhaps an omen. Ralph Cooper and the Popkin Brothers were not thrilled to find that the slim adolescent of the Cotton Club was now a plump new mother. *The Duke Is Tops* was, according to *Variety,* the story of a "girl-boy performer team having to split up when gal gets a N.Y. break. Boy goes down, gal goes up, and then sags. Get together for finale, when combined efforts put them into the big time." There were two elaborate nightclub sequences, as well as other musical numbers— none memorable, although critics did like Lena's "I Know You Remember." And although the picture got made, no one got any money for it. It seems that Harry Popkin had neglected to raise the funds before shooting began. In mid-production Louis ordered Lena to come home at once, and they had a terrible quarrel on the telephone. But Lena refused to quit. The Popkins promised to pay the actors out of the film's profits, and the picture was finished on time. It was scheduled for a Pittsburgh NAACP benefit opening —in honor of the home-town girl—but when Lena came home from Hollywood, Louis revealed his second thoughts about moviemaking and forbade Lena to go to the opening. (When Lena went to Hollywood again, the Popkin Brothers re-released *The Duke Is Tops* and called it *Bronze Venus,* but Lena still never got paid.)

. . .

According to *Fortune* magazine 84.7 percent of American blacks supported
FDR. The New Deal was the best thing for blacks since Reconstruction.
Frank Horne, who was moving up in the "Black Cabinet," was now assistant to Robert Weaver in the Office of Race Relations, United States Housing Authority. In March 1938 he posed for an official group photograph;
among the others in the picture were Mrs. Bethune, Robert Weaver, and
Frank's old Fort Valley boss, Dr. Hunt. (I first saw this photograph of my
great-uncle with the "Black Cabinet" some thirty-five years later, blown
up, on the wall of the old Smithsonian in Washington, not far from the
Spirit of St. Louis, the McCormick reaper, and other artifacts of American
history.)

In the fall of 1938, when I was about nine months old, Lena got another
call from Harold Gumm. This time Lew Leslie wanted her for his new
revue, *Blackbirds of 1939.* Leslie had discovered Florence Mills, who had
also starred in *Blackbird* shows. (*Blackbirds of 1928* was the longest running
all-black show on Broadway.) Since Leslie remembered Lena from the Cotton Club, no audition was necessary. Once again the offer was too tempting
to turn down.

Leslie could have been a theatrical producer invented by Hollywood:
lovable, full of grandiose schemes, and always one step ahead of his credi-
tors. He inserted a special footnote in all of his playbills: "Program Subject
to Change Owing to Magnitude of Production." Leslie's *International Revue*
of 1930, with Gertrude Lawrence and Harry Richman, was successful. But
two later *Blackbirds* had failed. *Blackbirds of 1939,* starring Lena, the Hall
Johnson Choir, and comedians Fletcher and Markham, tried out in Boston,
and once again Lena had her unofficial Harvard fan club. Leslie was pleased
with Lena's progress. He was grooming her—a dream come true, at last—
to be "another Florence Mills." "Be tender, Lena," he would urge as he
coached her singing. In November he gave an interview to newspapers:

"BLACKBIRDS" HAS A NEW DUSKY "FIND"

Lew Leslie, who discovered and developed such dusky stars in the
past as Florence Mills, Bill Robinson, Ethel Waters, Adelaide Hall
and the Berry Brothers, believes he has another theatrical "find" in
Lena Horne, the songstress, featured in the sixth edition of "Blackbirds" opening at the Majestic Theatre Nov. 7. Leslie first saw her

in the chorus of the Cotton Club three years ago and has been developing her ever since.

"In my opinion," asserts Leslie, "Lena Horne comes closest to the talented Florence Mills of any Ethiopian actress I have ever seen. She can sing, dance and read lines with great comic spirit. In addition to all of this, she has youth and beauty."

In typical Leslie fashion, *Blackbirds* was three months late coming to Broadway, and Leslie's wife, the singer Belle Baker, had to pawn her jewels to pay the bond. On February 13, 1939, when the show finally opened, Brooks Atkinson, of *The New York Times,* wrote:

After two months of heroic promoting the indomitable Lew Leslie has flown his "Blackbirds of 1939" as far south as the Hudson Theatre, where they opened on Saturday evening. When Mr. Leslie goes blackbirding he does not spare the horses. . . . He puts himself heart and soul into keeping the pace hot and terrific.

Among those present is a radiantly beautiful sepia girl, Lena Horne, who sings "Thursday" and "You're So Indifferent" in an attractive style, and who will be a winner when she has proper direction. . . .

A week later "Walter Winchell on Broadway" reported:

The First Nights: Lew Leslie, who has often snagged some pow'ful talents out of Harlem, must have roamed Lenox Avenue on a dark night when recruiting for his new "Blackbirds." Except for some greased light'ning hoofers and a radiant songstress called Lena Horne, the show, the inspectors thought, was almost as so-so as the run of revues. . . .

The 1939 theatrical season that Lena almost became part of was wonderfully star-studded: Merman and Durante, Walter Huston in *Knickerbocker Holiday,* Tallulah Bankhead in *The Little Foxes,* Raymond Massey's *Abe Lincoln in Illinois,* and Ethel Waters in *Mamba's Daughters* (which Lena saw).

When Louis came up from Pittsburgh for the closing of *Blackbirds* (after nine performances), he again played the heavy and wouldn't allow Lena to attend the cast party. And once again there was an enormous quarrel—ending, on Lena's part, in tears and sulking. When they returned home to Pittsburgh, Lena decided that she'd had enough of marriage. Teddy was furious. "What about your child? You have no money!" he said. But Lena announced that she would rather starve than live with Louis a moment longer. A family meeting was called to discuss the situation. It was agreed that Lena was young, therefore liable to mistakes, and that Louis must learn to forgive. On the other hand, Lena must also try harder to be a good wife and mother.

Looking around, Lena realized that she had no place to go. Teddy refused to take her in. Edna and Mike, with war at hand, had returned to Cuba (Batista had pardoned his former enemies). In the end Lena agreed to give marriage a second chance.

Around the time of Lena and Louis' reconciliation, Teddy took Irene, Lena, Louis, and me to see *Gone With the Wind*. I remember not the movie, of course, but an enormity of darkness, flashing colors, and people. It must have been my first step into the real world.

Edwin began to weaken that summer. In June Teddy and Irene went to Brooklyn to visit him (Teddy also found time for Yankee Stadium). In July Edwin gave Burke his power of attorney. A few days later he died, with his three surviving sons around him. He had never really recovered from his stroke. He may also not have recovered from the lonely surprise of outliving three wives. He had enjoyed (almost to the day) the "5 years more life" that he had wished for in a 1934 letter to Ted and Irene. And he had managed to reach eighty and to "beat the pension period."

Before her second pregnancy (the happy result of Louis and Lena's reconciliation was my baby brother) Lena began to earn money singing at private parties. Louis approved because Lena sang with fellow Bridge Circle member Charlotte Catlin, an elegant black pianist, who knew rich white Pittsburgh. The money was excellent and the social stratum of the party givers—Mellons et al.—was rarefied. To Louis, it wasn't like show biz. Lena and Charlotte would arrive in evening dress, toward the end of dinner, to entertain. The guests would gather around the piano, some of them sitting on the floor, while Charlotte played and Lena sang "Copper Colored Gal of Mine," "The Man I Love," and "On the Sunny Side of the Street." After the performance Lena and Charlotte would be served dessert and coffee, along with the compliments of the guests, before they went home. No cash ever changed hands, but a substantial check would always be delivered to Charlotte the next day.

When my brother was born in February 1940, he was given the names of his late great-grandfather—Edwin Fletcher—and was called little Teddy, to distinguish him from big Teddy, his grandfather. Little Teddy had his grandmother Edna's green eyes. I, a passionate doll keeper, thought he was a great big doll.

Little Teddy's birth marked the end of an already deteriorating marriage. Lena had made up her mind: she would get out of this marriage if it was the last thing she did. She now understood that she had married Louis only to get away from Edna—and he was beginning to seem more and more like her mother, wanting "perfect" behavior. This time Lena went to her canny stepmother, Irene, and asked to borrow a large sum of money. She needed enough to live on until she found a job, and she needed money to pay someone to live at Louis' house and take care of the children until she came back. Irene knew Teddy would be furious, but she also understood that Lena was desperate. Louis, for his part, was so taken aback by the utterly serious tone of Lena's announcement that he was nearly speechless. The only thing he said that really mattered was "If you go, you can come back for Gail, but you'll never get Teddy."

Thanks to Irene's generosity, Lena was able to check into Harlem's Theresa Hotel. She then went immediately to the Apollo Theater to see Clarence Robinson, the ex–Cotton Club choreographer. She wanted to know if there was an opening in the Apollo chorus line, and she wanted to try to find Noble Sissle. Clarence gave Lena Sissle's itinerary but was sorry to say there were no openings at the Apollo—a lucky miss for Lena. She then called Harold Gumm. "Well, there's a benefit coming up at the Apollo, you can do that," said Gumm. Lena agreed, figuring that a job without money was probably better than no job at all. "Come and see me," added Gumm. Lena was frankly terrified by the proposition. She had never gone on her own to see an agent, or anyone else, about a job. She had been totally sheltered from the realities of show biz life. Fortunately, Harold Gumm was a relatively good-hearted sort for a slightly unsavory agent. He genuinely liked Lena and thought she "had something." He wouldn't sully her with non-class surroundings—but he did advise her that he, as her agent, was entitled to 20 percent of her earnings. How was Lena to know any better? Portly little Harold Gumm, with his bullet-shaped head and his horrible eau de cologne, was the only agent Lena had ever heard of.

One producer told Gumm that Lena was not his idea of a colored singer. George White, of the *Scandals,* reiterated, "Don't say she's Negro. . . . Let her learn a few Spanish songs, give her a Spanish name, and I'll put her in." But Lena put her foot down at being Spanish. It was not merely the idea of "passing" that she disliked; she didn't like being reminded of her hated stepfather.

Rehearsing for the Apollo benefit, Lena ran into Noble Sissle, who had last seen her as a new bride and who, unfortunately, didn't need a girl singer at the moment. But it didn't matter. As she sang "Yes, My Darling Daughter" (a Dinah Shore hit record), "Good for Nothing Joe" (from the Cotton Club), and "Down Argentina Way" (from a Betty Grable movie), she wore one of the two new dresses Irene had sent her from Pittsburgh's best department store. Lena was a huge success at the benefit.

The next day—let down, depressed, and fearful—she slunk off in the middle of the afternoon to the comforting darkness of the Victoria movie theater, on 116th Street. Suddenly there was a commotion in the aisle— voices, and a flashlight. It was Clarence Robinson and an usher, looking for her. "Come on! Come out," Clarence was gesturing frantically. Once in the street, he explained: "Charlie Barnet is at the Windsor Theater in the Bronx. His girl singer got sick, and he called the Apollo looking for a replacement. Charlie's a great guy—you've got to go up there!" Charlie Barnet was indeed a great guy, widely known to be a liberal. Like John Hammond, he was a rich man's son who loved jazz. And Harlem loved Charlie Barnet's hit record of "Cherokee." But as she descended into the subway for the Bronx, Lena was dubious.

"*Wow!* Who are you?" were Charlie's first words to Lena as she approached him backstage at the Windsor. When she explained that she was there at Clarence Robinson's suggestion, Charlie apologized, saying that he was just about to go on. But why not "hang around" until he was finished? After the show Charlie took Lena to the rehearsal room with his pianist, and she sang a couple of the songs she had done at the Apollo benefit. Charlie's immediate response was "Do you want to work in the next show?" Lena went back into the subway, picked up her new dresses at the hotel, and returned to the theater in time for the next show. That night she called Pittsburgh to report on her new job. The following morning she moved into the YWCA at 135th Street and Seventh Avenue. For the next few weeks, when she wasn't working, she spent most of her time in her room at the Y listening to the radio. She would sometimes call "Stan the Milkman," of "Milkman's Matinee," to request Artie Shaw's recording of "Stardust." (Unbeknownst to Lena, the "Stardust" arrangement that she liked so much was by Lennie Hayton, someone who would later be very important in her life.)

Being on the road with Charlie Barnet was very different from traveling with Noble Sissle. Charlie, unlike Sissle, didn't try to fit Lena into a mold but encouraged her to find her own vocal personality. He also recorded with Lena: "Good for Nothing Joe" and "Love Me a Little." Even more important for Lena than the musical experience was the racial one. When she traveled with Sissle, they were all black together. When she traveled with Barnet, things were never predictable. Most hotels said "No blacks allowed." Sometimes they relented in the face of Charlie's threat to pull all twenty-five room reservations—and sometimes they did not. When that happened, Charlie and at least some of the boys would walk out with Lena to find a hotel that would take them all. Sometimes, at college dances, Charlie would be told that Lena's presence was unacceptable, and Lena would get the night off with pay. Other times she would be permitted to sing but not to sit on the bandstand, so she would wait in the bus and some of the boys would keep her company. When the band set off on a long Southern tour, Lena was given a vacation with pay.

At this time there was a traumatic reunion with Louis in Pittsburgh, and a long, tearful consultation with Teddy and Irene. Louis was adamant. She could take me, but he wouldn't give up little Teddy. Lena had already decided to quit Barnet's band, much as she liked Charlie. She needed a permanent home for her children (or child), and Teddy agreed to give Lena the Chauncey Street house to live in. He also advised her to go to Chicago to see newly widowed cousin Edwina: why not ask Edwina to come and live with her in Brooklyn and help take care of little me?

I remember quite vividly leaving Pittsburgh, forever, with my mother —of course at the time I didn't know it was forever. I remember being dressed up in my pink coat and hat, and I remember being surrounded by grown-ups' knees. I might even have clung to my father's trousers. I hadn't seen my mother for six months, after all. We set off for Lena's beloved Brooklyn; Edwina would join us soon. While Lena waited for Charlie Barnet's return, she landed a recording job with Artie Shaw on the strength of her "Good for Nothing Joe" record with Barnet. The new record, "Don't Take Your Love from Me," was quite well received.

Charlie Barnet took the news of Lena's imminent departure in typically generous Charlie fashion. Why not sing with the band, at the Paramount, while she looked for a job? It was the best possible showcase for job-hunting. Lena had to give up a couple of her songs, since Dinah Shore was the star attraction, but the Paramount opening coincided with the release of the Artie Shaw recording. And John Hammond called Barney Josephson at Café Society to say, "There's a girl singing at the Paramount with Charlie Barnet. You should see her."

Hammond was responding to Lena's plaintive call of several weeks earlier. She was "tired" of being "chased through hotel corridors by Charlie Barnet's musicians." Could John help her find another job? Hammond had liked Lena in *Blackbirds,* and he thought she might be ideal for Café Society, where they were always looking for "sophisticated" performers. Hammond also thought that Lena might learn something from Teddy Wilson, who ran the Café Society orchestra. So early one spring day in 1941 Barney Josephson went to a matinee at the Paramount, and he saw this "gorgeous creature" (he couldn't tell whether she was black or white) sitting on a chair in front of the band. Later he went backstage, introduced himself, and said, "How would you like to work at Café Society?"

Café Society was America's first political cabaret and one of New York's most successful nightclubs. According to insiders, it was started as a money-raising vehicle for the American Communist Party. Barney Josephson, the owner of the club, had joined the Young People's Socialist League before the Russian Revolution. In 1917 he had been a teenaged pacifist (older YPSL-ites went to Mexico to escape the draft). In 1938 Barney was given some money—not a lot, but enough to rent a $200-a-month basement on Sheridan Square, in Greenwich Village, to open the nightclub that would be unlike any other in America. It would be political and interracial. And it would be a "people's" nightclub—no fake palm trees, no velours draperies, no chorus line, and no hat check girls selling gardenias. Some unemployed WPA artists—William Gropper, Adolph Dehn, Syd Hoff, and Ad Reinhardt—painted the club's witty murals (which poked fun at Cholly Knickerbocker's "real" café society). The painters each worked for $250 in food and drink. In years to come, the walls would be worth millions.

Helen Lawrenson, a chic, glamorous, and funny writer of the 1930s and '40s (she wrote *Latins Are Lousy Lovers*) helped make Café Society popular with the rich midtown crowd. At the suggestion of Earl Browder of the American Communist Party, who informed her of the party's nightclub plans, Helen got all her *Vogue* and *Vanity Fair* pals to give the club free publicity and advice. It was Clare Boothe who said to Helen, "Tell Barney to call it Café Society." Helen's journalist friends contributed just the right irreverent tone. The matchbook covers at Café Society read "The wrong place for the Right people." And the cigarette girls called, "Cigars, cigarettes, wolfhounds?"

John Hammond was the club's musical expert and chief talent scout.

Café Society opened on New Year's Eve 1939 with a show featuring Billie Holiday, Teddy Wilson, comedian Jack Gilford, and a boogie-woogie combo.

Café Society's patrons, like its backers, were an eclectic group: left-wingers, jazz lovers, debutantes, labor leaders, and celebrities—white and black—from Eleanor Roosevelt to Paul Robeson. And the club's talent discoveries were extraordinary: Billie Holiday, Hazel Scott, Zero Mostel, Josh White, Betty Comden, Adolph Green, and Judy Holliday. It was the only unsegregated nightclub in New York outside of Harlem. Within two years the club managed—with occasional financial help from Hammond, or from his brother-in-law, Benny Goodman—to make enough money to open a branch farther uptown.

Lena almost blew it at her first rehearsal. She asked the pianist to play "When It's Sleepy Time Down South." Barney was aghast. "How can you sing such a song? Don't you know what they do to Negroes in the South?" he said. (Billie Holiday's big Café Society song "Strange Fruit" was about Southern lynchings.) Chagrined, Lena quickly switched to "Down Argentina Way." She managed a few bars, but Barney shook his head in despair. "No, no, Lena," he explained more in sadness than anger. "There are all these Jewish girls from Brooklyn who are giving themselves Latin names and singing Latin songs. You are unique—as yourself you'll have no competition." Lena was dismayed. She was finally allowed to proceed with "The Man I Love." Barney then appointed himself Lena's coach and mentor. First of all, she was much too beautiful and regal to be called Lena. She must go back to her Sissle name, Helena Horne. ("Over my dead body" was Hammond's response to the name change. But Harold Gumm, who was hopping with glee over Lena's good fortune, went along with "Helena.") Barney also planned Lena's repertoire: "You should sing nothing but standards—and in every show do one blues number." At this, Lena balked. "I can't *sing* blues. I don't even *know* any blues," she said. But Barney insisted. He told her to learn "Billie's Blues." Lena, out of her depth, decided to confer with Billie Holiday.

Lena went to visit Billie backstage at Kelly's Stable, another Village nightclub. Billie was delighted, in her low-key way, that Lena was doing her song. And she pooh-poohed Lena's fears about her vocal inadequacies. While Lena had never been permitted to *listen* to blues, she had certainly *overheard* them. To Lena the blues seemed a question of *size*. Her voice, not to mention her frame, would never be "big" enough. But Billie herself had disproved this idea; if the feelings were "big" enough, anyone could sing the blues.

Lena and I walking on Chauncey Street in Brooklyn, 1941

Helena Horne, a Cotton Club alumna who wowed 'em at Carnegie last night.

Blues Singer Brings Uplift To Village's Cafe Society

The New York press takes notice of "Helena's" 1941 performances at Café Society and Carnegie Hall

Lena and Billie liked each other. Lena saw, with Billie, a side of black life that was new to her. Billie was such a "victim," even then, exploited by everyone around her; no wonder she felt that her little dogs were her only friends. Lena, of course, loved dogs, too, and this became even more of a bond with Billie than music. Lena found Billie "pathetic"; she wanted to take care of her. And Billie found Lena "naïve"; she wanted to give her good advice. Billie herself was a living advertisement against drug abuse and dreadful men. If Barney's old-left puritanism—which insisted that reefer smokers would be fired—was not enough to turn Lena against drugs, the sight of Billie was. The only reason Lena never tried marijuana was because she didn't even know how to smoke a cigarette.

For her Café Society opening Lena sang, with Teddy Wilson's band, Billie Holiday's "Fine and Mellow," "The Saga of Jenny" (from Kurt Weill's *Lady in the Dark*), "The Man I Love," and "Summertime." Barney was coaching her. "What is a song, Lena?" he would ask. "A song is a song," said Lena. (Barney was beginning to remind her of Cora Horne.) "No, Lena," he said, "it's a story with music—you must listen to every word, and feel every word." Then he told her to "think of Gail and little Teddy" whenever she sang "Summertime." The next night she sang "Summertime" and heaved a tremendous sigh right in the middle of it. The audience was rapt. They burst into applause almost before she was finished.

Shortly after her Café Society debut in the early spring of 1941 Hammond recorded Lena, with Teddy Wilson, singing "Out of Nowhere" and "Prisoner of Love." A few weeks later Café Society hired Carnegie Hall for a jazz concert to benefit Local 802 of the American Federation of Musicians. The highlight was an enormous jam session featuring Teddy Wilson's band, Count Basie's orchestra (flown in from Pittsburgh), Bunny Berigan, Max Kaminsky, Charlie Barnet, and Henry "Hot Lips" Levine. Hazel Scott, who had moved to the uptown Café Society when Lena started at Sheridan Square, was the nominal star of the show. But Lena's photograph was used in most of the reviews: "Helena Horne, a Cotton Club alumna who wowed 'em at Carnegie last night." In June she was featured in *PM* newspaper:

"HELENA HORNE, WHO IS GIVING
THE VILLAGE A NEW THRILL":

Late this spring things took a turn for the better at Café Society Downtown. Word had spread that Barney Josephson, presiding genius . . . had uncovered an exciting talent, a singer who came in as

Lena Horne and stayed on as Helena Horne. The old guard drifted back to hear Helena Horne and having heard her—and seen her—stayed. Business is better now at Café Society Downtown than it has been in a long time, and it's getting better. The management makes no secret of the fact that Helena Horne is responsible for the change. At 23, Helena is snowballing to fame. . . . She is now featured at the "Cats 'n' Jammers" program on WOR. . . . Her "Summertime" is becoming a Café Society spécialité de la maison.

Lena loved her life. She was making seventy-five dollars a week and felt like a millionaire. Louis had even permitted little Teddy to come to Brooklyn for a long visit. Lena slept late, then spent the afternoons playing with her children under the same cherry tree that she had played under as a child. After she gave us dinner, she would leave us with Edwina and get on the subway for Sheridan Square. She enjoyed being back in Brooklyn, and she saw members of the old crowd regularly. Burke and Frank were also frequent visitors to Chauncey Street. Frank had now succeeded Robert Weaver as director, Office of Race Relations, United States Housing Authority, and he often came to New York on government business.

Café Society was the favorite night spot of the intellectual black middle class, and Lena was now meeting Frank Horne's friends for the first time as an adult. There were painter "Romie" (Romare) Bearden; painter "Spinky" (Charles) Alston and his wife, Dr. Myra Logan of Harlem Hospital; and Myra's brother, Dr. Arthur Logan. (The Logans were children of Cora Horne's girlhood friend Adella Hunt Logan.) There was also the Washington triumvirate of Ralph Bunche, E. Franklin Frazier, and Sterling Brown. Sterling, who was working on the WPA's Federal Writers' Project (nurturing such new talents as Richard Wright and Ralph Ellison), had very definite ideas about black life and culture. America might be a segregated world, but the black world was not necessarily inferior. "They have Kate Smith, but we have Bessie Smith," he used to say. He also believed that the purest example of "interracial harmony" was Hammond's brother-in-law, Bennie Goodman, and his quartet (blacks Teddy Wilson and Lionel Hampton, with whites Goodman and Gene Krupa).

Lena liked Sterling. She told him that she had never met a "briefcase Negro" who knew so much about music. He told her that she had a "clarinet" voice. Sterling went back to Café Society several times, and one night he stayed around until closing and took Lena home to Brooklyn. Edwina was waiting up, but Sterling and Lena talked until dawn. It was not a romantic conversation. Lena asked Sterling serious questions about life and the world, treating him like her Uncle Frank, which Sterling thought was a pity.

Café Society conversation was terrific. Barney Josephson basically considered his nightclub to be a seminar with drinks and entertainment. Lena was awed and flattered that Frank Horne's important friends were treating her like a peer. Walter White riveted his blue eyes on Lena and pronounced her a "winner." Her "responsibilities," he said, would be great. Lena was not quite sure what Walter meant, but Sterling explained that it meant Walter's approval—Walter spoke only to "winners."

Lena knew when Paul Robeson was in the audience at Café Society, because it was all that anyone talked about backstage. Paul's effect on any gathering was electric—he was the kind of man people stood on chairs to see in crowded rooms. He was physically enormous, and beautiful. And his voice was like gently rolling thunder. Paul had no public and private sides (except, perhaps, in his love life). He had been brought up in a very straightforward, old-fashioned way, as the son of a runaway slave who became a Presbyterian minister. When opponents crushed his bare fingers with cleats on the football field, Paul became a Walter Camp All-American. When he was given half the time of his white classmates to take an exam, he got the highest marks.

For the sake of our great-grandmother, Cora Horne, who had helped him get his scholarship to Rutgers, Paul came to Brooklyn to see me and Teddy. He bounced us on his knee and sang Russian folk songs. And he greeted the neighbors who had gathered outside when word spread of his arrival. As far as Lena was concerned, Paul belonged to the ages. Any romantic thoughts would have been a form of blasphemy. Other women were not that scrupulous, however. Sterling Brown said, "Paul must certainly *love* women—because women love him so much."

Anyway, Lena had a secret boyfriend: Joe Louis. Teddy Horne, who was an insider in the champ's circle, a pal of the big shots who "handled" Joe's finances, played Cupid in a way. On Easter Sunday, 1941, he took Lena and some friends to visit Joe Louis' Pompton Lakes, New Jersey, training camp. There were patches of snow on the ground; it was a blustery, sparkling early spring day. Lena wore a fetching Dutch bonnet hat and a silver fox jacket, another present from Teddy. In the photographs taken that day, Lena appears to be shivering in her silk stockings and open-toed, high-heeled pumps. The romance must have blossomed at once. Joe Louis became—when he wasn't fighting or training or with his wife—Lena's

Lena and Joe Louis at his New Jersey training camp in the spring of 1941

constant suitor. By June, John Hammond was one of the very few in on the secret. (In retrospect, forty years later, Hammond said it reminded him of DiMaggio and Monroe—only Joe and Lena were the Brown Bomber and the Sepia Songstress.) The night of Joe's big fight with Billy Conn, Hammond drove around and around Central Park with Lena, listening to the fight on the car radio. It was a tough fight; Joe didn't come through until the very end. The next day Hammond's arm was black and blue where Lena had punched him. In the end, however, the Louis-Lena romance was as brief as it was exciting. They had little in common besides youth and celebrity, and there were too many real complications.

After the spring and summer of 1941 little Teddy was sent back to our father in Pittsburgh. One day soon after that, Harold Gumm turned up at Café Society to tell Lena that Felix Young, a well-known composer and impresario, was planning to open a new nightclub in Hollywood. It would be called the Trocadero—and Felix wanted Lena for the first show.

CHAPTER · 6

LENA

In the late summer of 1941 Lena, Cousin Edwina, and I all got on the train and rode across the country to California, just as Lena's father and Edwina's brother had done twenty years earlier. As the train pulled into Los Angeles' Union Station, we were singing "California, Here I Come!" at the top of our voices, to the indulgent smiles of people passing our open compartment doors.

That transcontinental journey was the first of many. I would soon become a seasoned juvenile traveler. I loved trains. I loved sleeping in trains —the soothing chill of starched linen railway sheets, the wafer-thin blanket that was always just enough cover. I would lie awake at night with the shade up, the sheets and blanket gleaming blue in the eerie night light, and watch the towns go sliding by, fewer and fewer as we went West. I loved the railroad plumbing: the shiny chrome basin that descended from the wall, the toilet disguised as a seat. "Passengers will please refrain / From flushing toilet while the train / Is standing in the station / I love you . . ." we sang. When Lena and I traveled together we usually shared a compartment or a drawing room. When I traveled by myself I rode in a snug roomette. I loved the Pullman porters, with their beaming faces and snowy white jackets. We were treated like royalty by these kings of the road. One of them always knew Teddy Horne. And the dining car waiters, who were usually college graduates, knew Frank or Cora. In 1941 Lena, Edwina, and I were enjoying the benefits of a recent Supreme Court ruling: *Mitchell* vs. *U.S. Interstate Commerce Act,* which required the Pullman Company to provide equal accommodations for blacks. Congressman Arthur Mitchell of Chicago had sued Pullman and won.

Our westward journey began in Grand Central Station, where redcaps rolled heaps of luggage down a length of Art Deco carpeting to a sleek silver bullet called the 20th Century Limited. We boarded the train in the early evening, just in time for drinks (if you were a grown-up), dinner, and bed. Chicago, an enormous ugly city that was always too hot or too cold, materialized early in the morning. From there the Super Chief, the train of movie stars, politicians, and VIPs, would take us to California. As towns became hamlets, and hamlets became prairie and desert, the train never stopped. It hurtled through the night like a whistling star.

Albuquerque, New Mexico, was our long-awaited oasis after a day and a half of nonstop travel across what clearly was the "Badlands," limitless horizon and flat dry earth. The Fred Harvey restaurant, where most of the passengers enjoyed a drink, was segregated, but that didn't concern me. Albuquerque was where we bought comic books, movie magazines, and silver bracelets with turquoise stones from serape-wrapped artisans who sat by the side of the roadbed. Native Americans were not allowed into Fred Harvey Houses either.

Technically, California begins with the desert towns of Needles and Barstow. But our California—the real California—began with orange groves (in the winter ringed with smoky smudge pots), oil derricks, and dusty-violet, snow-capped mountains against the sky. This California no longer exists; it's been replaced by exhaust fumes and highway.

We later learned that no one who is anyone in the movies got off the Super Chief in downtown Los Angeles. Movie people disembarked at Pasadena, or San Bernardino (known as San Berdoo). On that first trip West, unbeknownst to me, Marlene Dietrich and Jean Gabin were in the drawing room down the corridor. They got on together in Chicago and did not emerge, even once, until Pasadena. Lena was incredibly impressed.

Our California trip had been a matter of great concern and discussion among the Horne family at large, with most of them opposed to it. Lena herself had been somewhat dubious about the Hollywood job, even before she left New York. Barney Josephson, of course, was furious. But Café Society's Teddy Wilson, and the boys in the music combo, had encouraged Lena, as had the rest of the black Café Society crowd. Walter White said that Hollywood "exposure" would be good for her. And Duke Ellington— inimitably—told Lena "not to be selfish," to let "the whole world benefit" from her "incredible radiance." Teddy Horne, by phone from Pittsburgh, said, "Go on! You can always come back."

Our new Hollywood home was at the lower end of a street called Horn Avenue—a happy omen. The apartment had been leased by Felix Young. Blacks were not permitted to live in that neighborhood, but Edwina was "white," Lena looked "Latin," and I was vaguely something or other in between. Anyway, no one seemed to care too much about our cosmopolitan ménage, and we settled in.

War—and the imminent Japanese invasion—were favorite topics of conversation among California grown-ups, and as far as Lena was concerned, invasion might not be so bad. California could certainly use a little excitement. In typical impresario fashion, Felix Young was having money problems trying to create his glamorous new Trocadero nightclub. What he had envisioned was a sort of Cotton Club "West": the opening show would feature Duke Ellington, Ethel Waters, Lena Horne, and the Katherine Dunham Dancers. But Ellington and Waters had already dropped out, and Lena sat around for weeks with nothing to do.

Two things saved Lena's sanity: the Dunham Dancers, and a Duke Ellington musical called *Jump for Joy*. The Dunham Dancers, who were probably the original show business gypsies, had a commune down on Sunset Boulevard, and they welcomed Lena into their cheerful *vie de bohème*. Nothing cast a pall over long, sunny afternoons of music, gossip, cooking, and the endless domestic chores peculiar to dancers. Dunham herself, the great Gypsy Queen, sometimes left her tribe temporarily in the lurch; but it was only to scrape together enough money to send for them. Dunham was beautiful, eccentric, and autocratic, ruling her dancers, and her English artist husband, with an iron hand—fortified by a Rosenwald anthropology fellowship, two University of Chicago degrees, and the knowledge that hers was the only company for *serious* black dancers. Dunham's dancers were some of the best modern dancers, black or white, in America, among them Marie Bryant, an indelibly blithe spirit, who became one of Lena's best friends. Marie had recently left Dunham to become the assistant, at 20th Century-Fox, of Jack Cole, the sinuous and charismatic dancer-choreographer whose students included Bob Fosse, Carol Haney, and Gwen

Verdon. When you asked Marie what she did for Jack Cole, she said, "I teach Betty Grable to shake her buns."

Jump for Joy was a jolly liberal joke on the death of Uncle Tom. It opened to critical success in Los Angeles in the summer of 1941 with Dorothy Dandridge, Herb Jeffries, and Ivie Anderson. The music was by Ellington and the lyrics were by Paul Francis Webster:

JUMP FOR JOY

Don't you grieve, Little Eve
All them hounds, I do believe
Have been killed.
Ain't you thrilled?
Jump for joy!

Ellington invited Lena to a performance. As the overture began and the house lights dimmed, a small man in owlish horn-rimmed glasses slipped into the empty seat next to her. "I'm Billy Strayhorn," he leaned over to say. "I've been sent to see if you're all right." It was the beginning of a lifelong platonic love affair. Strayhorn, called Billy or "Swee' Pea" (after Popeye's baby), was universally adored, an angelic man with whom Lena formed the first intimate friendship of her life. She found a soul mate and he found a sister. They became a couple.

Billy Strayhorn was a composer-arranger, and he wrote, among other songs, "Take the A Train," "Lush Life," and "Chelsea Bridge." He was Ellington's right hand. Lena, who like many others felt that a selfish genius lurked behind Ellington's protestations of universal love, thought that Billy was also Ellington's heart. Lena and Billy talked the days and nights away, and Billy made new arrangements for Lena. They often went to Brothers, a black Los Angeles nightclub popular with the movie crowd. Meanwhile Felix Young kept telling Lena not to worry, she was going to be *seen* in Hollywood. On Pearl Harbor Sunday Lena and Billy were rehearsing at a friend's house when they heard the news. They stared at the radio in shock. Lena's first thought was "Everything's over."

The war put an end to Felix's dream of a big nightclub, but it also turned Hollywood into a boom town. Felix was able to open a tiny club on the Sunset Strip next door to Adrian's (the MGM designer's) elegant dress shop. It was called the Little Troc, and it offered an extremely exclusive gambling den on the second floor. Lena and the Dunham Dancers opened the show, but the nightclub floor was infinitesimal and the dancers' big Haitian petticoats were constantly sweeping customers' drinks into their laps. On the third night Dunham said, "Enough!" and the dancers quit. Lena, all alone in Felix Young's chic new night spot, had her basic Café Society repertoire plus some new songs arranged by Billy: "There'll Be Some Changes Made," "When the Sun Comes Out," "Blues in the Night," and "Honeysuckle Rose." She was a word-of-mouth sensation. An early newspaper clipping reported:

> Felix Young's "Little Troc" . . . at the moment it is a big attraction because Lena Horne, a singer from the Downtown Café Society in New York, is being hailed as another Florence Mills. She has knocked the movie population bowlegged and is up to her ears in offers. She came out here unknown. . . .

Roger Edens, one of the talented people who made MGM musicals the best in the world, had seen Lena at Café Society. Now he came again and again to the Little Troc, as did Cole Porter, Marlene Dietrich, and John Barrymore (who kissed Lena's hand). Garbo came, with Mercedes D'Acosta (of "the international set") and Dorothy Arzner, Hollywood's only female director.

Around this time Cole Porter invited Lena to a Sunday afternoon pool party for the cast of *This Is the Army,* an integrated show. Again Garbo, the idol of Lena's childhood moviegoing, was there. She sat on the piano bench and smiled enigmatically while Lena sang. Of course, Lena was expected to sing for her lunch, just as *This Is the Army* cast members were expected to show their best profiles as they cavorted in the pool. Porter's parties always included Hollywood newcomers as well as old guard. The very young Lauren Bacall (called Betty) was another guest. Lena liked Betty Bacall immediately; she was so un-Hollywood. All in all, Lena enjoyed the party. But soon after, another Porter party changed her mind about free entertainment. Miriam Hopkins, a Southerner, sidled over to Lena to ask why she, Lena, was "not like the others," and therefore allowed in polite society. And Grace Moore, a Metropolitan opera diva and quasi–movie star, was, to say the least, extremely condescending. Lena decided that night to confine her socializing to people with whom she could feel totally secure.

■ ■ ■

Roger Edens—tall, amused, with a magnolia-and-moonbeams Virginia drawl—became one of Lena's intimate Hollywood friends. At first, however, he was merely her champion. He felt in his bones that MGM should hire her. Roger was the assistant—and general *éminence grise*—of MGM's "Freed Unit," run by Arthur Freed, who had masterminded 1939's *The Wizard of Oz,* as well as the successful string of Judy Garland–Mickey Rooney teenage musicals. Roger Edens first came to Hollywood as Ethel Merman's pianist and vocal arranger, and Freed had the perspicacity to keep Roger on despite Merman's lukewarm Hollywood reception. It was Roger who wrote "Dear Mr. Gable" for thirteen-year-old Judy Garland to sing at MGM's birthday party for Gable, electrifying the studio bosses, and it was Roger who told Felix Young that he wanted MGM to see Lena. Lena informed Harold Gumm, who—fortunately for everyone concerned—had no entree at Metro. Felix and Harold then asked Louis "Doc" Shurr to represent Lena. (Lena was now required to pay 20 percent to *each* agent, which Gumm told her was customary.) Although Arthur Freed was a very busy man, "Doc" Shurr was a popular Hollywood figure and Freed agreed to give Lena fifteen minutes.

Harold Gumm and Al Melnick of the Shurr office took Lena out to Culver City, where Roger met them and led them to Freed's office. Roger played—and Lena sang "More Than You Know" (Shurr knew that Freed was contemplating a Vincent Youmans picture) and "Everything I Have Is Yours." Suddenly Arthur Freed was terrifically unbusy. "We must take you to L.B.," he pronounced. Lena then went back to Roger's office to wait for the meeting with "L.B."

Roger was glowing, the agents were hopping up and down, and—happy coincidence—Vincente Minnelli dropped in to say hello. Vincente, a former art director and designer who was trying to become a second-unit musical director, had been one of Lena's biggest Café Society fans—he and Broadway producer Vinton Freedley had talked of starring her in a musical version of Max Beerbohm's *Zuleika Dobson.* Vincente was thrilled with Lena's news. "Wouldn't it be great if we could do something together!" he said. At that point Lena was whisked off to sing "More Than You Know" for Louis B. Mayer.

Mr. Mayer, short, chubby, and avuncular, sat behind a colossal desk. When Lena finished singing, he smiled, got up from his desk, and boomed, "I've got a surprise for you!" He opened a side door in his office to reveal Marion Davies (as William Randolph Hearst's girl friend, she was the power behind the former power behind the MGM throne) who had been listening from an inner room. Marion Davies was a shining white vision, platinum from head to toe. She advanced upon Lena, smiling and stammering, "L-l-lovely, my dear." Then Mayer called in Eddie Mannix, and it was all over but the signatures. Back in Roger's office the group was met by "Doc" Shurr—news traveled fast in Hollywood. "They want to sign you," he announced, as if he himself had twisted L. B. Mayer's arm.

Over the next few days everyone started talking about Lena as if she weren't there. What "to do" with her remained the only problem. Vincente and Roger badgered Freed to badger Mayer to let Vincente direct *Cabin in the Sky,* which MGM owned, with Lena in the second female role (played on Broadway by Katherine Dunham). Mayer, despite some grumbling from yes men, agreed, and Lena was offered a seven-year contract plus a guaranteed leading role in *Cabin.* Everyone except Lena was altogether ecstatic, but by now she loathed Hollywood with the abiding hatred of the transplanted Easterner. She did not know how to drive a car; no one walked; the place was impossible. Confused and isolated, Lena called her father and asked him to help her make the decision. She also consulted Walter White, who was thrilled with the contract. His only concern was the time before *Cabin* got made; he was afraid they might force Lena to play a maid, or some "jungle type." She was not to make a move without consulting him at every step. "It is essential that you establish a new kind of image for black women," said Walter—and Lena agreed.

The NAACP had been waiting twenty-five years for a weapon like Lena. They would strike while the iron was hot. Now was the time to force changes in Hollywood's traditionally pejorative treatment of blacks. The NAACP announced that the 1940 Republican presidential candidate, Wendell Willkie, would represent the organization in negotiations with Hollywood studio heads, and Willkie gave clout to what otherwise might simply have been seen as a nuisance campaign. Several of the more liberal studio heads, including Selznick and Zanuck, agreed to follow the new racial guidelines when depicting black characters, and to use blacks as extras whenever it would be realistic to do so. They also promised to begin the arduous job of integrating blacks into studio technical and craft jobs. *Variety* bannered "Better Breaks for Negroes in H'Wood." In 1942 Wendell (named for nineteenth-century abolitionist Wendell Phillips) Willkie attended the NAACP's Los Angeles convention, and Lena posed prettily at his side in a white suit and knitted snood. "You're our test case, Lena," said Walter White.

Teddy Horne, however, cast a suspicious eye on the whole situation. It

*Lena with Wendell Willkie
at an NAACP convention
in Los Angeles, 1942*

*The Freed Unit at MGM, c. 1945. From left to right: Robert Alton,
Kay Thompson, Lennie Hayton, Lucille Bremer, Arthur Freed,
and Jerome Kern*

is difficult to kid a kidder. He suddenly saw his lamb among the Hollywood wolves, and he flew out to California for Lena's next Freed-Mayer meeting. The studio executives were no doubt as impressed with Teddy's studied coolness as they were with his Sulka tie and handmade shoes. "Mr. Mayer," said Teddy, "I have very few illusions about the movie business." He studied his perfectly manicured nails. "The only Negroes I ever see are menials, or Tarzan extras. I don't see what the movies have to offer my daughter. I can hire a maid for her; why should she act one?" L.B. was both sincere and conciliatory. "Mr. Horne, I can assure you that we would never allow anything to embarrass either you or your daughter."

An item appeared shortly afterward in Louella Parsons:

> We did rave over Maxine Sullivan, the Negro blues singer, when she was in Hollywood, but even better than Maxine is Lena Horne who has just been put under contract by M-G-M. Louis B. Mayer and Arthur Freed, who were at the benefit for the Jewish Home for the Aged Sunday night at the Biltmore, have decided to find a picture for her as soon as possible. Lena is "different," she comes from the West Indies and has a personality that sparkles and how she can put over a song!

Lena's contract was also noted in the black press. The Pittsburgh *Courier* was both laudatory and incorrect:

> MGM signs Lena Horne for Hit with George Raft—Lena Horne received a six-month contract with Metro-Goldwyn-Mayer Pictures this week and will start work on "Panama Hattie" with George Raft in the near future. Lena Horne's entry in movies is the highlight of a career that has carried her into the nation's top niteries and has given her almost international repute.

Lena's first screen test, after the contract signing, was opposite Rochester, as a comic servant love interest in a Jeanette MacDonald movie. So much dark make-up was smeared on Lena's face in an attempt to match her skin color to Rochester's that she began to look like Al Jolson singing "Mammy." At that point Max Factor himself was summoned to confront the problem. How could they make Lena look black, but not blacked up? The Factor chemists soon came up with a coppery-caramel-colored pancake make-up, to be applied to the skin with a wet sponge. It did wonders for

Hedy Lamarr in *White Cargo,* a part that Lena longed for (though surely Walter White would have called it a stereotype). Ethel Waters eventually got the part that Lena had screen-tested for.

Lena, meanwhile, was becoming a member of the Freed Unit family—a position on the MGM lot with distinct cachet. Among the contract players who appeared in Freed Unit pictures were Judy Garland, Mickey Rooney, Gene Kelly, and Frank Sinatra. The Freed Unit was considered "Eastern" and sophisticated. Besides Roger Edens and Vincente Minnelli, there were chic, blond Kay Thompson (vocal arranger); Berlin-born Dietrich lookalike Lela Simone (expert on musical cutting); young composers Hugh Martin and Ralph Blane ("The Trolley Song"); choreographers Robert Alton, Charles Walters, and Eugene Loring; Conrad Salinger (musical arranger) and handsome, slightly saturnine Lennie Hayton (arranger, conductor, composer, who worked for the whole studio, not just the Freed Unit). The Freed Unit considered itself superior to the rest of Culver City. Its wits (most of the writers were New Yorkers) were rudely competitive, making up irreverent musical in-jokes about everyone on the lot. Freed Unit nicknames universally stuck: Jeanette MacDonald and Nelson Eddy were known as "the Iron Butterfly" and "the Singing Capon"; June Allyson was "Prune Venison"; and Fred Astaire was "Nervous Nellie."

Lena enjoyed the merriment, but she wasn't truly content until she finally had a movie to make. Her scene in *Panama Hattie* was partly the result of pressure on MGM by Paul Robeson and Walter White. "What are you going to do with this girl?" they kept asking Mayer and Freed. The Red Skelton–Ann Sothern version of Cole Porter's Broadway hit had bombed in previews (maybe because neither of MGM's stars was Ethel Merman, the original Hattie). Then Pearl Harbor had temporarily shut down all shooting, and *Hattie* was shelved. Roger was convinced that Lena might be able to help the picture—at least she couldn't hurt it—and he arranged for Vincente Minnelli to be given his first directing assignment. Together they shot a nightclub scene in which Lena wore a gardenia in her hair and sang "Just One of Those Things."

Lena was busy on more than one front. Her new career had put her in political hot water. An unofficial but influential group of black Hollywood actors had decided that she was a threat to the status quo. These actors controlled all work for black extras—they owned a kind of stock company of stereotypes. Walter White and Paul Robeson wanted to break the power of this group, but it was Lena who came face to face with them at their "protest" meeting: "You're making it impossible for us to get work!" was the gist of their argument. There would be no more "jungle" or "old plantation" parts. They would all starve. Lena was unstrung.

"Pay no attention to these people," said Paul Robeson. "It's the Pullman porters—the people farther down the line—whose opinion of you really matters," he said. But Lena had two major allies among Hollywood's black inner circle: Rochester, a radio star who didn't need the money and didn't give a damn; and Hattie McDaniel, the first black Oscar winner (*Gone With the Wind*). Hattie McDaniel stood up for Lena at the meeting and later invited her to visit her elegant house. "I'm nobody's fat black mammy," said Miss McDaniel, "but it's how I make my money." She told Lena to take charge of her own life and do what was best for *her*.

Lena felt she had to get away. She was so homesick that she broke her terror-sworn oath never to fly again and took off for New York. I vividly remember my mother's look of apprehension as she peered through the round window of the airplane to wave good-bye to us on the edge of the tarmac. Even then it looked like a toy plane.

New York brought a tearful reconciliation with Barney Josephson. All was forgiven. And Barney, ever the socialist hero, decided to bust Lena's MGM contract, which represented capitalism run amok. Lena had signed a seven-year contract at $350 per week, for forty weeks a year guaranteed, and a $100 a week raise per year. She was also "permitted" to play such Loews theaters as the Capitol on Broadway (affiliated with MGM) for $700 a week. And she had twelve weeks on her own to make money. This was a standard studio contract; Clark Gable's was not much better. So Barney told columnist Leonard Lyons that Hazel Scott (not a Metro contract player, but managed by Barney) would be working at MGM for $5,000 a week, while Lena (the famous black contract player) was making only $350. Lyons printed Barney's story and managed to embarrass MGM so thoroughly that Lena's salary was raised to $900 per week, with the same $100 weekly annual raise. But Lena still didn't want to go back to Hollywood. She spent most of her New York trip in tears. One weepy scene took place in the lobby of the Theresa Hotel, where Count Basie told Lena to pull her socks up and stop feeling so sorry for herself. "They never *choose* us," he said, "but they've chosen you. You have to go back so that other people can have your opportunities." Cora Horne would have approved.

Lena returned to Metro to find everyone high on *Panama Hattie*. She was soon given two numbers—"Honeysuckle Rose" and "Brazilian Boogie," both directed by Vincente—in *Thousands Cheer,* an all-star patriotic musical. Lena was beginning to feel better about herself and Hollywood. She decided to celebrate by going shopping at Magnin's, where she bought herself a little silk afternoon dress with the words "Good Luck" printed all over it in various languages, and she wore it for her first informal MGM photo session. Walter White took one look at the dress and had a fit. "You must never wear a dress with writing on it!" he admonished.

Panama Hattie got lukewarm reviews, but the critics all asked about Lena: "Who is the girl who does 'Just One of Those Things'?" And the studio fan mail arrived: "Who is the new Latin girl singer?" Lena was now accused of trying to "pass," although it certainly wasn't her fault that MGM made her nameless and creditless. (They were probably trying to see if they could palm her off as Latin.) And it wasn't her fault that her and Vincente's scene had been the only memorable moment in the whole flat and tiresome movie.

Still waiting for *Cabin*, Lena went to work at the Mocambo, another Sunset Strip nightclub, to even more rapturous reviews than she had received at the Little Troc. In July 1942 Ted Le Berthon of the Los Angeles *Daily News* wrote:

> The stars that have looked down . . . upon warships and bombing planes . . . looked down upon the exclusive Cafe Mocambo on the Sunset Strip. . . . Hollywood history is being turned topsy-turvy. . . . Cops have had to shove back crowds made up of screen stars—on one night a friend of mine counted 62 big names in a mob of several hundred niftily habilimented people—who had tried futilely to get into the Mocambo to see and hear Lena Horne. And, well, who is Lena Horne? . . . An exquisite olive skinned, 22-year-old beauty of the Negro race whom anyone might mistake for an aristocratic and exciting Latin American senorita, with inkily dark gleaming eyes. She wore a sea green evening gown and stood there with a powerful smile of quiet affection. And then she began to sing. And before the evening was over, all of us . . . had seen and heard the greatest artist in her field in our time in history. We heard a great singer who is something more than that—a great actress; and something more than that, I suspect—a great soul. . . . Nothing sexy. No appeal to innuendo. Just the high mystery of art, of the more complete individual. Just some of God's excellent workmanship. And so decently humble in bows after storms of handclapping. And members of the movie colony present deserve a tribute. They so obviously recognized and acclaimed her as an artist of a stature

far beyond themselves . . . if she were white she'd go beyond Bette Davis, Colbert, Shearer, Garbo, Crawford and all the rest. She has a bigger presence. And she's so beautiful it hurts. . . . I wondered what would happen if a Negro party came out on "The Sunset Strip" to see and hear their own incomparable Lena Horne.

By now Lena had made enough money to move her small family into a new home. We moved across Sunset Boulevard to the other end of Horn Avenue and the top of a steep hill. Our house, which rested against the side of a mountain, was a typical Southern California Mexican-style house with white stucco walls and a terraced terra-cotta roof. There was the smell of eucalyptus everywhere—and azalea, bougainvillea, and red and pink geraniums. The nights were cold and the crickets were thunderous. Little Teddy came to live with us for a while. I thought he was adorable, as long as I was allowed to rule the roost. At the same time he stood up for me against other children. (I was considered "thin" and un-rugged.)

My best friend at the time was Olivia, a little French war refugee who lived next door. Her family belonged to Hollywood's international refugee colony. She had bright eyes and rosy cheeks, and she didn't speak any English. Our single word in common was *"poupée"* (doll), which she taught me. I was a *poupée* freak. I had an enormous family of them with whom I slept. After saying my prayers I would carefully ease myself into the sliver of bed that remained, next to my favorite, a large red-haired doll named Millicent.

When we first moved into our new house, some local bigots passed a petition to have us removed from the neighborhood. Fortunately, our allies were stronger than the bigots. Humphrey Bogart, with his wife Mayo Methot, lived directly across the street. When the petitioners rang Bogart's bell, he told them to get off his property or risk being shot at. (Bogey was also our air raid warden.) Peter Lorre, who lived at the bottom of our hill, also told the bigots to buzz off. And Vera Caspary, author of elegant thrillers *Laura* and *Bedelia,* who lived in the middle of the hill, was outraged.

The Horn Avenue hill was a celebrated automobile trap. It was so steep that cars would slide, silent and driverless, to the bottom and lumber into a ditch (usually in one piece). At the foot of Horn Avenue was the Gala Restaurant, an elegant supper club whose owner, John Walsh, was a smooth, silver-haired New Yorker. The Gala bar was an extremely discreet homosexual meeting place that featured only what was new, exciting, or avant-garde. It was also quietly integrated. The after-hours parties at the Gala were famous, with stars singing around the piano and everyone letting his hair down. Lena would sometimes drop in for a nightcap with friends and wind up singing at the piano with Walsh, who was a former New York supper club singer. She even managed, between *Panama Hattie* and *Cabin,* to squeeze in a week at the Gala, headlining a show that featured Zero Mostel and the Jack Cole Dancers. There were lines of customers down the Strip, and the regulars, including Tyrone Power and his wife, Annabella, were furious because they could not get in.

My first real California memory is a visit from Grandfather Teddy, who took us all to a dude ranch. "Murray's Overall-Wearing Dude Ranch" in Victorville, California, was owned and run by blacks, for a black clientele. It offered "tennis, croquet, softball, horseshoes, basketball, swimming and riding" ("Bring your own rackets and clubs") at "$18 per week for adults— $10 per week for children." But Lena left us in mid-vacation. She had to resolve her divorce situation.

Louis and Lena's divorce had turned nasty just before Lena began performing at Café Society. It was noted at length in the black press, particularly the Pittsburgh *Courier*:

> Beautiful Lena Horne was sued for divorce here Thursday by her husband Louis Jordan Jones, charging desertion. The pretty singer, now featured with Charlie Barnet's Orchestra, failed to accept service on the libel when in Pittsburgh last week, as she left town the very night of the day the papers were issued. The Jones have two children, Gail, three and Edwin Fletcher, one.

The story featured a picture of Lena in her Noble Sissle band costume (the one that wowed the Harvard boys). The *Courier* gossip columnist covered the story more informally:

> Tellin' It to the Judge . . . The Louis Jordan Jones (Lena Horne). Lena was in town the first part of the week, but missed service on the libel. She is in Chicago this week with her dad, the well-known Ted Horne, and Mrs. W. A. (Woogie) Harris. The party left Thursday night. . . . Ada went to the station to see Lena and Ted off. . . . But Woogie pushed her on the train. . . . All aboard! He sent her bags the next day. They are having a grand time in the big town.

Now my mother was calling, long distance, to speak to me at the ranch. She was crying when she asked me whom I'd rather live with, her or my father. I remember distinctly not wanting her to feel worse than she obviously did. "You," I said. And then I cried and cried, and Grandfather and Edwina and all the grown-ups tried to console me.

We went back home to Hollywood and I learned to read a McGuffey Reader, sitting on my mother's lap. She always sang me to sleep with two songs: "The Owl and the Pussycat" and "Long Time Ago" ("Once there was a little kitty, white as the snow / In a barn she used to frolic, long time ago . . ."). It was about this time that I created an imaginary playmate, a basic survival technique for California kids. Playmates were hard to find if you lived in the Hollywood Hills. Domestic animals were good stand-ins for human companionship. We eventually accumulated a family of six: three dogs (two dachshunds and a Labrador) and three cats (a pair of Siamese and a nondescript gray tom).

My California was pre-freeway and pre–coaxial cable. I can see the field of orange-red poppies that grew wild at the end of Sunset Boulevard, where one road led to Culver City and the other to the beach. I can still smell the drive to the beach in an open car, the wind and sun smacking our faces. Grown-ups always wore sunglasses and scarves. The pre-smog climate was Edenic. Our lemon trees produced fruit the size of grapefruit, and gardenias bloomed by the garden door.

Below our hill was Hollywood and the Strip—Disneyland before its time. There were restaurants in the shape of sombreros, bowler hats, and old shoes. There were Swiss chalets, Bavarian schlosses, Kentish cottages, Spanish haciendas, and the Garden of Allah, which looked like Christmas in Bethlehem. (Christmas in Hollywood was often more exotic than traditional. Beverly Hills pioneered the dyed Christmas tree—usually shocking pink, or gold.) Most of the buildings on the Strip had enormous façades, with tiny rooms inside—as if they had been built for Munchkins by moonlighting MGM set decorators. (MGM's art department dismantled Loire Valley châteaux and Tibetan monasteries in pursuit of on-screen verisimilitude and decorated movie moguls' houses with the leftovers.)

My brother and I would walk down the hill, across the street, and down another hill to school, carrying our lunch boxes with wax-paper-wrapped sandwiches. We were the only black children in the school. Once, at nap time, a little girl asked me why my arm was so brown. I remember examining my brown arm in honest confusion. "I don't know," I replied. Lena gave Teddy's teacher "what for" for reading *Little Black Sambo* to his class.

Natalie Wood, another refugee, was briefly in my class; her name was Natasha, and she was very tearful and spoke only Russian. On Sundays we walked down the hill to church, a place of dark shadows and deep boredom and relieved only by the mesmerizing flicker of candles in dark blue glass.

On the wall of my bedroom, opposite my bed, was a picture of, I think, St. Thérèse of Lisieux. I had a ruffled tulle dressing table and a musical jewel box with a twirling ballerina on top. The jewel box held silver barrettes engraved with my name, a gold heart pin that read "To Gail—Love Daddy," and a tiny gold ring with a tiny diamond, a christening present from my godmother, one of Louis' beautiful sisters-in-law. I wore overalls or play suits to school, depending on the weather, and lace-up brown shoes that I detested (the laces were always breaking). I also had Mexican skirts and blouses, and soft woven leather sandals called huaraches. My party clothes were triple-sleeved organdy pinafores over pale cotton dresses, with horrible shoes that fastened with a button hook. I was small and thin and had two long braids that were often looped over my ears, like Margaret O'Brien, MGM's waif-like Mexican-Irish child star.

My favorite movie stars were Abbott and Costello, especially Costello. Once I saw Lou Costello, in person, at the Hitching Post Theater on Hollywood Boulevard, where we went on Saturdays to see cowboy movies. He was walking up and down the aisles in a cowboy suit, talking to kids in the audience. We all squealed and yelped. We had heard that Lou Costello's little boy had drowned in a swimming pool. This was another occupational hazard of California kids. Teddy was constantly being fished out of people's pools. I had a couple of close calls myself, both at the beach and in people's swimming pools.

Movie star mothers were loving, but somewhat ephemeral. Here today, with hugs and kisses and *Winnie-the-Pooh*; gone tomorrow, to return somewhat later with no freckles, false eyelashes, vermilion lipstick, and a deep suntan, all courtesy of Metro make-up. MGM used the "spare parts" make-up technique: Garbo's eyebrows and Crawford's lips were liberally distributed. I loved to watch my mother bead her eyelashes. She used a little can of Sterno that made a blue flame. The liquid soot that congealed on the lashes, and made them spiky, was applied with a matchstick. My mother's bedroom and bath were awash in Chen-yu lipsticks, Guerlain perfumes, prescription pill bottles from MGM's Dr. Feelgood, and books by Agatha Christie, Edna Ferber, Pearl Buck, and John O'Hara.

When, at last, shooting began on *Cabin*, Vincente and Lena were inseparable. The coincidence of their simultaneous Hollywood careers strengthened their natural bond of sensitivity. *Cabin* was the third picture for each, and their first whole movie. (The next year Vincente would direct *Meet Me in St. Louis,* with his future wife, Judy Garland.) They dined together every night while *Cabin* was in preparation. Lena carried her lonely childhood everywhere, and Vincente gave her, once again, the kind of brother-sister relationship she needed so badly. She was thrilled with Vincente's *Cabin* concept. She thought he was a genius. He wanted to shoot the picture in sepia—to make it gleaming, lush, and dreamlike.

Cabin would be a lark. Roger Edens was musical director, and Katherine Dunham's dancers and Duke Ellington's orchestra were also in the cast. Everyone was happy—everyone, that is, except Ethel Waters. Reports were coming in via Dunham's "talking drums" that Ethel had it in for Lena. Because of her own background, Ethel Waters absolutely despised educated or light-complexioned blacks. Moreover, Miss Waters considered herself, quite rightly, to be an enormous star and regarded Lena as an upstart, and her enemy on every front. Lena herself stood in awe of the Waters reputation. Anybody who could make Katherine Dunham cry had to be one very tough customer. But Lena felt no real reason to worry; she and Ethel had only one scene together near the end of the schedule.

Lena was merry as a grig in her scenes with Eddie "Rochester" Anderson, a growly elf of a man whose wry comedy came as close to modern humor as was then possible for black actors. Jack Benny and Rochester had a master-servant relationship as old as Beaumarchais, or at least Bertie Wooster and Jeeves. Benny's outrageous wimpishness allowed Rochester to be the "brains" of the partnership, and Rochester found most of life infinitely amusing. Life on the set was great fun.

Lena had no big-picture anxiety. Having made two pictures on the lot, she was already a favorite of the technical crew. There was a rollicking two-day scene in "Hell," with Louis Armstrong as a trumpeting imp of Satan. And there was Lena's favorite scene, the bubble-bath number, "Ain't It de Truth"—in which she got the full movie-star bubble bath treatment: upswept hairdo, backlighting, and a cascade of bubbles. Both "Hell" and the bubble bath were eventually cut from the picture. (The bathtub scene wound up in a Pete Smith MGM short; and the song, "Ain't It de Truth," reappeared in Lena's 1957 Broadway musical, *Jamaica.*

The first Ethel Waters storm exploded in the sound department. When Ethel heard Lena's recording of "Honey in the Honeycomb," she accused Lena of parodying her singing style. By now Lena was getting a bit nervous. It was almost time to shoot her scene with Ethel. She was, in fact, rehearsing the big dance number that introduced their scene when she fell and broke her ankle. Rochester swore that he had seen Ethel making voodoo signs right over the spot where Lena fell. Lena only half laughed. She was shot full of dope by the MGM doctor and sent to Los Angeles to be X-rayed and plastered.

The next morning she hobbled onto the set to film the reworked scene. Ethel's entrance would now immediately follow a solo close-up of Lena singing, instead of the big group dance number. Lena was propped up on the bar of the nightclub set, her refurbished costume hiding the cast. Vincente had said to her, "Be real small. You can never be stronger than Ethel. Just be vulnerable and coquettish." In the first rehearsal Lena got a big laugh on her first line and, simultaneously, a prop man put a cushion under her plastered ankle. At that point Ethel Waters went into orbit (or as Duke Ellington might have put it, "My dear, she wrote the history of jazz . . ."). She flew into a semicoherent diatribe that began with attacks on Lena and wound up with a vilification of "Hollywood Jews." You could hear a pin drop. Everyone stood rooted in silence while Ethel's eruption shook the sound stage. She went on and on. Freed, Mannix, and Ethel's agent all appeared on the set. She was still more or less raving when Vincente dismissed the company and suspended shooting for the day. Lena was shaking; she had felt like a pinned butterfly on top of the bar. All the black actors eyed one another nervously and spoke among themselves in whispers. The next day, however, the scene was rehearsed and shot impeccably. There was little conversation beyond dialogue, and only Rochester continued to be amused. Lena and Ethel never spoke again. And Ethel—because of her vocal anti-Semitism—was a very long time between pictures.

Lena ended *Cabin* with a well-autographed leg cast, and Hollywood no longer seemed such a lonely place. She was enjoying life on the lot. Metro's "more stars than in heaven" were, all things considered, a relatively civilized and intelligent group of people (no studio with Hepburn and Tracy could be all bad). Only Warner Bros. had more card-carrying liberals, but they had learned their liberalism the hard way—fighting Jack Warner. The MGM leadership encouraged an elitist atmosphere. They were not crude or openly racist like the lowbrows at Republic or Paramount. With Lena's contract, MGM stood in the vanguard of democracy. The first day that Lena had appeared for "hair and make-up," an assistant had refused to work on her, whereupon Sydney Guillaroff, the gentlemanly head of Hairdressing, announced that he would personally take care of Miss Horne in the future. Jack Dawn, head of Make-up, made the same announcement to

A publicity photograph for <u>Cabin in the Sky</u>, 1942

At a <u>Cabin</u> rehearsal with Vincente Minnelli, Lena wears the "Good Luck" dress that shocked Walter White.

The bubble-bath scene in <u>Cabin</u> made Lena feel like a real movie star. It was later cut out of the picture.

The nightclub finale of <u>Cabin in the Sky</u> (its filming was interrupted by Ethel Waters's explosion of fury). Eddie "Rochester" Anderson is standing between Ethel and Lena.

his staff. Major trouble was averted; and because of Lena, a couple of black non-union assistants were hired. Louis B. Mayer remained a distantly benevolent figure: Lena was invariably greeted with "Good girl!" and a pat on the shoulder. Once L.B. sent down a request that she make a recording of "I'll Get By," a song purported to make the great man cry. So Lena and a one-hundred-piece orchestra recorded the song for L.B.'s private weeping enjoyment.

In late 1942 Lena got another lucky career break. Ivan Black, Café Society's publicity agent, suggested to Dick Dorso of New York's Savoy-Plaza Hotel that he hire her. Black knew that Lena was waiting for *Stormy Weather* to begin shooting, and that she was homesick for New York. MGM approved the plan. In November, *The New York Times* noticed her imminent arrival in an article by Barbra Berch:

SCORE FOR MISS HORNE
THE CAREER OF A SINGER FROM BROOKLYN
PROVES THAT IT PAYS TO STRIVE

Lena Horne is a light-brown, soft-spoken young Negress who came to Hollywood straight from Brooklyn, the Cotton Club, Noble Sissle's Band and Café Society Downtown. . . . She opened quietly at the Little Troc, a few months ago, in a plain white dress and one soft light. She came on without an introduction and started to sing without even announcing her number. Everybody stopped doing nothing and listened. . . . She just sang "The Man I Love" and "Stormy Weather" and a few other daisies that had been laid away by singers long before Lena ever got out of Girls High School. . . . She stayed on at the Little Troc for weeks, and people who never went to nightclubs pushed their way into the place four or five times a week to hear Lena Horne sing straight versions of a lot of numbers they'd been hearing for years. . . . Last May she changed her address to the Mocambo, another nightclub down the street, and gave out with the same act for her bosses that when contract time came up again they gave her a bracelet . . . and asked her to stay around and keep bringing in the money. . . . Finally, Metro-Goldwyn-Mayer curled a finger at her and lured her out to Culver City to give their pictures the type of class she was handing the Mocambo. . . . She lives in a five-room duplex in Beverly Hills with her four year old daughter and an aunt. And singing offers come in faster than she has time to refuse them. Right after finishing "Cabin in the Sky" she was torn between two class A dates—the Waldorf's Sert Room and the Persian Room of the Savoy Plaza. She chose the Savoy and is written down as the first Negro girl to play the room. They stopped clanging silverware for her in Hollywood—so it's conceded she's good for anybody's cover charge.

I was really almost five, and Edwina was technically Lena's second cousin.

Lena, Phil Moore (the Little Troc pianist whom Roger had persuaded Metro to hire), and Lena's new friend Nuffie O'Neill all checked into the Theresa Hotel. (Nuffie, like many of Lena's college-educated friends, was a researcher for Gunnar Myrdal's black American study, *An American Dilemma*. A young black woman who looked white, she had once almost married John Pinkett of Washington, one of the richest and most eligible bachelors of the black middle class. Now she was keeping company with Cab Calloway.) The Savoy-Plaza had offered Lena a room to rest and change, but she couldn't spend the night. There was no hotel outside of Harlem that accepted black guests. But Lena liked the Savoy-Plaza neighborhood, Fifty-eighth Street and Fifth Avenue. Mabel Mercer, lovely and regal, was singing around the corner at Tony's to integrated audiences that sometimes included Billie Holiday or Dizzy Gillespie.

The only real question in Lena's mind was what to wear for her opening night. MGM had promised to send dresses, but they hadn't arrived yet, so she and Nuffie decided to go window-shopping, even though Lena had no money for a new dress. At Bergdorf Goodman, right across the street from the Savoy-Plaza, they found a red lace dress that was perfect, and Lena looked divine in it. The Bergdorf saleslady happened to have a soft heart. "Wait a minute," she said. Fifteen minutes later she returned, accompanied by courtly young Mr. Andrew Goodman, the owner of the store. "I understand that you're opening at the Savoy-Plaza and have nothing to wear," he said. "We wouldn't want our Savoy neighbors to be disappointed. Why don't you take the lace dress? Charge it, and pay for it a little bit at a time." Lena nearly swooned with gratitude. She would forever be devoted to Mr. Goodman's store.

The Savoy-Plaza Hotel was an elegant smaller version of the Plaza. The Café Lounge on the lobby floor where Lena would appear was a long, narrow room with perfect acoustics. Lena sang without a microphone. The opening night audience included Cole Porter, Ethel Merman, Richard Rodgers, and fifteen-year-old Carol Marcus, who spent more time in nightclubs than

Top: *This photograph—from the pages of Marshall Field's newspaper,* PM—
accompanied an article celebrating Lena's success.
Below: *A newspaper advertisement for Lena's Savoy-Plaza Hotel engagement, 1942*

LENA HORNE

Young Negro with haunting voice charms New York with old songs

Each year in New York's after-dark world of supper clubs there appears a girl singer who becomes a sensation overnight. She stands in the middle of a dance floor in a white dress and a soft light, and begins to sing. The room is hushed and her voice is warm and haunting. Her white teeth gleam, her eyes move back and forth, and her softly sung words seem to linger like cigaret smoke.

This year that girl is Lena Horne, young Negro who has been appearing at the Savoy-Plaza's Cafe Lounge

(see left). Born in Brooklyn, she started her career at 16 by dancing in the chorus of Harlem's Cotton Club Review. Since then she has been heard in night clubs, traveled across the country as vocalist with orchestras, and appeared briefly in the recent screen version of *Panama Hattie*. Soon she will be featured in the all-Negro musical *Cabin In The Sky*. Singing without a microphone, Lena Horne makes old song favorites sound new and exciting. Below, with words and gestures, is her treatment of Cole Porter's *Let's Do It*.

COLD CAPE COD CLAMS 'GAINST THEIR WISH DO IT

EVEN LAZY JELLYFISH DO IT

ELECTRIC EELS, I MIGHT ADD, DO IT

GOLDFISH, IN THE PRIVACY OF BOWLS, DO IT

PEOPLE SAY, IN BOSTON, EVEN BEANS DO IT

LET'S DO IT—LET'S FALL IN LOVE

21

A page from a January 1943 Life magazine story about Lena. Her celebrity had reached a new height; the same week feature articles about her appeared in Time and Newsweek.

school (she would grow up to marry William Saroyan and Walter Matthau).
The Savoy newspaper advertisements showed a smiling Lena in her
"good luck" dress (and Lena wondered whether they might provoke
another lecture from Walter White). By the second night, however,
dresses no longer mattered—Lena was a smash hit and an overnight
sensation.

PM, the afternoon daily, owned by NAACP board member Marshall
Field, did stories on Lena at every opportunity. It now reported her Savoy
success:

LENA HORNE STILL ON WAY UP

Last year PM reported that Lena Horne (then Helena), talented
Negro songstress, was hauling them in at Café Society Downtown
and thereby making the management of that bistro very happy. This
year she's doing exactly the same thing for the snazzier Savoy-Plaza
Café Lounge—only more so. Since her November 26th opening she
has attracted capacity houses every single night and, once or twice,
the management had had to turn away up to 500 guests. This, by
the way, is the first time that the Savoy-Plaza has given Negro
entertainers a chance. . . . Despite piles of fan mail and an average
of six invitations a day to play benefits, she still talks of learning how
to sing. She got a letter asking her to come down and talk over a part
in a musical comedy, but never heard of the guy who sent it—fellow
named George Abbott. When singing, she can turn on the sophistication. . . . She was more interested in a delegation from her alma
mater, Girls High School in Brooklyn, than in the slew of celebs
who came to hear her sing.

Lena's future is pretty well taken care of in Hollywood, where
she's under a seven year contract to MGM, but she'll be coming
back to New York, now and then, for personal appearances. If the
present trend continues, she'll need Madison Square Garden for her
next stand.

Lena was in fact delighted to be reunited with the old Junior Debs—whom
the management of the Savoy-Plaza permitted to visit Lena in her suite, but
not to see the show.

The week of January 9, 1943, Lena hit the publicity jackpot when *Time,
Newsweek,* and *Life* all did features on her. *Time* wrote:

Manhattan's quietly swank Savoy-Plaza Café Lounge was last week doing the biggest business in its history as a nightspot. Its Mondays had begun to look like Saturdays. No opulent floor show was packing in the customers. The attraction was the face and shyly sultry singing of a milk chocolate Brooklyn girl, Lena Horne.

Unlike most Negro chanteuses, Lena Horne eschews the barrel house manner . . . conducts herself with the seductive reserve of a Hildegarde. But when Lena sings at dinner and supper, forks are halted in mid-career. Flashing one of the most magnificent sets of teeth outside a store she seethes her songs with the air of a bashful volcano. As she reaches the end of "Honeysuckle Rose" . . . her audience is gasping. . . .

And *Newsweek*:

Lena Horne would be the last person in the world to claim she has a great voice. She says she's still learning to sing. Nevertheless she is the biggest New York nightclub sensation since Libby Holman opened at La Vie Parisienne in October. What Miss Horne will admit—and what any member of her nightly SRO audience at the Savoy-Plaza Café Lounge will testify—is that she knows how to sell a song. So well, in fact, that she has broken every Savoy-Plaza record —and that includes such top flight attractions as Hildegarde, Jean Sablon and Morton Downey. . . .

A week later, Lena—in MGM lamé and tulle, with an orchid in her hair—was the cover girl for *PM*'s weekly magazine:

How a girl from Brooklyn became this season's biggest nightclub hit. . . . And how she's quietly using her unrehearsed success to win respect for her people.

• • •

Stormy Weather was made on loan-out to Fox—and very quickly. Andrew Stone, the director, was no Minnelli. The title sequence gave him the most trouble. "For God's sake!" he complained to Cab Calloway. "Talk to this girl, see if you can get her to show some emotion!" Cab's idea of a pep talk was to tell Lena that she was stupid and untalented: "Only white people are dumb enough to think you've got something," he said. Lena was meant to be crying real tears in "Stormy Weather" because her boyfriend, played by Bill "Bojangles" Robinson, had left her. Since Lena loathed Bill Robinson and nearly everything connected with *Stormy Weather,* it was difficult to evince the kind of emotion the director had in mind. *Stormy Weather* was very loosely based on the careers of James Reese Europe, Adelaide Hall, and Noble Sissle. As far as Lena was concerned, nothing—not even the moveable feast of the Dunham Dancers or the cuddly bearishness of Fats Waller —could make up for Bill Robinson. Robinson was a male Ethel Waters, and the biggest Uncle Tom in show biz. He carried a revolver, was poisonous to other blacks, and truly believed in the wit and wisdom of little Shirley Temple.

One day at MGM, before shooting began, Benny Thau (known on the Metro lot as "everybody's procurer") said to Lena, "The big man at Fox thinks you've got a great future." Lena had no idea who "the big man" was. She had never heard of Joe Schenck. But about twenty minutes after she arrived on the Fox lot the message came down: "Would Miss Horne join Mr. Schenck for lunch?" Lena went to lunch in slacks, full make-up, and a red beaded fez that was part of one of her costumes.

"Are you happy?" asked Mr. Schenck.

"Yes, Mr. Schenck," said Lena.

She had nothing to say, and his conversation was certainly uninspired: "How old are you?" and "What do you like to do?" were about the extent of it. Lena found Schenck ridiculous and boring, but agreed to join him for dinner "with friends" the following week. The "friends" turned out to be Thau, Mannix, and some fellow MGM starlets. After an extremely formal dinner during which the men discussed grosses, the butler passed coffee and cognac and everyone settled down to watch a movie. Joe Schenck beckoned Lena to sit next to him on the sofa and reached for her hand. Lena pretended that her hand did not belong to her and stared stonily at the movie screen until it was over. She went home unmolested and never received another Schenck invitation, but after this occasion she thought Schenck was repulsive. The big men at MGM never made passes, though rumor had Mayer simultaneously in love with Jeanette MacDonald (the "Iron Butterfly") and Greer Garson. As far as Lena was concerned, the most persistent bottom pincher at MGM was gentlemanly Walter Pidgeon.

Cabin in the Sky opened in New York at the Capitol Theater, with Lena and Duke Ellington as the stage show attractions. Both the picture and the show were a smash; there were lines around the block. Even Ellington was

*Lena with Bill "Bojangles" Robinson
in a scene from <u>Stormy Weather</u>, 1943*

*Lena wearing her "Digga, Digga, Doo"
costume from <u>Stormy Weather</u>*

A publicity photograph for <u>Stormy Weather</u>. Lena poses in the fez she wore one day to lunch with Joe Schenck, "the big man at Fox."

impressed. From New York Lena went on to a week's engagement, on her own, at Washington's Howard Theater—next to the Apollo, America's most famous black theater. At first the audience failed to turn out; it seems the prices were too high. When Lena then discovered that her agents had refused to cut her salary for a black house, she volunteered a pay cut and the audience poured in. Lena found wartime Washington exhilarating. She had a wonderful time, not only because of the personal success she enjoyed there, but also because she was able to spend time with old family friends and her beloved Uncle Frank.

Box office response to *Cabin* was excellent, but some of the more serious critics had reservations. *Newsweek* wrote:

> The forthcoming cycle of films that will exploit the nation's sizeable reservoir of Negro talent is the direct result of plainspoken hints last summer from Wendell Willkie, Lowell Millett of the Office of War Information and others, that now was the time to give the Negro his place as a dignified, responsible citizen. First in the cycle—and Hollywood's first all-Negro production since 1936 and "Green Pastures"—Metro Goldwyn Mayer's "Cabin in the Sky" can now be recommended as a warm, engaging entertainment chiefly on the merit of the players involved though hardly what Messrs. Willkie and Millett had in mind. . . . Lena Horne, as the seductive menace, is an eye-filling excuse for Little Joe's downfall.

Time magazine agreed that *Cabin* was still full of stereotypes, but called Lena "handsome and luscious voiced." *Variety* announced that "Lena Horne is a definite click, both vocally and dramatically as fatal Georgia Brown."

When I went to see *Cabin in the Sky* I had to be dragged from the theater in tears. Lena, who played the "wicked" Georgia Brown, appeared at the end of the picture to be one of the victims in the general destruction of the nightclub. She had to be called long distance, in New York, to assure me that she was still among the living.

By the middle of 1943 Lena was tenth on the list of black America's favorite movie stars. And A. E. Lichtman, who owned twenty-six black movie houses, told *Variety* that Lena had "dynamite star potential." Lena got more star treatment when Al Capp briefly featured a character based on Lena's Georgia Brown in "Li'l Abner." By mid-1943 many little black girls, and some little white girls, regarded Lena Horne as one of their favorite movie stars. My own personal favorites were Sonja Henie and Esther Williams—as a California kid, I admired jocks.

In May 1943 Lena visited Kaiser Shipbuilding's Yard Number One, in Richmond, California, to christen the liberty ship *George Washington Carver,* whose captain was black. The black press took extensive notice:

> The ship is second in a series of three, bearing the names of outstanding Negro Americans. Lena Horne will christen the ship and Beatrice Turner, one of the 6,112 Negro workers in the four Kaiser shipyards, will be matron of honor—both were chosen by the United Negro Labor Committee.

Lena, asked to comment on the event, might have said the following, but the words could also have been those of MGM's Publicity Department:

> It is such a high honor to have even the slightest part in this tribute to a great American and outstanding Negro genius and patriot that I am speechless with gratitude. To be privileged to christen the Liberty ship named after him will become one of the most inspiring moments of my life.

Barely six months into 1943, Lena had, without anyone planning it, become a girl of the year. It was coincidental saturation: *Time, Life,* and *Newsweek* all in the same week, and three movies all released in the first six months of the year. On the black fighting front alone, Lena was a revelation. "Now we have someone we can pin on our lockers," the black GIs wrote to MGM. And she was a crossover pinup as well. Richard Basehart, the movie actor, told Lena that he carried her picture all through the Battle of the Bulge. And a future Texas oilman said, "Some people fought the war for Dwight Eisenhower, but I fought it for Lena Horne." In the States *Cabin* and *Stormy* were shown only to black units. The British, however, showed them throughout the fleet, and as a result Lena would have many fans when she went to London after the war.

Blacks were 9.8 percent of the American population and 10.3 percent of the American armed forces. Black engineers built Burma's Ledo Road, China's Stilwell Road, and the Alcan Highway; and black transport troops supplied all fronts. There were 165,000 black sailors (all messmen or stewards), 17,000 black marines, 5,000 black Coast Guard, and 4,000 black WACs and WAVEs. The only integrated service was the Merchant Ma-

Lena at the christening of the liberty ship _George Washington Carver_ in May 1943. The event was widely publicized in the black press.

The "Queen of the 99th" poses with members of America's first squadron of black combat pilots, Tuskegee, Alabama, c. 1943.

TO CHRISTEN NEW SHIP

LENA HORNE

Lovely and talented young screen and stage star, who will christen the new Liberty ship, S.S. George Washington Carver, at Richmond, Calif., on Sunday. The vessel was recently completed at the Kaiser Shipbuilding Yards and is the latest addition to the United States merchant marine.

Lena Horne To Launch S.S. Carver On Sunday

rines. Generals Patton (in Europe) and MacArthur (in the Pacific) were among the very few to accept black combat troops. (Blacks in the Pacific suffered discrimination and violence; in one month the NAACP received $3,290 from a single black unit on Guam.) The Battle of the Bulge was America's first integrated battle of World War II; the blacks, along with the Japanese-Americans, were volunteers.

In 1941 the Army Air Corps established a training school for black pilots at Tuskegee Institute. (The training school was in response to a legal suit filed by a Howard student.) The first Tuskegee graduates formed the nucleus of the 99th Pursuit Squadron, the first squadron of black combat pilots. Lena was named "Queen of the 99th," and when Lena went by train to Tuskegee to accept her "queenship," it was the first time that she had been in a Jim Crow car since childhood. At Tuskegee she was greeted by Frank Horne's pal Otto MacLaren, the Howard professor, who was the 99th's public relations officer. And Sterling Brown was there, writing a series of articles on black GIs in the South. According to Sterling, the place went wild when Lena appeared. The officers were all over her, but she spent her time with the men. The 99th served in Italy and North Africa. It won 95 Distinguished Flying Crosses, 1 Silver Star, 1 Legion of Merit, 14 Bronze Stars, 744 Air Medals and Clusters, and 8 Purple Hearts.

On the home front, Lena entertained troops for both the segregated USO and the integrated Hollywood Canteen—wartime show business was more liberal than the general population. The Hollywood Victory Committee, whose chairman was Bette Davis, stipulated that Hollywood's canteen be integrated, as was Broadway's Stage Door Canteen. The USO ran only all-white or all-black clubs. I knew whenever Lena was going to the canteen because she always wore a particular suit (on loan from Irene, the MGM designer) that was my favorite article of clothing. It was violet wool, with a little purple beaded patch pocket. Over this she donned a red, white, and blue apron in which to serve coffee and doughnuts to the boys.

A USO-sponsored junket to Camp Robertson, Arkansas, stopped Lena in her tracks. She was scheduled to give two performances, one for the white officers and another for the black men. She was surprised at the second performance, however, to see another sea of white faces. "Who are these soldiers?" she asked. "They're not soldiers, they're German prisoners of war," was the reply. "But where are the Negro soldiers?" Lena asked. "They're sitting behind the German POWs," was the answer. To that Lena replied "Screw this!" and walked out of the auditorium to find her black driver and say, "Take me to the NAACP!" The NAACP's lone Little Rock representative was a woman, Daisy Bates, future heroine of the 1950s Little Rock school crisis. After Lena and Daisy drafted a statement of protest regarding Camp Robertson, Lena returned to Hollywood—and hot water.

First the USO censured her for refusing to perform. Then the Screen Actors Guild got involved. Dick Powell, a board member from Arkansas, just didn't believe that such a thing could happen in his home state, although his wife, Joan Blondell, also a board member, was on Lena's side. Ultimately Lena was more or less kicked out of the USO. But she went on visiting black army bases at her own expense, wearing dresses borrowed from Fox or Metro.

Teddy Horne was enjoying the reflected glow of his daughter's success. As usual he spent August 1943 "Idling at Hot Springs," as his picture in the local papers was captioned. Teddy also saved two other newspaper clippings that month: a photograph of a Brooklyn Smart Set "Get Together" (childhood friends, now middle-aged, among them Francis C. Holbrook, Charles R. Scottron, George W. Lattimore, and Ferdinand J. Accooe), and a newspaper column by the conservative white columnist Westbrook Pegler. The Pegler piece was about a "Negro boy" who had enlisted in the army, only to take abuse from white Southern civilians:

> . . . Now, assuming that this boy comes back from the war to a victorious country, what status will he come back to? Will he be Niggerized again and restricted to menial jobs, Jim-Crowed and driven back to the dreadful Ghettos of our cities, or will he be treated as an American?
>
> . . . We will accept foreigners from Europe and organize leagues to protect their rights, we welcome them into all our residential districts with no more restraint than that of snobbery, and all our professions and trades are open to them. But the Negro who was born among us and fights for the United States, when the war is up is told to stand aside because he is a Negro. . . .
>
> If I were a Negro I would live in constant fury and probably would batter myself to death against the bars enclosing my condition. I would not be a sub-American or a sub-human being, and, in docile patience, forever yield up my rightful aspiration to be a man, to work, to progress and to move out of the slums. . . .

To me, almost seven, it seemed that there had always been a war, just as there had always been FDR, Mrs. FDR, and Joe Louis. I loved uniforms.

With my brother, Teddy, in Hollywood, 1944

AT THE "GET-TOGETHER" of Brooklyn's Smart Set AC last Saturday the above members posed for

My grandfather Teddy kept track of his boyhood friends with clippings such as this newspaper notice of a Smart Set "Get-Together" in Brooklyn, 1943.

I wanted the war to last long enough for me to become a WAVE, like our friend Harriet Pickens, who looked smashing in her Mainbocher uniform. I wanted that serious shoulder bag and smart little tricorn cap.

I wanted desperately to be part of the Youthful War Effort. Girls were taught infant care, and boys learned auxiliary fire and police training. "Teenager," like "juvenile delinquent," was a wartime neologism. Juvenile delinquents were "acting out war fantasies." Even worse were the outcroppings of wild teenage girls, whose mothers were in factories and fathers away at war. They were called "bobby soxers." They wore ankle socks, saddle shoes, "sloppy Joe" sweaters, and gobs of passion-red lipstick. And they squealed for crooners. I could not wait to be a teenager.

We younger children did have responsibilities, too, however. We could collect library books and phonograph records for GIs, distribute anti–black market pledge cards or "War Worker Sleeping" signs, sell war stamps, and collect waste pulp. I saved old newspapers and silver cigarette paper—of which I had an enormous ball, mostly from Edwina's Luckies. Teddy and I also made a Victory garden; I think we grew carrots and radishes.

Lacking a WAVE uniform, I wanted at least to be a Brownie. But the Brownies were segregated, and my mother would not bus me to Los Angeles' black Brownies. The distance between Hollywood and Los Angeles might as well have been that between New York and Chicago, they were that far apart, in mentality if not in miles. But I enjoyed my rare forays into the Los Angeles black bourgeoisie. There were occasional visits to some older Smith family third cousins, who lived in a big dark house, with a wide front lawn, on a palm-tree-lined West Los Angeles street. Their house had a garden with an apricot tree, a big, cool kitchen, and a back porch where we shelled peas from the garden, eating every other one.

The Smith cousins sometimes took me to a church in whose basement Sunday school we heard Bible stories and stared at the large picture of blond, blue-eyed Jesus hanging over the blackboard. When the Sunday school put on a "Tom Thumb" wedding, I was chosen to be the bride. Local mothers and daughters must have been furious. My wedding dress was beautiful, however (it was probably made at MGM).

One day on the lot, Lena ran into L.B., who clapped his hands and said that luck must have brought them together, because he had been meaning to ask Lena, "as a personal favor," to do "something" for a friend of his in Chicago. What L.B. asked was that Lena play the Chez Paree nightclub in Chicago—for less than her normal fee. Lena, unable to refuse, went to Chicago and proceeded to break all house records. The grateful management rewarded her with an enormous star sapphire ring. In Chicago Lena felt like a real "movie star" almost for the first time. She sang for black Coast Guardsmen at the Great Lakes Naval Station and made a movie star entrance on the arm of a tall, handsome black officer named Reginald Goodwin, another old Horne family friend. Lena wore a Helen Rose creation, a bare-midriff top and slinky sarong skirt, with a hibiscus in her hair —and the Coast Guard went berserk. The Chez Paree engagement led to a flood of nightclub offers for her. At last she could make some money and afford to live like a movie star.

Lena now had good friends in Hollywood: Billy Strayhorn, Vincente, Roger Edens, Marie Bryant, and Kay Thompson. She also made early morning make-up pals with sweet and slightly insecure Kathryn Grayson, bubbly and skittish (from all those Metro diet pills) Judy Garland, acerbic and witty Ann Sothern, and two beauties, Lana Turner and Ava Gardner. Naturally, they discussed men. Everyone was in love with Joseph L. Mankiewicz. Artie Shaw was known as "Mr. Know-it-all." And Turhan Bey, the Turkish star, was considered "cute." Orson Welles, who was preparing *Jane Eyre,* had pursued Lena all through *Cabin in the Sky,* but she was much more interested in Orson's mind, and the sound of Orson's voice, than in Orson himself. He told her that MGM make-up must be mad to cover up her freckles.

Lena had begun to socialize, on a fairly regular basis, with members of the "Eastern liberal group": Gene and Betsy Kelly, Frank and Nancy Sinatra, the John Garfields (he was called "Julie"), and the Richard "Nick" Contes. Lena's friends mostly entertained at home. Romanoff's was the only top Hollywood restaurant that permitted blacks—most of whom, including Lena, could never afford it. When Barney Josephson came to Hollywood for a visit, he took Lena to Trader Vic's, which was notoriously segregated but the one place Lena really wanted to see. As they came into the restaurant they met and joined a group that included Humphrey Bogart and Robert Benchley, either one of whom would have vociferously discouraged the management from asking Lena to leave.

When the actor Canada Lee, an old acquaintance of Lena's, was making Hitchcock's *Lifeboat,* Lena visited the set. Tallulah Bankhead, the star of the picture, greeted Lena with open arms—and with the words "My daddy had a beautiful little pickaninny just like you." Lena was so bowled over by the sheer audacity of Tallulah, who had been one of the great theatrical stars of the 1920s (as well as a famous "free spirit"), that all she could do was laugh. And she laughed the rest of the afternoon. Tallulah was no bigot

—she was, in fact, one of show biz's great liberals. In her world there were simply Alabama Bankheads (her "daddy" was speaker of the House of Representatives), Democrats, and the rest of the human race, none of whom were less equal than others.

Paul Robeson had said, "The artist must speak out"—and Lena had listened. In 1941 she was elected to the board of the Hollywood Independent Citizens Committee for Arts, Sciences and Professions (HICCASP would be a major target of 1950s Red Baiters). Lena also made appearances with Assemblyman Augustus Hawkins to promote a Fair Employment Practices Commission in California, and she joined the ranks of Hollywood's activist liberal Democrats, a group that included Bette Davis, Myrna Loy, James Cagney, Joan Blondell, Helen Gahagan and Melvyn Douglas, and Bogart.

In early 1942 Lena began work on *I Dood It*, Vincente's second feature-length movie. Like their lucky *Panama Hattie*, it starred Red Skelton. Lena loved making *I Dood It*. She was finally learning to sing. Kay Thompson, the chic whirling dervish of the Freed Unit, was teaching Lena breath control, and Lena was finding notes she didn't know existed. Kay, one of Fred Waring's original singing Pennsylvanians, was teaching Lena simply to open her mouth and sing. Kay had been known to have her students sing along with Ethel Merman records. *I Dood It* also brought Lena face to face with her old Café Society rival, Hazel Scott. On the first day of rehearsals Lena turned up, California style, in pigtails, slacks, and loafers. Hazel, fresh from New York, was dripping silver fox. The next day Lena wore her Irene canteen suit, and Hazel appeared in slacks. Everyone finally laughed, and a more or less permanent truce was effected. They rehearsed Kay's wonderful arrangement of "Joshua Fit the Battle of Jericho," which Kay thought suffered from unimaginative musical direction. She kept saying, "If only Lennie were doing this we would have been finished days ago." Lennie Hayton—a staff composer, arranger, and conductor—was in constant demand, though Lena was not one of Lennie's fans. "He's too sarcastic," she said to Kay. "He's not sarcastic," Kay replied; "he just has a dry sense of humor." But in any case Lennie was tied up with another MGM musical, *Best Foot Forward*.

One day while *I Dood It* was shooting, Lena and Vincente were lunching in the commissary when Lennie stopped at their table to say hello. He was not sarcastic at all, Lena realized, except for the usual Freed Unit Mickey Rooney jokes. And slowly, through the next few weeks, Lennie Hayton began to turn up wherever Lena happened to be. One night they were part of a large group at Lucy's restaurant, a favorite MGM hangout.

Lennie started to play the piano, Lena and Hazel started to sing, and no one stopped until the wee hours.

It became a serious romance. Lena soon learned that Lennie was a widower—his wife had died suddenly of a cerebral stroke. He had a teenaged stepdaughter, Peggy Husing, whom he adored, and a mother, sister, and brother-in-law, all of whom he knew would adore Lena. The Haytons were bourgeois Russian Jews to whom music and the arts were sacred. Lennie had the looks of a soulful nineteenth-century Russian Georgian: a long thinly chiseled nose, slightly Asian eyes, and prematurely silver hair, which he wore longish, musician-like. Of medium height, he was as clothes-conscious as his friend Fred Astaire: Charvet silks, cashmere blazers, and soft flannels. Later he grew a little Van Dyke beard, and through the years became even more distinguished-looking. He always wore the dark blue cap of a New York Yacht Club commodore, which he had received as a gift from a sailor friend. The cap kept the wind out of his hair while he drove one of his many convertible sports cars. (Lennie's only sailing was on ocean liners, where the cap naturally received special attention.)

Lennie and I were introduced for the first time during one of my interminable naps. I knew he must be important: naps were rarely interrupted. From that moment on, Lennie was indulgent, devoted, fatherly, and fun. He added Camel paper to my foil collection. He took us for long drives in his MGs and Jags, all of which had steering wheels on the "wrong" side. (Nobody in Hollywood drove American cars—not since Valentino's Hispano-Suiza and Gary Cooper's Duesenberg.) We drove everywhere: to Santa Monica, to Palm Springs, and to beautiful Baja California.

Lennie was devoted to the art of food and drink, and it was apparent even in the way he rubbed the garlic clove around the inside of the wooden salad bowl, the way he made curried eggs. He daily consumed, without a change of expression, a cold beer (or two) at lunch, several martinis at sunset, a bottle of Bordeaux at dinner, and some Hennessy and soda after dinner—not to mention four packs daily of Camel cigarettes. And he *never* appeared any the worse for wear. He came of age in Prohibition. But Lennie's consuming life's interest was music, to the point where Lena would scream, "I hate musicians!" And Lennie would reply, "I hate girl singers." He was in fact merciless in his appraisal of Hollywood's girl singers. The very young Debbie Reynolds, the last star MGM made, once sent him a Christmas card signed "Debbie 'No Voice' Reynolds." At least Debbie had a sense of humor; some of the others did not.

Lennie had begun as the classically trained protégé of the great Serge Koussevitzky, but he fell in love with jazz while still in his teens and became pianist-arranger for Paul Whiteman. In 1924 Whiteman had billed himself as the King of Jazz, much to the disdain of blacks. Whiteman's orchestra was extremely popular. It combined the sounds of Jim Europe's Clef Club Orchestra and Duke Ellington, jazz-cum-proto-swing. Whiteman, hugely fat, was a nationally known figure, and his band attracted all the great white jazz artists. When Lennie was Whiteman's pianist, his orchestra colleagues included Bix Beiderbecke, Bunny Berigan, Frankie Trumbauer, Jack Teagarden, Red Norvo, and the Dorsey Brothers. There was also a singing trio called the Rhythm Boys, whose lead baritone with the buttery vibrato was Bing Crosby. In 1929 a very young Bing and a very young Lennie recorded a piano-vocal duet of "Sweet Sue." The result still seems, more than fifty years later, the bubbling essence of great jazz-swing.

In the 1930s Lennie became a "name" in the relatively new medium of radio—first as leader of the Fred Allen Show orchestra, then as "Maestro" of the "Hit Paraders and Lucky Strike Orchestra" on NBC's popular "Hit Parade" show. The "Hit Parade," which featured the ten top tunes of the week, might be where Lennie developed his aversion to girl singers. He also rather scorned popular music—his idols were Bartók, Ravel, Stravinsky, and Richard Strauss. Luckily for me, Lennie seemed to enjoy it when I banged impressionistically on the piano, trying to imitate Sir William Walton's *Belshazzar's Feast.*

■ ■ ■

Nineteen forty-four was an election year. The Reverend Adam Clayton Powell, Jr., became New York's first black congressman. And Lena took violets instead of the customary orchids when she called on Mrs. Roosevelt in the White House (Mrs. Roosevelt was clearly pleased—she apparently wasn't that fond of orchids). Eleanor Roosevelt was, as far as Lena was concerned, Mom, Flag, and Apple Pie all rolled into one. As for FDR, Lena —like her contemporary Helen Lawrenson—confessed to romantic dreams about that father figure in the White House. Nevertheless, and as usual, it was the Republicans whose racial platform did not mince words:

We pledge an immediate Congressional inquiry to ascertain the extent to which mistreatment, segregation or discrimination against Negroes who are in our armed forces are impairing morale and efficiency. . . .

My brother, Teddy, 1944

Lennie Hayton, c. 1930. My stepfather was classically trained, and was a protégé of Serge Koussevitzky.

Myself as a California kid, 1944

With cousin Edwina at our house in Hollywood

The Democratic platform was, in Wendell Willkie's words, a "splinter."

By 1944 I had turned my cinematic attention from Abbott and Costello to Van Johnson in Jimmy Doolittle's air corps. But though I was a Hollywood kid, I was not a Hollywood princess. I made only three visits to MGM in my life. When I went to watch the shooting of *Anchors Aweigh*, Frank Sinatra knelt by my chair in the commissary, and no one had bluer eyes. I watched a scene on the remake of *Little Women*; I thought Peter Lawford was beautiful. And I spent a day on the *Singin' in the Rain* set watching Debbie Reynolds pop in and out of a cake in the big Hollywood party scene. The studio was my idea of heaven. It was a maze of bungalows, barracks, and airplane hangars. In one of those numbered concrete alleys, on my first studio trip, I met Clark Gable. He was walking ahead of us, and when Lena called, "Clark! Say hello to my little girl," he turned to zap us both with that incredible Gable grin.

Besides movie star worship, my pursuits were mainly serious, artistic, and school-related. I studied ballet and piano. And I played with the children of such Hollywood liberals as Gene Kelly and Ella Logan. The little Sinatra children were shy, and wore white gloves, whenever they came to visit; and their mother was nice. (*Everybody* knew that Joan Crawford's children, who also wore white gloves, had a weird mother.) Later I had good Hollywood friends: Adrian McClure and Judy Chaplin, both daughters of musical MGM fathers, and my step-cousin (Lennie's niece) Michele Hart. Adrian had red hair, green eyes, and a wonderful singing voice. Judy, who danced like a muse and played the piano like a dream, was the funniest person in the world. And Michele, a miraculous product of Southern California, could ice-skate like my idol Sonja Henie. We were all star-struck.

Many of my best childhood friends were grown-ups: Roger Edens, Kay Thompson, Conrad Salinger of the Freed Unit, Billy Strayhorn, and Marie Bryant. There was also Edmund Kara, the beautiful young man who designed Lena's nightclub dresses and lived just down the hill with his equally beautiful model sister.

Matching mother-daughter outfits were a wartime rage, and my mother and I wore them once in a fashion show for the opening of a new black USO. When the fashion show was over, Lena was onstage singing, and suddenly (just like in *San Francisco*) the lights began to dim and the room began to shake, rattle, and roll. It was a big earthquake. I was nowhere to be seen (I had skipped down to the ground floor to buy a Coca-Cola), and Lena was in a panic. She had vivid pictures of me lying in rubble, like a child victim of war. She was about to run offstage when a Cora Horne instinct stopped her short and helped avert general panic. She spoke into the microphone: "We've got a lot of men here who are trained to act in emergencies. I suggest we let them take over and lead the rest of us out of the building. Okay with you, soldiers and sailors?" And the military calmly led the civilians out of the building and into the street. Lena found me waiting outside.

I thought earthquakes were fun. At the time I also liked roller coasters, Ferris wheels, and storms at sea. I was much more frightened by fantasy than by real life. When Lena acted on "Suspense"—the radio show produced by Kay Thompson's husband, Bill Spier—I was so frightened by the Nazis stalking her in the program that I hid under a glass coffee table (the way we did under our desks at school), much to the contemptuous amusement of my little brother. That same night Air Raid Warden Bogart came rapping on our door to say that a light was shining through the blackout curtains. As far as I was concerned, real life was just like the movies.

Lena made two movies in 1944: *Two Girls and a Sailor,* in which she sang "Paper Doll" and "hated" it ("It's a *boy's* song," she complained), and *Ziegfeld Follies,* the all-star extravaganza in which every MGM player except Lassie had a part. Vincente codirected *Follies* with George Sidney, and Lennie was musical director (Lennie and Vincente had just finished *Meet Me in St. Louis*).

In the fall of 1944 Lena achieved another Hollywood first: she appeared, in upswept hairdo and Joan Crawford lips, on the cover of October's *Motion Picture* magazine. The cover announced, "Step right up and meet that enchanting flash of lightning—Miss Lena Horne. First of a series of *Motion Picture* cover stars by famed Hollywood writer Sidney Skolsky." Skolsky's interview was straightforward:

> Lena Horne is a unique person. She is unique because she is the only colored actress who has sustained a career in Hollywood without being a comedy character or portraying servants. . . .

There was a photograph of Lena standing in front of the Horn Avenue fireplace, wearing a Chinese robe and holding a glass of milk: "Daytimes Lena appears around town in classic suits. At home, she bursts out in wild pajamas. Wears striped ones to bed." And another photograph of Lena at her dressing table, brushing her hair: "Lena lives very simply in a little home in Hollywood, often cooks for her guests. Her Aunt Eddy helps her keep house."

In October 1944 Lena became the first black to appear on the cover of a movie magazine. _Motion Picture_ later reported that 80 percent of the mail was "congratulatory."

The elaborate "Liza" number from _Ziegfeld Follies_, 1944. The scene was later cut from the picture.

The issue of the Spanish-language magazine
Sensacion that sent my grandmother Edna
rushing from Havana to Los Angeles.

Edna and Lena at a National Council of Negro Women tea in Los Angeles, 1944

Skolsky went on to reveal Lena's philosophy of life:

> Her great ambition is to use her talent and her success to win respect
> for her people. . . . Lena has great admiration for Marian Anderson
> and Paul Robeson. Her great desire is to continue their good work
> for the colored people. She has.

A month later Lena was featured in *Movieland* in an article headlined
"Tootin' Lena's Horne," which ended on a serious note:

> Lena is a forthright and intelligent champion of her people. She is
> proud of the strides they have made so far, and constantly stumps
> for greater educational opportunity for them. Only through educa-
> tion can their hopes for a better heritage for their children and their
> children's children be realized, she firmly believes. That better her-
> itage she defines as financial security, economic equality and a cul-
> tural background.

Lena was beginning to sound more and more like Edwin Horne.

All of Lena's good news was bound to reach Edna, of course, and when
Lena appeared (sporting her *Ziegfeld Follies* hairdo) on the cover of a Cuban
magazine, Edna managed to get from Havana to Los Angeles in record time.
She stayed at a downtown Los Angeles "whites only" hotel, and Lennie had
to pick her up to take her to see Lena. At once Edna announced the purpose
of her visit. She was tired of Cuba, and she wanted to resurrect her acting
career. (Edna was by now a stylishly stout matron, but her hair and make-
up were still Clara Bow; 1924 had been Edna's "best" year.) She wanted
Lena to speak to her "producer friends"—to help find acting jobs for her.
Lena was beginning to wonder if her mother had any grasp of reality at all
—she could never get her mother a job, although she could (and would)
give her financial help. Meanwhile Lena played Hollywood hostess to Edna.
They posed together at a National Council of Negro Women tea. Soon after
that Edna returned to Havana, careerless but apparently satisfied. A few
months later, however, Lena got a note from Hedda Hopper. "I get so many
of these . . . ," it began. Attached was a letter from Edna castigating Lena
as a selfish and neglectful daughter. It took Lena another twenty years to
forgive her mother.

In 1945, after he had made *The Harvey Girls,* for which he was nomi-
nated for an Oscar as musical director, Lennie and Lena worked to-

gether on *Till the Clouds Roll By,* an all-star Jerome Kern musical biography. MGM was roundly derided for *Clouds,* especially the "all-white" finale in which Lena leaned against a pillar in a white Grecian gown to sing "Why Was I Born?" and Frank Sinatra, in snow-white tails, sang "Ol' Man River."

Hollywood days remained mostly long, golden, and boring for those too young to be wartime teenagers. Moments stand out, however: VE Day, when all the cars on the road to the beach were honking, and people were laughing and yelling, "It's over!" The death of FDR is memorable because all the grown-ups stood around weeping, and my brother and I couldn't go to see *Snow White and the Seven Dwarfs* (Teddy called them "seven drawers").

The next time we went to the movies we saw the atom bomb. The Age of Anxiety must have dawned in a million movie theaters that week. As we sat in the dark, the billowing, molten fire seemed close and overwhelming. The mushroom cloud unfolded—looming over us—and you could hear a pin drop. It was not really frightening, just awesome and ominous. Then I read in a magazine about a little Japanese girl whose skin came off in strips, and about shadows left behind by people who were no longer there. I added "bomb" to my litany of bedtime intercessions: God save us from mud slides, brush fires, earthquakes, rattlesnakes, and atom bombs. In a way, the bomb was why my family would spend a great part of the next decade in Europe. The Age of Anxiety had a Red-Baiting effect on grown-ups.

As if to italicize the point, in October 1945 the Hornes (minus Lena) gathered as a clan in the Grand Ballroom of New York's Biltmore Hotel to see their great friend Paul Robeson receive the NAACP's thirtieth annual Spingarn Medal, "for the highest achievement of an American Negro." The Spingarn was sort of the black Oscar and Medal of Honor rolled into one. The Pittsburgh *Courier* later reported that Robeson's Spingarn speech "shocked his several hundred listeners by voicing frank and pronounced preference for Soviet principles—economic, political and social." The *Courier* wrote:

In pointing out that the Russians have shown what backward peoples can accomplish in one generation of endeavor, Mr. Robeson said, "Full employment in Russia is a fact, and not a myth, and discrimination is nonexistent" . . .

Marshall Field, Chicago editor and publisher, made the presentation to Robeson. . . . Mr. Field pointed out the difficulty a white man experiences in grasping and appreciating the cost of outstanding accomplishment by an American Negro. "It is little wonder that the Negroes who have accomplished what is symbolized by the Spingarn Medal have had such thrilling and incredible life histories. In many cases they have endured trials that few white Americans can imagine, and even fewer have ever experienced," he said.

There is a panoramic photograph of the gathering in the Biltmore Ballroom. There are ladies wearing hats like powder puffs, a few uniforms, and a sea of mostly black faces. The Hornes are seated together, with uniformed Harriet Pickens, her white WAVE cap shining like a beacon. Ted Horne—slim, tanned, and balding—is dapper, still sporting pearl stickpins. But the circles under his eyes make him look haggard. His expression is almost professionally serene. Frank Horne wears a scowl, the successful but personally unhappy public servant (at the time Frankye was known to be terminally ill). Burke, perpetually overwhelmed by his older brothers, seems to be enjoying his brief "engagement"; it is the time when he and Harriet were flirting with the idea of uniting their old Brooklyn names. (Fifteen years earlier, Harriet's best friend Yolande Du Bois, daughter of W.E.B., had briefly married Countee Cullen with more or less the same idea in mind.) But Harriet later broke the engagement. (Not only did she look smashing in uniform, she "found" herself in the navy.) And Burke, who had ended the war a sergeant in the 369th, eventually married a Kentuckian who claimed descent from Henry Clay. (Cora would have approved.) Burke's son became the last Horne to live on Chauncey Street.

It is significant that Lena is missing from this "family" portrait. There are actually two families represented here, the immediate one and the extended one. There are the surviving Hornes of old Brooklyn, gathered to celebrate the peace and to honor their friend Paul—probably the last time that they were captured together on film. The picture acknowledges both their own brotherhood and their place in the larger tribe. The other family —the family of the black bourgeoisie—is also here in force. The Spingarn was a bourgeois tribal rite, like the Comus or the Smart Set summer meets. Here they are, all together. But not Lena. She had left the quiet waters of the black bourgeoisie for the perilous open seas of "white" life. Many things had already distanced Lena from those middle-class roots—show business, Hollywood, politics. Now it was love. Lena and Lennie had decided to marry. She was preparing to take a step that would further isolate her from the world in which she had grown up.

My mother and I therefore entered the great "white" world, where we lived not *as* white people, but *like* white people. We breathed the rarefied international air of "stardom," where billing is more important than color. Lena was the first black Hollywood star—a title of great symbolic value, though she actually did very little in movies. But as long as she *existed* as a symbol of black aspiration and American brotherhood, Hollywood was not racist. This may have been enough for the NAACP, the propagandists of the Office of War Information, and possibly the black GI, but it could hardly have been enough for Lena. She had no roles to play because the only roles open to blacks in pre-1947 Hollywood were demeaning ones. So Lena shone brightly—everyone knew she was *there*—even if the position was mostly ceremonial. It took a long time for her to overcome feelings of being trapped behind the role model, and feeling "unworthy" of the part at that. On the positive side, being "symbolic" may have saved her from the ordinary pitfalls of Hollywood life, the stuff of Hollywood Babylon. She was never permitted the common mistakes, bad habits, or ego trips; there were too many people watching—all those Pullman porters, for example.

In the first half of the twentieth century, only a handful of American blacks were stars of *anything*. (The turbulent nineteenth century was richer: Toussaint L'Ouverture, Frederick Douglass, Harriet Tubman, Sojourner Truth, valiant old "Uncle Tom," et al.) Before 1947, and the desegregation of American sports, few twentieth-century blacks were American household names. Certainly Jack Johnson, Jesse Owens, and Joe Louis. Possibly Booker T. Washington, Bessie Smith, Louis Armstrong, Duke Ellington, Paul Robeson, Marian Anderson, Eddie "Rochester" Anderson, and Lena. World War II created new opportunities for a handful of black specialists. They were not household names, but they were known in the corridors of power. They were Generals Benjamin O. Davis, Sr. and Jr., of West Point; Federal Judge William H. Hastie, civilian aide to the Secretary of War; and (in war's aftermath) future Nobel Peace Prize Laureate Ralph Bunche (known in the Belgian Congo as "the white black man"). World War II also inevitably caused the civilized world to examine racism, however obliquely. Lena, as Hollywood's first black glamour symbol, was practically a "token" of a token. Lena paid the dues for all the black stars who came after her, but she never felt free to enjoy herself as a performer, or to step out of her symbolic persona. (Thirty years after her initial "stardom" we went to see Bette Midler on Broadway. Backstage, Bette Midler said to Lena, "You're so *tasteful*." To which Lena replied, "I'm *tired* of being tasteful.")

At the Horne family table (clockwise from top):
Teddy, Burke, Harriet Pickens, and Frank

The Springarn Medal dinner, October 1945

SPINGARN MEDAL
AWARDED ANNUALLY FOR THE HIGHEST ACHIEVEMENT
OF AN AMERICAN NEGRO
BY THE NATIONAL ASSOCIATION
FOR THE ADVANCEMENT OF COLORED PEOPLE
THIRTIETH AWARD
TO
PAUL ROBESON
HOTEL BILTMORE OCTOBER 18, 1945

PART TWO
THE NEW HORNES

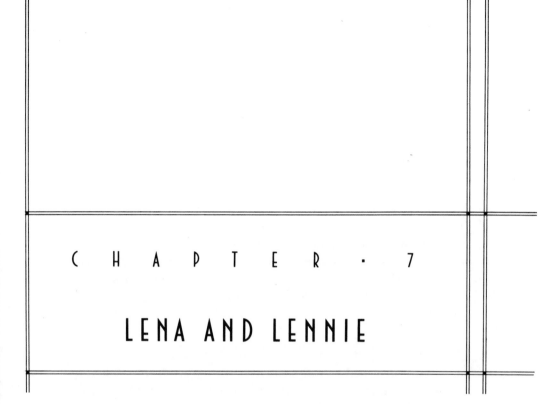

C H A P T E R · 7

LENA AND LENNIE

The year 1946 was a transitional one. The prewar and the postwar orders were fighting it out, and Lena was now a soldier in the new order. Billie Holiday's advice to the contrary, Lena responded to every issue. How could she not? She was Cora and Edwin's grandchild, Frank Horne's niece, and the political protégée of two of the most powerful and persuasive black men in America, Paul Robeson and Walter White. I received my first political lesson in 1946 at the time of a local housing discrimination conflict. A disabled Japanese-American veteran was trying to buy a house in a restricted Los Angeles neighborhood. Emotions were high, and a rally was held to support the vet. Lena told me all about it when she came home. She described the nisei vet—in a wheelchair, with both legs off at the knee. Then she started to cry as she described the tears that streamed down *his* face as she sang "America the Beautiful."

There were some meaningful political victories in 1946. The NAACP won a major Supreme Court ruling in *Morgan* vs. *Commonwealth of Virginia*, which determined that segregation on interstate buses was an unreasonable burden on interstate commerce. At the same time, voter registration was increasing in the South; 100,000 blacks voted in the Georgia primary. But three days later five blacks were lynched, including one veteran, Macio Snipes, the *only* black voter in Taylor County, Georgia. A sign was posted on a black church: "The first nigger to vote will never vote again." There was comfort to take in less baleful aspects of American life. "Sugar" Ray Robinson, the most elegant black boxer in years, became the new welterweight boxing champion. And for those who craved stability, Satchel Paige pitched 64 straight scoreless innings for his team to win the Negro World Series.

America might be starting to change, but Teddy Horne was a man whose life-style was at home in the status quo. It had not altered during the war—why should it change in peace? He continued to make money (and to lend money to friends), he still traveled, and he still had fun. His small Pittsburgh hotel was a center of black life. And he was entrenched in the local Democratic machine, with friends and contacts in all the right places; he had learned at the knee of Tammany, after all. Teddy was a perfect member of the demimonde. He was only "shady" around the edges —hardly noticeable in his world of big-time sports, ward heelers, and gay divorcées. He still saw his boyhood pals, all respected members of the bourgeoisie: doctors, lawyers, businessmen. Teddy never hid what he was, and was never ashamed of anything he did, and his only god was money— he saw money as the only sure protection against white racism. In essence, he took half of his father's 1875 advice to black men: make money and get an education. But he went on scorning all other middle-class values and pretensions.

In June 1947 Teddy went to Cleveland for the World Welterweight Championship match between "Sugar" Ray Robinson and Jimmy Doyle. In October, instead of the Negro World Series, he went to New York for the "Subway Series" between the Yankees and the Brooklyn Dodgers. Jackie Robinson had become the first black in major league baseball when he had signed with the Dodgers that April. (That same April the Congress of Racial Equality had sent the first group of "Freedom Riders" to the South, but much less attention was paid to that event.) Teddy got so excited by the Robinson phenomenon that he caught pneumonia and was hospitalized in New York.

We were still in California. After the war we had moved from Horn Avenue to Nichols Canyon, up in the Hollywood Hills. My brother Teddy had gone back to live with our father, and we saw each other only on infrequent holidays. At the time I had no idea that Lena and Lennie's impending marriage was a momentous event. I had no idea that it was illegal in California, in 1946, for blacks and whites to marry each other. In the summer of 1947 Lena, Lennie, and I went East. Although we kept our canyon home, we now began to live like Eastern nomads, pitching our tents from hotel to hotel.

August 21, 1947, was Lena Horne Day in Brooklyn. There was a motorcade tour of Bedford-Stuyvesant, and a citation from Girls High School: "In grateful recognition of the achievements of one of its distinguished daughters . . . ." Lena sat on the back of an open convertible in an enormous pink Mr. John hat. She was disappointed that MGM publicity hadn't thought to notify any of the old Junior Debs, but she did see many of her old friends at the Capitol Theater, where she was appearing in vaudeville for Loews and breaking all house records.

It was my first New York summer. I don't remember if there was air conditioning in 1947, but in the upper reaches of the now extinct old Broadway hotel where we stayed the heat and noise of the street seemed very far away. I took to hotel life like a duck to water—all kids do. Hotels represent luxury, magic, and freedom—all those corridors, elevators, and opportunities for solo missions. My life was excitingly similar to that of "Eloise," the little girl (created by Lena and Lennie's great friend Kay Thompson) who lived at the Plaza Hotel. "This is me, charge it please!" And up would roll club sandwiches, with dill pickles, and Coca-Cola; French toast with maple syrup; or roast beef, baked potato, and apple pie à la mode. There was magic in the folding tables, with their starched white cloths, and all the steamers, burners, and domed utensils of room service cookery.

My mother and I kept more or less the same hours. In the late morning we walked to the theater. I would see the Clark Gable–Lana Turner movie for the hundredth time, then watch the orchestra rise from the pit, with its blare of trombones. Between shows (with Lena still in make-up) we might go to Longchamps, for chicken à la king and stuffed celery; or to Saks, for summer dresses and white cotton petticoats. Or we might go up to F. A. O. Schwarz, where you could buy a "Sparkle Plenty" doll, or some *Dr. Doolittle* and *Oz* books. In those days, before behemoth stuffed animals, you could sit on the floor at Schwarz to read a book. My favorite restaurant was Lindy's, because old Mr. Lindy himself served us strawberry cheesecake. Lindy's was often the scene of meetings between Walter Winchell and J. Edgar Hoover. They could be seen, cheek by jowl, plotting over their black coffee. Lena told me they were villains. To me they both looked sort

My grandfather Teddy (at right) near the end of World War II, characteristically intense at a sporting event

Little Teddy and I in our mother's dressing room at the Copacabana, New York 1947. We had just met Charles Boyer.

of waxen, as if they wore a light pasty make-up. Celebrities, restaurant dinners, room service, and ocean travel were quickly becoming my young way of life.

Lena and Lennie began their travels by sailing to Europe in October 1947. London was still "war-torn" and in rubble. *Everything* was either rationed or nonexistent. The city was freezing, but Londoners were the warmest people in the world. James Mason's mother brought eggs from the country so that Lennie could have a proper breakfast. James Mason, the first postwar European movie idol, sent his American press agents into a tailspin when he said that Lena was the most beautiful woman in Hollywood. Lena was appearing with Ted Heath's orchestra at the London Casino, a theater owned by one of the Grade brothers (then small agents, later titans of British show business). The Royal Navy had seen *Cabin in the Sky* and *Stormy Weather,* and English music fans knew Lena's prewar Charlie Barnet and Artie Shaw recordings. As one of the first American performers to play in postwar London, Lena was an enormous critical and popular success. Fleet Street took notice, and Dylan Thomas declared drunken devotion. London was not a place where Lena and Lennie could be quietly wed.

Paris—not war-torn at all—was full of black-market chic and such new American friends as Auren Kahn (of the Joint Distribution Committee refugee service), John Galliher (former Foreign Service officer), Art Buchwald of the *International Herald Tribune,* and the war photographer Robert Capa. Lena opened at the Club des Champs-Élysées, just off the Arc de Triomphe, and made new French friends: Yves Montand, Simone Signoret, and Edith Piaf. The French press was appreciative, but somewhat confused on the subject of Lena. She was not exactly *their* idea of a black American —but she was beautiful, beautifully voiced, and *chic*. She was a *succès d'estime.* Paris was a fine place for a wedding. Lena and Lennie were married by the lady mayor of the 16ᵉ *arrondissement,* who concluded the ceremony with a gracious speech on Franco-American friendship. Lena wore a new black dress from Balenciaga (she was married in black both times). Auren Kahn was best man.

Lena and Lennie sailed home, secretly married, on the S.S. *America.* There was a tense labor-race situation on board. Lena, taking the side of the black stewards and stewardesses, refused to sing at the captain's gala. It was not a pleasant voyage. Toward the end of the trip Lena and Lennie called America on the ship-to-shore telephone to tell me that they were married, but I was not allowed to tell anyone about it.

America was still a quasi-apartheid country in 1947. The NAACP appealed to the United Nations at Lake Success, New York, with a "Statement on the Denial of Human Rights to Minorities in the Case of Citizens of Negro Descent in the U.S.A. and an Appeal to the United Nations for Redress." No action was taken on the petition. Henry Wallace, a Democratic presidential hopeful, repeated Wendell Willkie's prewar statement that America's attitude toward blacks, Jews, and recent immigrants made the world laugh at United States pretensions to democracy. Less than 3 percent of the adult black populations of Alabama, Louisiana, and Mississippi were able to vote. There was, however, an important victory in the old Calhoun province, where, in a case argued by Thurgood Marshall, a heroic federal district judge upheld the right of blacks to vote in the South Carolina Democratic Primary.

The bad news was that Lena and Lennie were coming home just in time for blacklisting and the Hollywood Ten.

Most of the ten—each of whom invoked the Fifth Amendment before J. Parnell Thomas's House Committee on Un-American Activities—were or had been Communist Party members. The party had begun to infiltrate Hollywood in the 1930s; one of its most sophisticated operatives was John Howard Lawson, a founder of the Screen Writers Guild, whose recruits included some of Hollywood's smartest people. Among the ten were the writers, producers, and directors of some memorable movies: *Woman of the Year, Crossfire, This Gun for Hire, Action in the North Atlantic, Objective, Burma!, Sahara, Destination Tokyo, Thirty Seconds over Tokyo,* and *The Pride of the Marines.* Clearly, Hollywood Reds fought Hollywood's war against the Fascists. (Two of the Hollywood Ten were stepfathers of friends of mine.)

The black list began in late 1947 when a large and important group of movie executives announced that Communists and other subversives would never "knowingly" be employed in Hollywood again. Producer Dore Schary was the only Hollywood figure to correctly call the black list illegal. The black listers had enormous resources at their disposal, including those of the United States Government and William Randolph Hearst. And they had a powerful hold on the media through such newspaper columnists as George Sokolsky, Walter Winchell, Jack O'Brien, and Hedda Hopper, all of whom both "named" and "cleared" suspects.

Two magazines, *Red Channels* and *Counterattack,* both "listed" and "cleared" names for a fee. Names were listed because of support for so-called Communist-front organizations. Lena was listed for her support of (among other organizations) the Hollywood Independent Citizens Committee, the Joint Anti-Fascist Committee, and W. E. B. Du Bois and Paul Robeson's Council on African Affairs. Lena was considered, if not a Communist, at least *prematurely* anti-Fascist.

In 1948, while Lena threw herself into progressive politics, I was settling into both a progressive New York school and a progressive New York family. My hosts, Dick and Aileen Morford, were actually transplanted midwesterners, and a merrier left-wing family could hardly be imagined. They both had white hair, bright blue eyes, and hearty midwestern laughs. They lived near Columbia University with their two daughters, Linda, who was my age, and Susan, who was about to go to Radcliffe. Dick, an ordained Protestant minister without a regular church, was also president of the Council on Soviet-American Friendship. The Morfords read Soviet magazines and listened to Paul Robeson's "Songs of Free Men." One of their few frivolous records was the original Broadway cast album of *Oklahoma!* and by now I was in love with the theater, collecting playbills, *Theatre Arts* magazines, and autographs.

The Morfords did not go to the theater much, although we did go to Easter Sunrise service at Radio City Music Hall to sing the "Hallelujah Chorus": the household politics were radical, but the faith was orthodox. On Sundays we often went to the celebrated Brooklyn pulpit of Dick's best friend, the Reverend William Howard Mellish, who was considered a very red reverend indeed. And on May Day we went to Union Square to see Paul Robeson.

The best thing about progressive education was Pete Seeger. To have grown up without Pete Seeger is to be a deprived child. I never mastered long division, English grammar, spelling, or fractions, but I could sing "Talking Union" and "Joe Hill." My New York school was like "Auntie Mame's" nephew's. We called our teachers by their first names and had coed viewings of Walt Disney sex education movies. (My mother, always reticent on the subject, gave me a book, *The Stork Didn't Bring You.*) The school was totally integrated, with the possible exception of the children from a family of thin vegetarians, who gnawed their carrots in grim isolation while the rest of us ate hot dogs. But progressive as our school was, the Morfords, the Corliss Lamont children, and I were among the few children there who supported Henry Wallace. "Win with Wallace!" "Let's Put Henry Wallace in the White House!" we sang along with Wallace's folksinging running mate. In 1948 the Democratic Party was split into three parts: on the left were Wallace and the Progressives, on the right were Strom Thurmond and the Dixiecrats, and in the middle was Harry Truman. Robeson led the parade of stars—including Melvyn Douglas, Katharine Hepburn, and Lena—to the Wallace band wagon. Robeson had laughed when reporters asked him if Wallace was a Communist; according to Robeson, Wallace was a "progressive capitalist." The Progressive Party platform called for federal antilynching and antidiscrimination action, as well as the desegregation of Washington, D.C. Unfortunately, the real Communists got a hammer lock on the campaign, and Wallace's natural populist constituency of farmers, workers, and liberals (Lena among them) abandoned him for Truman.

It is amazing that more blacks were not Progressives, or even Republicans. The Republican civil rights plank could have been written by Robeson himself, while the Democrats had only three weak references to "full and equal political participation," "equal opportunity of employment," and "equal treatment in service and defense of the nation." Weak as this platform was, the South went into orbit. Thirty-five Southern Democrats, led by Strom Thurmond, stormed out of the convention and wrote their own racist civil rights platform:

> We stand for segregation of the races . . . oppose elimination of
> segregation in employment . . . favor home rule, local self-
> government and minimum interference. . . .

A. Philip Randolph, however, was able to convince a Democratic president to do something good for blacks, if only to salvage political skin. In June 1948 Randolph formed the League for Non-Violent Civil Disobedience Against Military Segregation, urging blacks to resist induction until the armed forces were desegregated. In July Truman issued Executive Order 9981, desegregating the army. It was at this point that Lena left the Wallace campaign for Harry Truman.

Truman was grateful. Lena was invited to sing at the Inaugural Ball in (still-segregated) Washington, D.C. For the occasion Lena unveiled her New Look, which—like everyone else's new look—involved short hair and long skirts. Sidney Guillaroff, at Metro, had cut Lena's hair for *Words and Music*, the all-star movie biography of Richard Rodgers and Lorenz Hart. Lennie was musical director of *Words and Music* as well as of three other big 1948–49 pictures: *Good News*, *The Barkleys of Broadway*, and *On the Town*—for which he won his first Oscar. Betty Comden and Adolph Green stayed in our Nichols Canyon house while they were writing *On the Town*.

Lena with Paul Robeson, 1947

Lena with Walter White, c. 1950

At Truman's Inaugural Ball, January 1949. Lena is third from left. Others who are recognizable: Edgar Bergen, Joan Davis, Margaret O'Brien, George Jessel, Dorothy Maynor, President Truman, Phil Harris, Alice Faye, Jane Powell, and Gene Kelly.

(Lennie won his second Oscar for another Comden-Green opus, *Singin' in the Rain.*)

The house in Nichols Canyon was still our only permanent home, though I was seldom there except for summers and holidays. Like the house on Horn Avenue, it hugged the side of a mountain. Consequently, in rainy seasons Lena and Lennie held ditch-digging parties to save the house from mud slides. Also, as on Horn Avenue, neighborhood bigots tried to drive us out, and once again movie people shut them up. This time the good neighbors were Larry Parks, Jane Greer, and one of Lena's best friends, Ava Gardner.

The house in Nichols Canyon was postwar modern and had been decorated from top to bottom by Lena's friend and designer Edmund Kara. I loved it, and my bedroom was my favorite room in the house. Like Lena's old room at Uncle Frank's, in Georgia, it doubled as the library, so I slept next to a wall of books. Every night at bedtime I took the cats, a dish of Wil Wright's chocolate-pistachio ice cream (or a piece of lemon meringue pie made by Cora, the cook, from our own lemon tree), and a good book to bed with me.

But despite such pleasures, life in California seemed somewhat primitive now, compared to New York. Lena complained that life in California was only about getting in the car and driving all day to find the perfect avocado for dinner. Since there was no TV, and, of course, no theater, we listened to the radio and played records. Lennie liked board games, chess and Scrabble; he, Billy Strayhorn, and my brother, Teddy, would play for hours. (I couldn't spell well enough to play Scrabble and I was hopeless at chess, although Lennie and Teddy both tried to teach me.) As Hollywoodites, we rarely went to the movies. We *saw* movies, however, at the homes of our friends James and Pamela Mason (she had the wickedest wit in Hollywood) and Gene and Betsy Kelly (where a group of regulars played volleyball on Sundays). Lennie was working with Gene on his magnum opus, *An American in Paris.*

We were all about to become Americans in Paris ourselves. In June 1950 we sailed to Europe on the French liner *De Grasse,* the very same ship that had taken my great-grandmother Cora on her 1929 grand tour. It was a busy June. The Korean War broke out, Lena was "named" in *Red Channels,* and Lena and Lennie revealed their 1947 "secret" French marriage.

Like my great-grandmother before me, I was convinced that abroad was better. America remained a segregated country, although not everything at home was bad for blacks in 1950: Frank Horne's friend Ralph Bunche became the first American black Nobel laureate, poet Gwendolyn Brooks became the first black Pulitzer Prize winner, and the American Medical Association accepted its first black delegate. But I was a terrible anti-American snob, the incarnation of Jules Feiffer's "What, you haven't been to Europe!?" cartoon. The Compagnie Générale Trans-Atlantique was the only way to go. I sailed on every ship of the French Line—just saying their names reminds me of blasting horns and confetti: *De Grasse, Flandre, Liberté, Île de France,* and *France.* We never sailed American because the line discriminated, and we rarely sailed British because it wasn't as much fun. I thought, in fact, that we left home for "fun." We actually left home because of race and politics.

There was a song—a shimmering, nostalgic song by Charles Trenet—called "La Mer" that was played every night, by every ship's orchestra, throughout the 1950s. For the French, and Europeans in general, it was a hymn of rebirth after the German nightmare. When I began to travel I was a ghastly preteen, too old for the nursery and too young for nightclubs, but every night at sea I would watch the grown-ups dance, and "La Mer" was the song that was played. "La Mer" is actually my personal 1950s. My children are amazed that I preferred Piaf to Presley, and Gérard Philipe to *Beach Blanket Bingo.* Young people, when I was young, were "seen" but "not heard." We were not permitted to speak, but we certainly looked and listened. We were practiced "voyeurs."

Ocean travel in the 1950s was dedicated to the proposition that getting there was half the fun, and Lena and Lennie played glamour travel to the hilt, from Lennie's monogrammed bar case to Lena's Vuitton trunks. Their entourage normally included me and, sometimes, little Teddy—all of us in first class. Irene Lane, who guarded the dogs and the jewelry, went second class, with two or three musicians. Lena and Lennie would usually sleep late; Lennie would appear at lunch and Lena usually appeared around teatime. We took our meals at the second sitting, theoretically when civilized people ate, although I maintained that it was a ploy to make kids starve. Lena and Lennie looked wonderful at night: Lennie in black tie and commodore's cap, Lena usually dripping ermine and incredibly chic. Their friend Ludwig Bemelmans once said that Lena always made her entrance down the staircase of the first-class dining room like the ex-queen of a Balkan country. (Lena loved reading Central European biographies and novels.)

Paris in the 1950s meant American expatriates, bookstalls, bridges, trees, the river, tall windows, Notre Dame at sunset, and beautiful clothes.

I was confined to being a voyeur about fashion, since in those days you wore white socks and patent leather shoes until you were fourteen years old. One of Lena's best friends was the English-born *directrice* of the House of Balmain, Ginette Spanier, whom Lennie called "Muggsy" (for Muggsy Spanier, the jazz musician). We all went to fashion shows—and Lena poured herself into Balmain's beads, Madame Grès' jerseys, Jean Dessès' chiffons, and Maggy Rouff's hats—all at celebrity prices. We all loved hats. Lena wore enormous cartwheels, or tiny feathered helmets that clung to the head with combs. I thought her prettiest dresses were by Jacques Fath. When Lena and Lennie announced their 1947 marriage, *Life* magazine photographed them at a sidewalk café looking almost like newlyweds. Lena was the essence of 1950s Paris chic in her quadruple pearl choker, Jacques Fath suit, and seriously frivolous French hat.

The best fashion show, to my young eyes, was Monte Carlo (we international travelers called it "Monte"), where every other summer Lena sang at the Sporting Club's Red Cross Gala. The audience was notoriously impossible, and Lena was one of a handful of stars in the world who could shut them up. (The rest of the handful were Sinatra, Piaf, Noel Coward, Judy Garland, and Marlene Dietrich.) This audience did not appreciate music, but they understood chic—and Lena was chic. Gala night in "Monte" was my big voyeur moment. I sat in the lobby of the Hôtel de Paris after dinner and watched the fashionable ladies descend. The Begum Aga Khan and the Maharani of Baroda wore pearls the size of ostrich eggs. The "golden" Greeks draped themselves in Ionic chiffons by Jean Dessès. And rich South Americans wore Fath dresses with skirts so voluminous they could barely fit into their cars. And the rubies, emeralds, and diamonds that flashed from necks, wrists, and ears were rivaled only by the aftershow firework₃ display.

Most of my time in Paris in the early 1950s was spent going to the movies (I saw *Gone With the Wind* for the first time since 1939—when, of course, I did not really "see" it) or to the American Embassy for chocolate-marshmallow sundaes. I despised sightseeing, however, and went through the Louvre in fifteen minutes. I preferred fashion-watching or celebrity-watching, and cherished the hours spent with Lena's friend "Muggsy" and her French doctor husband, Paul-Emile, who kept open house on the Avenue Marceau for a moveable cast of celebrity pals: Noel Coward, Marlene Dietrich, Beatrice Lillie, Laurence Olivier and Vivien Leigh, Art Buchwald (of the Paris *Herald–Tribune*), Irwin Shaw, and Robert Capa. Lena, like everyone else, had a crush on war-photographer Capa. And I idolized Noel

Coward, the nicest and funniest of grown-ups, who gave me a signed photograph and an inscribed copy of his collected short stories.

We were in London when the Korean War started, and although there was an American rush to go home, we stayed put. I went to the newsreel movies with a young draft-age friend of a friend whose hands literally began to shake, and his teeth to chatter, when the war footage came on. Lena was singing at the Palladium, where in her queen-sized dressing room I was introduced to my favorite English actors, Trevor Howard, Jack Hawkins, and Richard Todd. London audiences and critics loved Lena, and she was a favorite of the "Princess Margaret set." London always liked sophisticated black entertainers, from Florence Mills to "Hutch" (Leslie A. Hutchinson, the handsome black man in white tie and tails who sang Cole Porter songs in the 1930s—he was the debs', as well as the married ladies', delight). Above all, the British adored Robeson. Every family in the British Isles with a record player had Paul's recordings. In the 1920s he had been the toast of London in *Othello* and *Showboat.* In the 1930s he made *Sanders of the River* and *The Proud Valley,* with the Welsh miners. And in 1937—from the stage of the Albert Hall—he made his famous "the artist must take sides" speech, on behalf of Republican Spain.

Lena toured Britain enthusiastically. The sun never shined, but the audiences were the warmest in the world. Glasgow was the toughest, gloomiest town of all, but the audience stamped and whistled, and mounted police were sent to guard the stage door. In Edinburgh we were taken up by the local artistic community and were entertained with haggis, Highland dancing, Robert Burns, and more Paul Robeson records. And we were greeted with equal warmth when we made our way, by train and boat, to Scandinavia.

We would spend alternate summers throughout the decade in Europe. I often crossed the ocean by myself, armed with detailed instructions and secret envelopes of cash from Lena's manager, Ralph Harris, my favorite surrogate uncle. I rarely saw California. My home away from Europe was now a Quaker boarding school in upstate New York, chosen by Lena and Lennie for two reasons: the Quakers' abolitionist history and their policy of integration. The Quaker schools and one or two progressive, proto-hippie schools in Vermont were the only American boarding schools that accepted black female students.

Boarding school was a study in international brotherhood. My favorite teacher was Japanese, and it was because of his English course that I read *Moby Dick* nonstop, from cover to cover, on a cross-country train ride. One

On the Champs-Élysées. *Life* magazine used
photograph in 1950 when it announced that
Lena and Lennie had been married since 1947

*Lena, Lennie, and I enjoying a
New York snowstorm, early 1948*

Lena and Lennie on the Ile de France, 1950

My mother and I pose for a photographer aboard ship while Lennie (left) looks on, c. 1952.

Teddy and I in front of the George V Hotel in Paris, c. 1952

One of our family outings recorded by the press. Lennie, Lena, and I attend a movie premiere in New York, 1953.

THE WEEK'S BEST PHOTOS

of my classmates, from a Dutch Quaker missionary family, had been imprisoned by the Japanese in Java. To complete the circle, we were visited by the Hiroshima Maidens, hideously disfigured by the bomb. We were, naturally, pacifists. We sang "Onward, Christian *brothers,* marching on to *peace,*" and "We are climbing Jacob's ladder, *brothers* of the cross." The Quakers were also against capital punishment. There was a poster on campus of Ike's famous grin in which you saw, on close inspection, that every tooth was a tiny electric chair for the Rosenbergs. Sunday silent meeting was found to be the perfect time for boys and girls in a 1950s coeducational boarding school to discreetly size each other up, but my copy of *The Catcher in the Rye* was confiscated from my room by the housemother as "unsuitable" reading.

For five years dedicated Indiana Quakers tried to undo the damage progressive school had done, without much luck. I had no concept of math or science, nor could I spell. I was hopelessly literary and artsy-craftsy: pottery came second only to Pete Seeger in the progressive school lexicon. Plane geometry was not too bad—I liked to draw—but algebra was the end. There was also a loathsome, all-female course called "home economics" in which it took all year to make a laundry bag, a dish towel, and a pot holder, and in which we were required to memorize the correct order of dish washing: "glasses, silver, china, cutlery, cooking utensils," a totally useless litany I will know for the rest of my life. But I threw myself into French, English, field hockey, and cheerleading. In the autumn cheerleaders wore big wool sweaters, short circular skirts, and thick white socks that we glued to our legs so they wouldn't fall down when we did cartwheels.

We would be called the Eisenhower generation (though some of us were "madly for Adlai"), and we were extremely conformist and label-conscious about our clothes. We were owned by *Seventeen, Harper's Bazaar,* and Madison Avenue. We wore Haymaker blouses with Peter Pan collars, Bermuda shorts, and Brooks Brothers shirts. We wore Anne Fogarty or Lanz of Salzburg dresses, with Capezio ballerina flats. We also wore horsehair petticoats and instruments of torture called "merry widows," which pulled in the waist and pushed up the bust. We wore camel-hair coats in the winter, tan raincoats in the spring, Rose Marie Reid bathing suits in the summer, and "Fire and Ice" lipstick all year round. And we wanted Suzy Parker's looks. Suzy was a friend of Lena's, but I didn't talk about that much. I regretted that my mother was not like everyone else's. There were other celebrity parents: Walter White, Rex Stout, and Pearl Buck. And one of my classmates was the daughter of the president of America's biggest black insurance company. But most of the mothers wore cloth coats and bare New England faces. I was always embarrassed when Lena came to school in make-up and mink.

. . .

Lena and Lennie had, of course, come home to face the black list. In June 1950 *Red Channels* was being distributed to every radio and TV station in America, and to all advertising agencies with broadcasting accounts. Listing alone was tantamount to "guilt"—if not in fact, then by association. Those who were black-listed usually could clear their own names only by naming others. Ex–party members gave lists of names to the FBI. Non–party members, who had no names to name, could clear themselves by public repudiation of their pinkish pasts. In either case, the emphasis was on public humiliation. The careers of some performers, such as the musician Larry Adler and the dancer Paul Draper, were significantly damaged by black listing. The premature deaths of actors John Garfield, Canada Lee, Mady Christians ("Mama" of *I Remember Mama*), and Philip Loeb ("Papa" of *The Goldbergs*) were also blamed on the black list. John Henry Faulk, an iconoclastic Texas broadcaster, sued the black list, and although it took six years, won $3.5 million.

Our friend and neighbor Larry Parks was not so lucky. Larry lived down the road in Nichols Canyon with his wife, Betty Garrett, and their two small children. Larry had become an overnight movie star with *The Jolson Story*. He belonged to the Communist Party for four years during the war. In March 1951 he became the first black-listed Hollywood star to reluctantly name names, in order to clear his own. Larry had announced that he was willing to talk, but only about himself. The committee insisted, however, that the only way to be cleared was to implicate other people. Quid pro quo. After pleading that he did not want to "crawl through the mud like an informer," Larry ultimately broke down and named names. He had finally cooperated; nevertheless, he was finished in Hollywood. John Wayne immediately denounced Larry for testifying "reluctantly and late." Larry Parks went into real estate to support his family.

Lena's *Red Channels* listing was modest compared to some. No one ever "named" her a Communist, and Congress had no interest in her. The Hearst press and other serious black listers did, however. Hearst columnist Jack O'Brien used Lena to go after CBS (whose news department under Edward R. Murrow, with the blessing of William Paley, was vociferously anti–black list). O'Brien called Lena's TV appearance a typical CBS "pink tea." Lena, in this case, was probably more weapon than target. The black listers appeared to be much more aggressively anti-Semitic than anti-black.

HUAC preferred to use blacks rather than humiliate them. Only one black mattered, and that was Robeson. Blacks who were called to testify were not required to name names, only to denounce Robeson. In the summer of 1949 Jackie Robinson, in a move he later regretted, testified against Robeson's statement that American blacks would not go to war against Russia. In April of that year, at the Paris Peace Conference, Robeson had remarked (it was not a prepared statement) that it seemed "unthinkable" to him that American blacks would "go to war on behalf of those who have oppressed us for generations . . . against a country which in one generation has raised our people to full human dignity. . . ." At the same conference W. E. B. Du Bois stated that colonialism was the real enemy of world peace —and America, "drunk with power," was "leading the world to hell . . . and a Third World War." The world press went into various orbits— particularly over Robeson's remarks.

When Jackie Robinson was called to testify, the committee announced:

> . . . it is not the purpose of this Committee in conducting these hearings to question the loyalty of the Negro race. There is no question about that. It is an opportunity to you and others to combat the idea that Paul Robeson had given by his statements.

The chairman of the committee, a congressman from Georgia, stayed away from the hearings when Jackie testified. He was a member of the Ku Klux Klan and didn't want to have to call him "Mr." Robinson.

Lena's political ideas were not completely her own. Some she had inherited from the people she loved best, and in a sense she was now simply carrying on the family politics. It was a Horne *thing*—a responsibility she owed to her grandfather Edwin, who wrote so expressively about the Civil Rights Act of 1875—America's first. It was a something she owed to her grandmother Cora, who helped put Paul Robeson through college (and knew W. E. B. Du Bois when he was young "Willie"). And it was a responsibility she shared with her uncle Frank—formerly of FDR's "Black Cabinet." Unfortunately for Lena—granddaughter of Reconstruction and daughter of the New Deal—a great deal of her "family" politics was echoed in the party line. Lena knew perfectly well that communists were active in many of the causes she supported. She felt that most of those causes needed all of the help they could get. The Russians had been our allies, after all.

She never felt that she was aiding communism, she felt that communism was aiding her. Lena had been well advised by Robeson when he told her not to join the party. As a result, she was "tainted" only by her Du Bois and Robeson connections. And, of course, she *had* sung "The Four Rivers" on wartime radio. ("The Four Rivers" were the Thames, the Mississippi, the Yangtze, and the Don—a soggy United Front.) Since Lena was never "named" a Communist, she never had to testify publicly. Nor did she have to denounce Robeson, as Josh White and Canada Lee (both "named") had to do. But every time she appeared on television the Hearst press went after her. She was forced to clear her name for the sake of her income.

Although Hearst columnist Jack O'Brien was vocally anti-Lena, Dorothy Kilgallen, an equally important Hearst columnist, was not. Dorothy was, in fact, a good friend. Lena and Lennie had become part of the 1950s New York social scene, dining with such other famously first-named couples as Dorothy and Dick, Tex and Jinx, Jock and Betsy, and Bill and Babe. The first two couples (the Kollmars and the McCrarys) were media figures. The other two (Whitneys and Paleys) were media owners. And it did not hurt that Tex and Jock were important and highly visible Eisenhower supporters. Another big name in Lena's corner was Ed Sullivan.

Lena was fortunate in her friends. She didn't have to wait out the black list. Sullivan and McCrary arranged a tête-à-tête for her with George Sokolsky, one of the biggest "namers" and "clearers" of names. Ironically, she met Sokolsky in a building on West End Avenue where she and Lennie later, with much difficulty, bought an apartment. Sokolsky tried to put her at ease by explaining that he knew all about racism, because he had once been married to a Chinese. The meeting was painless enough. The Right, Sokolsky said, might have decided that Lena was as much a symbol to use as Robeson was to destroy. The black listers did not want to be seen as racists but as patriots. Sokolsky did most of the talking. He told Lena how much he "understood" her reasons for being "left." It was youthful misguidance, he said, and a lack of understanding of the true nature of the Red Menace. Lena kept quiet, letting Sokolsky read her political motives as he saw fit. Sokolsky even "understood" her loyalty to Robeson.

Lena cleared herself in *Counterattack* rather than *Red Channels*. The lists in both magazines were identical. Her manager, Ralph Harris, made a statement to the press:

> . . . to clear up once and for all the propaganda emanating from *Counterattack* charging her with having been associated with "sub-

versive" causes and implying that she was unfit to entertain Americans. . . . She's been given a clean bill of health. But she'll try to avoid groups which are *called* subversive.

Lena was now free to work on television. Her choices would be limited only by personal affinity—but no network would give a black performer her own show, and the only shows Lena really enjoyed were with people she considered friends: Ed Sullivan, Tex and Jinx, Perry Como, Steve Allen, and (her real favorite) "Kukla, Fran and Ollie."

Dorothy and Dick and Tex and Jinx and the rest of the pals were part of Lena's Waldorf "gang." She made a more or less annual late fall or early spring appearance in the Empire Room of the Waldorf-Astoria Hotel—to packed audiences and sold-out performances. Lena's friends and protectors were so loyal that they even forgave her remaining a Democrat. (She sang a song for Adlai Stevenson called "I Luv the Guv," based on "I Love to Love.")

By 1950 Lena was making an enormous amount of money in nightclubs. Nightclubs were rarely affected by the black list—the Mafia did not confuse politics and profits. Although nightclubs were Lena's bread and butter, she considered them all "toilets," especially the one in Vancouver, British Columbia, where she had to pass through the kitchen to reach the stage. One memorable night, in that Vancouver kitchen, Lena bumped into a woman patron looking for the ladies' room. "Hurry up, Lena, we're waiting for you!" the woman said, and then proceeded to throw up spaghetti and meatballs all over the billowing tulle fishtail of Lena's white gown. Lena's dresser, Tiny Kyle, had the presence of mind to douse the fishtail with a handy pitcher of water, but Lena's drummer, Chico Hamilton, laughed about the episode for days. So did Lena—later. If all nightclubs were "toilets," then all nightclub managements were "hoods." Some "hoods" (like the owner of a club in Lake Tahoe, Nevada) were not allowed to cross the threshold of her dressing room. Other "hoods" became good friends.

In the mid-1950s the Sands Hotel in Las Vegas was the premier nightclub in terms of salaries. Vegas was basically a one-street town. Along the Strip there were three or four large gambling hotels and many smaller gambling joints. The Sands was commonly regarded as the only hotel with "class," and Lena found the Sands a sort of "New York" oasis in the midst of the honky-tonk tackiness that was essentially Vegas. The Sands was actually New York's Copacabana, gone West. An early 1950s Sands brochure opens on a picture of Lena and the words "Jack Entratter presents in the Sands Copa Room 'Sophisticated Lady' starring Lena Horne . . . and the Most Beautiful Girls in the West. . . ." The back page of the brochure featured face shots of all the Sands performers: Milton Berle; Louis Armstrong; Peggy Lee; Sammy Davis, Jr.; Nat "King" Cole; Dean Martin and Jerry Lewis; Robert Merrill and Marguerite Piazza; Van Johnson; Rosemary Clooney; Sam Levinson; Peter Lind Hayes and Mary Healy; and Tallulah Bankhead. Only Lena, Sinatra, and Danny Thomas had their faces framed in stars. They were 1950s nightclub royalty. They guaranteed sell-out audiences—which, in turn, guaranteed a bigger and better class of gamblers. Lena worked in Vegas only at Christmas or Easter, the most profitable times. I used to lie by the pool in my Rose Marie Reid bathing suit reading seventeenth-century French plays and longing for high-heeled, open-toed, plastic mules (known locally as "fuck-me" shoes) like the ones the chorus girls wore. I was still a voyeur, however. Lena forbade them.

At night I enjoyed the nightclub shows—and I especially enjoyed my mother's shows. There would be the last-minute scurry of waiters (they were not permitted to serve while she was on). Then a drum roll, lights, anticipatory applause, and the upbeat introductory tune "Fine and Dandy," followed by "The Sands Hotel is proud to present Miss Lena Horne!" Then, in the midst of the smoke and the sudden stillness, my mother would begin to sing. There was always quiet, broken only by the odd tinkle of ice in a glass. As I toyed with my Shirley Temple, even *I* knew she was great. Between shows I roamed the casino with Jack Entratter's two daughters. We were allowed to play the slot machines, but not permitted to enter the Silver Queen Bar, where most of the chorus girls "mingled" between shows. After midnight was best for teenaged voyeurs. Other Strip performers and visiting VIPs gathered in the Sands' Garden Room for Chinese food, chili, and hot pastrami from the Chuck Wagon. The Entratter girls and I swooned over José Greco, the Spanish dancer, but Sinatra was the reigning Romeo. We watched Marlene pursue Frank, while Frank pursued "Copa Girls." We seen-but-not-heard teenagers listened, rapt, while Marlene complained to Lena that Sinatra "never slept." And we listened, agog, as Zsa Zsa Gabor described how Porfirio Rubirosa (the playboys' playboy) gave her a black eye.

All this was a far cry from Quaker boarding school.

. . .

In the spring of 1952 Lena and Lennie sent me postcards from Israel. They and their friend Auren Kahn had sailed from Naples to Israel on a refugee

Lena was nightclub royalty in the 1950s.

Performing in Europe, c. 1954

A newspaper ad for one of "Queen-a" Lena's
engagements at a New Jersey nightclub

ship. One postcard, with a view of old Jerusalem, had a special message for
the Quakers:

> Israel and the countries that surround it are not at peace—only an
> armistice exists. Anyone without a permit trying to enter the Arab
> section will be shot at—with *one* exception, a Quaker teacher. . . .

Back home the winds of race and politics were changing. I remember
Brown vs. *Board of Education* as if it were yesterday. That is, I remember a
beautiful May morning and bending over the front page of *The New York
Times* in the school library. The windows were open, and the room was
bathed in leafy sunshine. I remember feeling very grown-up (it was the end
of my junior year) because I was able to understand the incredible importance of the headlines. The beauty of the morning and the good news, in
black and white, combined to fill me with a sense of extraordinary well-
being. I distinctly remember thinking, It's over—we've won. Two months
later, white citizens' councils had sprung up all over the South, and another
decade of bloodshed followed. But from the ivory tower of boarding school,
all seemed serene.

■   ■   ■

The title of Ralph Ellison's *Invisible Man* correctly reflected the average
1950s black condition, but I always felt highly visible. Tokenism is conspicuous. Most people would prefer not to admit to racism. But they often
prefer the *theory* of racial toleration to its practice. Tokenism made it possible for people to *practice* toleration. (Many racists can be perfectly cour-
teous on a one-to-one basis.) The Hornes never hid their light under a
bushel, and there was no reason for me to be an exception to the rule, and
I didn't actually mind the public gaze that much, unless I had egg on my
face. Consequently, I always tried to remain as eggless as possible. I was
determined to be a successful teenager—I had been waiting since 1944,
after all. I made friends, I was "popular," and "nice" was my favorite word.
I was not a total Goody Two-shoes, however: I smoked cigarettes in the
boiler room of the girls' dorm and ostentatiously perused *The Red Badge
of Courage* in silent meeting. I also strove, whenever possible, to evade
Lennie's Draconian rules—no alcohol, no tobacco, no painted fingernails,
and no Shalimar perfume. Sex, of course, was the ultimate no-no, but boy-
friends were part of being a teenager. I liked good-looking young men who
played tennis, basketball, and soccer. For school dances I sometimes im-

ported Delany Hill, a handsome young member of the black establishment, who was enrolled at a nearby boys' school. Delany drove a convertible and wore white buck shoes—my standard criteria. Other times I went to dances with white schoolmates, a thing rarely done in the world beyond our "simple" Quaker boarding school. But the Quakers, naturally, paid little attention to the complicated practices of the outside world.

By the time I was in high school, I think I *knew* only two or three black boys my own age. I did not know very many black *people* after the age of nine or ten. I knew, and loved, some of Lena and Lennie's domestic and musical employees (especially Irene Lane, the long-time house-and-dog keeper). And I knew, and loved, a few old family friends who were Lena's best black friends: Myra and "Spinky" Alston; Alston's half-sister Aida Bearden Winters (related to the painter "Romie" Bearden, but, more important, a former Junior Deb); and Myra's surgeon brother, Dr. Arthur Logan. The Logan-Bearden families were typical of the interrelated, intergenerational friendship roots of the black middle class, but there were no children my age among them. Later, Arthur Logan's daughter Adele (who lived with her mother and not her father and stepmother) became a friend of mine almost by accident. I was by now a totally lapsed member of the black middle class. Lena's remarriage, as well as her postwar politics, caused her to re-examine the bourgeois life-style. She found it shallow and frivolous. She had no more use for black debutante balls than she had for white. As far as Lena was concerned, the "uplifting" bourgeoisie of Cora and Edwin's turn of the century black America, and the "creative" bourgeoisie of Harlem's 1920s and '30s, was now just black Babbittry.

My parents had had a bitter divorce. My father spent the war years on the East Coast. Then, when he moved to the West Coast, I went East again. My father's nephews and nieces are my only first cousins. (There was a torn and faded newspaper photograph clipping in my grandfather's trunk of one of my beautiful Jones aunts, and small cousin, my uncle "Buddy" Jones's wife and child.) The Jones cousins would have kept me in the tribe. But I no longer saw any Joneses. I was no longer attached to the black bourgeoisie because I was no longer attached to my father. I left him at a very young age, then saw him perhaps once or twice, in ten years, after that. My memories of him have become probably more mythic than real. I have a distant memory of someone who was gentle, kind, and strong. Then I have a less distant memory of someone who became a stranger. And I never saw enough of my brother. In those days, in bitter divorces, divided custody meant *divided* children. But at least I saw him for a month or two a year. I never felt as if I knew him well enough. (It is wonderful to *see* him in his children and my own.)

When Teddy and I were little at Hollywood "kiddie" parties, we were always the only nonwhite children. We were a reflection of Lena and Lennie's world. The upper reaches of postwar international entertainment were more or less color-blind. (This had been true even in 1910 when Bert Williams escaped the "black peril" ban.) When I began to actually notice color (midway between seven and ten), I began to have fewer black friends. Eventually, my encounters with the black bourgeoisie were so rare that I felt even less "different" among my overwhelmingly white schoolmates. Because Lena went beyond "mere" *achievement* to become a "star" (and because she married Lennie) I was doomed to be "different" among blacks as well as whites.

I grew up considering Lennie to be just as much of a *parent* as my real father, Louis. Lennie already had a nearly grown-up stepdaughter when I met him. Peggy Husing (daughter of radio pioneer Ted Husing) became a sort of big-sister figure to me. Peggy and I both felt lucky that our mothers had married Lennie. He was such a loving, happy, funny man. I *identified* with Lennie far more than I identified with Louis. I was not consciously rejecting blackness, the black bourgeoisie, *or* my father. I was simply reflecting the world in which I lived. I was even further removed from real black life than my great grandparents were.

Sociologists agree that the black bourgeoisie always tried to shield their children (especially females) from racial prejudice. Even a century ago, at the "nadir" of black American life, Cora and Lena Calhoun were protected from overt racial insults. Edna Scottron, sixty years ago, never faced overt racism until she left Brooklyn. Fifty years ago Lena also faced it only when she left Brooklyn. Now I, in Lena and Lennie's international white world, was such a stranger to racial discrimination that I would have recognized only the most obvious manifestations. My brother Teddy, like all black males, felt it more directly. Boys were less sheltered in every way.

I was sixteen years old when the Supreme Court school decision became the first "domino" in the collapse of institutionalized American racism. In a segregated world, I had always attended integrated schools. They were actually more *un*segregated than they were *in*tegrated. But there would always be a few other blacks in the school. As a typical teenage conformist, however, I went along with the crowd. And the crowd was usually almost totally white. By the time I was graduated from high school I was economically, culturally, and socially assimilated into the white world, a "beige bourgeoise."

I finished high school in 1955, the year that Rosa Parks refused to give her bus seat to a white man in Montgomery, Alabama. I paid no attention. Eleanor Roosevelt made the commencement address at school. I do not remember anything she said. I was much more excited by the prospect of later—when commencement was over. There was dinner on the Starlight Roof of the Waldorf. Harry Belafonte, in a mustard-yellow shirt open to the waist, was the star of the show. He came to our table afterward and asked me to dance. I was no longer interested in radical politics and the world situation, but I was definitely interested in being "worldly." Harvard was the ideal place for me.

CHAPTER · 8

GAIL

Harvard in 1955 was the definition of elitism. Harvard even held itself serenely above the rest of the Ivy League. Yale was muscular Christianity; Princeton was alcoholic Southerners; the rest were Babbitts and savages. Harvard tolerated more eccentricity and conspicuous individualism than other colleges. "Harvards" were more intellectual, more original, and much more effete than the other Ivy Leaguers. Harvard *naturally* preferred Piaf to Presley. Harvard already *knew* all about Vita and Virginia and Harold and Lytton. I felt at home. Harvard was a country of voyeurs. And Harvard, like myself, was somewhat patriophobic. Except for Humphrey Bogart, Fats Domino, and cheeseburgers, "abroad" was better. We were very "worldly" young people indeed. In terms of sex and politics, however, we were practically prehistoric.

The great trick at Harvard in the 1950s was never to be caught studying. You were meant to affect a pose of languid déjà vu toward all aspects of higher education. Displays of academic fervor, except for either the most erudite or the most simple-minded of subjects, were regarded as distinctly jejune. Every Cliffie knew the legend of Gertrude Stein and Professor William James. Gertrude, along with Helen Keller and Amy Lowell, was an illustrious old girl. At the final exam of Professor James's course Gertrude opened her blue book and wrote something like: "Dear Professor James, It is such a lovely morning that I am unable to concentrate on your examination. Sincerely, G. Stein." Professor James returned Gertrude's blue book with the reply: "Dear Miss Stein, I understand perfectly. A + ."

If the trick was never to be caught studying, then I caught on too well. I was guilty of enthusiasm, however, about some courses. I fell in love with American history. Professor Arthur Schlesinger, Jr.'s course in American intellectual history was fascinating and fun. And America's literature was as exciting as its history. Professor Kenneth Lynn told us that Huck Finn was the American alter ego: eternally adolescent, and free from sex and death; while Faulkner was the heart of American darkness, with all the dirty little secrets revealed. Unfortunately, as I was an erstwhile sophisticate, my major was French. I did not even wake up until the eighteenth century with Voltaire, and saucy novels like *La Vie de Marianne* and *Les Liaisons Dangereuses*. When I decided to write my thesis on Colette, the French Department was displeased because she was not dead yet. French literature became the tip of the iceberg of my future disillusion with Abroad.

A student of Professor Gordon Allport's sociology course—known as "Nuts and Sluts"—once dissected the Harvard social scene for a term paper. She decided that it was divided into three classes: "Clubbies," "Bohos," and "Other Ranks." Clubbies were the Anglo-Saxon scions of capitalism for whom the university was created. Bohos were literary, arty, Beat, and "acceptably" Jewish, black, or foreign. "Other Ranks" were the people from South Dakota, Sioux City, or the Bronx. Clubbies and Bohos interacted. The others were left to themselves. Jews were subdivided by class and money. There were so few blacks that most of us came under the heading of "foreign." Among my black contemporaries were poets, novelists, academics, and actors to be, as well as a future Secretary of the Army. In reality, everyone at Harvard who was *not* a postadolescent male WASP was some sort of "token."

Personally, I found that tokenism could be "fun." The iceberg of my social consciousness was still almost entirely submerged. I continued to give lip service to the Left, of course—I would rather be almost *anything* than far right. But the serious old Left (Paul Robeson and Pete Seeger excepted) was so *boring*. When I was a Red Diaper firebrand, my heroine had been La Passionaria, but now it was Julie Harris as Sally Bowles. In those days (before "radical chic") there was never any "fun" in issues.

Harvard Square and its radii were the universe. Boston was merely a place of special excursions: Symphony, the Ritz Hotel, rock and roll bars, and the museum where I always returned to Andrew Wyeth's hawk's-eye view of a farm. The rest of Cambridge (where "townies" lived) was the back of beyond—though it did have a colorful side. It was where the "Beatniks" "crashed" (I heard Allen Ginsberg, surrounded by a pack of hairy "Beats," read "Howl" from the stage of Harvard's Memorial Hall); where unknown Joan Baez sang in a coffee shop; and where young Professor Timothy Leary and company were creating LSD.

A major center of smoke-filled red-wine conversation was the Harvard Dramatic Club, where we discussed life, love, Chekhov, and success. Success was very important. Some of us were the children of very successful people. There was Chris Kazan, son of Elia. (We all called his father "Gadge.") There was Jamie MacArthur, son of Helen Hayes and Charles MacArthur. There was also Ruell Wilson, son of Mary McCarthy and Edmund Wilson. And my old friend Danny Selznick, grandson of Louis B. Mayer and son of Irene and David O. Selznick. Among my other HDC contemporaries were future composer Joe Raposo, future movie director Glenn Jordan, playwright Arthur Kopit, actor Richard Jordan, actor-director Andre Gregory (a great giggler and a terrible Macbeth), Erich Segal, and director Jean-Claude Van Itallie, who directed my prize-winning acting performance. I won the best acting prize at the 1957 Yale Drama Festival in Molière's *School for Wives*. My picture, circled in laurel leaves, appeared in the *Crimson*, with the caption: "This is the girl." I was not really an actress, but I *could* play slightly comic "naïves"; in many ways it was type casting. My other great part was the spaced-out heroine of Edna St. Vincent Millay's *Aria da Capo*.

. . .

Lena was treading the boards as well. Her new musical, *Jamaica*, opened on Broadway, after the obligatory Boston tryout, in November 1957. I spent my weekends at the Ritz while the show was in Boston. The *Sturm und Drang* was terrific—producer David Merrick and lyricist Yip Harburg called each other terrible names. Composer Harold Arlen waited patiently for the yelling to subside. Lena's old friend Noel Coward reported on *Jamaica* in his diary:

On stage in *Jamaica*

Lena with dancers from the Broadway show Jamaica, *1957. Alvin Ailey is at far right.*

On Monday evening I went to see a sorry spectacle: "Jamaica" with Lena Horne. . . . Lena was brilliant and Ricardo Montalban's chest was lovely. Apart from this the evening was a loss.

All the critics loved Lena, however, and the silly show was a hit. A newspaper column reported:

> . . . The premiere of Lena Horne's musical, "Jamaica," was the season's major gala. . . . The star alone guarantees a happy time with her larking. . . . The show came to town with an advance sale of $1,300,000. Queen Lena conquered One and All, with the New York *Journal-American*'s John McClain curtsying, "Lena plus music equals a BIG winner! . . ."

New York now offered as much fun as Cambridge. I spent Fridays and Sundays on the Yankee Clipper, smoking Pall Mall cigarettes and drinking whiskey sours. In New York we danced at Elmo's (El Morocco), and went to see Mabel Mercer, Bobby Short, and Nichols and May. I avoided the Stork Club, which discriminated against blacks. (Lena got into minor trouble with the NAACP when Josephine Baker, in the mid-1950s, was denied admission to the Stork Club. In the general outcry Lena merely wondered aloud why Miss Baker would want to go to a "joint" like that in the first place.) I also did a lot of hanging around backstage to see the stars. One who came was Marlon Brando. He was divinely beautiful, with charm that left one deaf and dumb for days. Brando's backstage visit almost eclipsed that of Robeson, for whom the entire cast lined up as if he were visiting royalty. Paul told Lena that it would be the last time that they would see each other for a long while. He would not subject his friends to the kind of harassment he knew would be forthcoming from the FBI. "Don't even try to contact me," he said. "I know you care." And he inscribed a copy of his book *Here I Stand*.

We went to Eddie Condon's for Dixieland jazz, or to Birdland for the late, great show of Count Basie and Joe Williams (Birdland was rumored to be a place where people actually smoked marijuana). Baby brother Teddy came to New York for the holidays. He was a freshman at UCLA that year, 1957, a track and field athlete, and a young Republican—he was very *cool*. Teddy sneered at Eddie Condon. His heroes were Miles Davis and the Modern Jazz Quartet. He also discovered Lenny Bruce before the rest of us.

Lena and Lennie had wonderful Saturday night parties on West End Avenue. Invitations went round to neighboring stage doors between performances. There was much singing at the piano, and enormous amounts of food and drink—with Noel and Bea, Chita Rivera, Gwen Verdon, Sybil and Richard Burton, Maureen Stapleton, the Robert Prestons, Pierre Olaf (of *La Plume de Ma Tante*) and all the gangs from *West Side Story, Look Back in Anger,* and *Jamaica.* And Arthur Mitchell taught everyone to dance the boogaloo.

I was now spending my summers at home in America. (Freshman year summer had been the last in Europe, when Lena and I took a trip alone, from Paris to Venice, on the Orient Express. We looked for spies and tingled to names like Zagreb and Ljubljiana. Coming out of the Adriatic marshland, Venice suddenly appeared, a baroque pearl resting on a shimmering, silvery-green sea. Never was any city so beautiful or romantic.) I had my first jobs. Sophomore summer I worked on the newspaper at Grossinger's resort in the Catskills. The Grossinger family were friends of Lena and Lennie's. The resort's daily paper was a sort of cruise ship handout: activities of the day, plus flattering gossip about guests and visiting VIPs (like Elizabeth Taylor and her fiancé, Eddie Fisher). Most of the summer staff were college students, and they made for a wonderfully irreverent crew. The next summer I worked in public relations for Air France, known to the other airlines as "Air Chance." (Air France called TWA "Try Walking Across.") And I went out with a young Frenchman whose best friend was married to Jean Seberg. The four of us used to double-date. Poor Jean was often berated by her French husband for her poor French accent and her lack of "chic."

Now and again, throughout the 1950s, I rejoined the black middle class. At Christmas 1957 I gathered with the other black princes and princesses for old Brooklyn's annual Comus Ball. We were not called "black" then— we were called "Negro" or, as my great-grandfather preferred, "colored." Going into the ball I was reminded of the famous Weegee photograph of the dowager at the Met (tiara and all) being given the raspberry by a 1930s bag lady. The crowd of onlookers outside Brooklyn's Academy of Music was mostly black. Now curious, and semihostile, dark faces stared at the parade of café-au-lait creatures passing through their midst in white tie and ballgowns. In 1957 the ancient gulf between field hand and house slave still had not been bridged. It would take the 1960s. This half-curious, half-hostile reaction to the old middle class en masse was not reserved for blacks alone. I saw the same look on the faces of white gravediggers as the mourn-

THE HARVARD CRIMSON

This is the Girl

The *Crimson* noted my performance in Molière's *School for Wives*, 1957.

A French newspaper reported on Lena's visit in 1959, when I was living in Paris. The journalist misspelled my name. I didn't buy the Dior dress.

La cantatrice U.S. Lena Horne a habillé sa fille Gal à Paris

Gal essaye une robe de cocktail en lainage et faille noire sous le regard admiratif de sa mère.

I'm one of the bridesmaids (holding two bouquets) at my Radcliffe roommate Susan Colt's wedding to Billy Doolittle, 1958.

ers filed by at Frank Horne's funeral. In both cases racism was only another aspect of the class struggle.

■ ■ ■

I saw the rest of life in Harvard's rosy glow. Cambridge was the last playground of our privileged youth, and Harvard's silver cord allowed us miles of leeway for getting into trouble. Sometime in 1958 Fritz Schwarz, whose family owned F. A. O. Schwarz, and who was engaged to my roommate Marion (Minnie) Lapsley, asked if I would join him in picketing the Cambridge Woolworth. I did not live in *total* isolation. I read the *Crimson* and *The New York Times*. I knew that people were picketing *Southern* Woolworths. But I simply could not see the Cambridge connection. "Why on earth would anyone want to picket the Cambridge Woolworth?" I asked incredulously. (In terms of 1960s confrontational dialectic, I was *not* an Oreo: black on the outside and white in the middle. If pressed, I might have called myself a vanilla Girl Scout cookie with a chocolate cream filling.)

In the autumn of 1958, at Harvard's Memorial Hall, John F. Kennedy campaigned for re-election to the United States Senate. He was actually running for the presidency. Minnie and I were there early, in the front row. Kennedy made a front-page speech about Algeria. He was not about to discuss anything so parochial as Massachusetts politics. He was a shoo-in; he only wanted to win *big*. Afterward we all crowded around him, trying to shake his hand. An entire generation was smitten, and the next morning we were all stuffing envelopes at his Boston headquarters. It was a split-personality campaign. In Cambridge, Kennedy was Harvard; in Boston, he was Irish. We loved the way he spoke of Camus on the one hand and James Michael Curley on the other. We worked hard for Kennedy, and he won *big*.

The following spring, at the Harvard commencement, Kennedy and Archbishop Cushing walked side by side in the parade. Kennedy was wearing the silk topper and morning coat of a Harvard overseer. After the parade I was standing in the crowd on the steps of Widener Library when the senator invited me to join him for a cup of coffee. I happily accepted and followed him through the yard among the old grads, where women were not permitted to be. Over coffee and English muffins, he asked me what I planned to do after graduation. I told the senator that I planned to be an expatriate, that I was going to get a job in Paris and probably stay there the rest of my life. "You'll come home," he said.

Nineteen fifty-nine would be the last of my lotus-eating European summers. I met my Radcliffe friend Liliane Solmsen in Rome, and from there we went to Capri—to sunbathe, eat fresh figs for breakfast, and paint our toenails "Windsor Pink." We bought gold chain sandals, ruffled bikinis, and silk trousers. And we were pursued by dirty old men. In Monte Carlo, where we met Lena and Lennie, I was a voyeur no more, grown up at last, and free to join the youngish rich at play. Our afternoons were spent at the Sporting Club, where a Greek tycoon gave me waterskiing lessons.

That fall we stayed in Paris. I got a job at *Marie-Claire* magazine, which was owned by *Paris Match* and seemed to be staffed entirely by widows of intrepid *Match* journalists, whose dying words were always the *Match* telephone number. It was not a bad job, the hours were short, there was little to do. There was also no salary. I shared a freezing antiques-filled apartment near the Musée Rodin with Sally Kuhn, another Cliffie. We lived on our allowances and were always broke. I pretended to augment my nonexistent *Marie-Claire* salary by selling ads for the *Paris Review*. Teddy came over to go to the Sorbonne, which is another way of saying he did not go to school at all. People never actually *went* to the Sorbonne unless they were studying law. Teddy and his friends listened to jazz in the Rue Saint-Benoit, smoked hashish with North Africans, and went out with much older women. I went out with Burt Bacharach, who was already a famous composer but was playing and conducting for Marlene at the time. Burt was the nicest man in Paris. All the Frenchmen you met turned out to have wives or girl friends at home.

Lena was appearing at the Olympia Music Hall. Even though I was twenty-one years old, she would still not allow me to go out with Prince Aly Khan, whom I met backstage. In those days there were rules about young women and playboys. (Today there are either fewer rules or fewer playboys.) Paris was beginning to lose its charm for me anyway. The French never invited you into their homes; all life was in restaurants. Worst of all, in the winter it was always much colder indoors than out. I was beginning to find the French people as wet and grim as their weather.

When I came back home to West End Avenue, Lena and Lennie were touring the clubs. Lena had wanted to do a Broadway show, but she had been told that the other lead actor was unwilling to play opposite a black. Whereupon Lena and Lennie took a slow boat to Brazil to forget American show business.

Lena was still queen of the nightclubs—an art form she detested. Walter Winchell reported in September 1959:

Lena Horne reportedly told London friends: "In two years I shall retire. I hate show business. I feel insecure, and I always have been. That's why I want to get out. . . ."

I, on the other hand, in the spring of 1960 was jumping into show business with both feet. The show was *Valmouth,* a new musical by Sandy Wilson (of *The Boyfriend* fame). *Valmouth,* based on the novella by Ronald Firbank, the aesthete's aesthete, had been a success in London. Now Wilson and Gene Andrewski (former advertising director of the *Paris Review,* now an off-Broadway producer) were bringing it to New York. Andrewski and Wilson wanted me to play Firbank's "native bride," despite the fact that I had no professional experience. Vida Hope, the director, was less keen. "You're pretty enough, I suppose," said Vida, "but you haven't your mother's voice at all." Vida was correct. I was a famous nonsinger. I was fortunate, however, to be coached by the world's greatest, Kay Thompson, who for friendship's sake gave me two or three sessions and then sent me home to sing along with Ethel Merman records. Kay and Merman made me fearless.

The cast was talented and bright, and rehearsals were fun. Publicity was fun, too. My picture appeared on the cover of *Theatre Magazine,* and I remember the singular feeling of passing a Fifty-seventh Street magazine stand and seeing my own face staring back—it was oddly embarrassing. We were set to open in Warner Leroy's little theater on York Avenue. The sets and costumes were by Tony Walton, an Englishman (married to the *The Boyfriend*'s Julie Andrews) totally in command of Firbankean whimsy. We all had high hopes; opening night was the most fun of all. Unfortunately, the reviews were mixed. The critics liked Tony's sets and costumes, one or two songs, and some performers, including me. But New York was not London—it didn't know Ronald Firbank from Oscar Wilde. Despite the reviews, we ran a few weeks; after all, there was the New York Firbank constituency to exhaust. I was not entirely grateful, however. Playing night after night seemed to me ghastly. I felt that I was stuck in a job while all of my friends were going to dinners and parties. Clearly I had been born a show business "civilian."

With a view toward free nights, I found a regular job (in early 1960 women still had "jobs" instead of careers) in advertising, which I hoped would at least be as interesting as *The Hucksters.* Thanks to Lena's good friend Kitty D'Alessio, who was vice-president of an advertising agency, I became an "assistant producer" of TV commercials. In my case, it mostly meant "assisting" the producer—who went to lunch at noon and came back (pie-eyed) at 3:30—not to be a total screw-up.

When a wire came from Kennedy headquarters requesting that I join a speech-making tour, I happily said farewell to Madison Avenue. Our group, led by old Horne family friend Frank Montero, was eclectic. Besides two or three well-known black athletes, there were Mrs. Willie Mays, Mrs. Chester Bowles, and me. We made flying stops to Kentucky, Ohio, Tennessee, and New Jersey, bumping around in a tiny propeller-driven plane. Mrs. Bowles, my tour roommate, whose husband had tried to become President himself after *giving up* advertising (he was the "Bowles" of Benton and Bowles), spoke to the elderly, and I was assigned the young. But with me they got two minorities in one. My campaign speech was short and simple: not only was a vote for Nixon a vote against minorities, a vote for Nixon was clearly a vote for a man who had never been young. As it turned out, Kennedy lost every state in which our little group appeared.

Turning away from both art (theater) and commerce (advertising), I decided to get a "meaningful" job. I went to work for the National Scholarship Service and Fund for Negro Students—known as NSSFNS, and pronounced "Nessfeness." NSSFNS sent me to Columbia University for postgraduate psychology courses. I became a counselor for black students seeking scholarships to predominantly white colleges. Using test scores, grades, and recommendations, I advised students on college applications and became their advocate with college admission directors. The work was always interesting and sometimes exciting.

In the summer of 1961 I was NSSFNS observer at the National Student Association congress held at the University of Wisconsin. An amazing group of young people was gathered there, and the most extraordinary among them were the members of the Student Non-Violent Coordinating Committee—known as SNCC, pronounced "Snick"—who were mostly Southern, black and white, "born-again" Christians, and passionate integrationists.

These were very "straight" revolutionaries (this was the time before "Black Power" and the "Days of Rage," before drugs, rock music, and sexual liberation), and they were the bravest people I had ever met. Many of them—black and white, men and women—had been beaten in Southern jails. They represented a cross section of the Southern population. Among them were the children of white landowners, black sharecroppers, and "red necks." Their only unifying factor was zealous Christianity (not the "Christianity" that is peddled on far-right television shows, whose motto is "Nuke

the Poor," but the old-fashioned kind that calls all men Christ's brothers).
SNCC members gave "witness" at the drop of a hat, describing how they
had been brought up to hate the other race, until Jesus Christ had shown
them the way. And they would argue nonviolence for hours. I remember
one drawling white farm kid saying, "You can't kill a snake by kissin' it to
death." As we all joined hands to sing "We Shall Overcome," I had a
religious crisis. When I returned to New York, I dreamed of wastelands,
my own spiritual ones.

"The Movement"—short for the Civil Rights Movement—had been
born in the spring of 1960 at Cora Horne's alma mater, Atlanta University,
with a full-page advertisement in the Atlanta *Constitution* headlined "An
Appeal for Human Rights":

> We the students of the six affiliated institutions forming the Atlanta
> University Center . . . have joined our hearts, minds, and bodies in
> the cause of gaining those rights which are inherently ours as mem-
> bers of the human race and as citizens of these United States. . . .
> We must say in all candor that we plan to use every legal and non-
> violent means at our disposal to secure full citizenship rights as
> members of this great Democracy of ours.

One month before the Atlanta *Constitution* ad appeared, black students in
Greensboro, North Carolina, engaged in the first sit-in. Instead of merely
marching outside of Woolworth's, they went inside and sat at the lunch
counter, until they were served or forcibly ejected.

The early 1960s came to belong to the Civil Rights Movement and its
martyrs. Eventually, in the late 1960s, after the assassinations of the Kennedy brothers and Martin Luther King, the Movement diverged on the
issue of black nationalism. And white veterans of the Civil Rights Movement went on to spearhead the anti-war campaign. By the early 1970s the
acorn of black civil rights had become the oak of everybody's rights. Out of
black pride came Cesar Chavez, Dennis Means, "Sisterhood Is Powerful,"
the Gray Panthers, and gay pride, as well as concern for the rights of the
unborn and the almost dead. But it all began with the Civil Rights Movement and the Kennedy presidency, which happened together. In my mind
they are permanently connected. Kennedy became the first American President to state publicly that segregation is morally wrong. His administration
made patriotism something more than the last refuge of scoundrels. (Half
of the Harvard class of 1959 seemed to be in the Peace Corps or the Justice

Department.) In the early 1960s the torch was effectively passed to a "new generation" of Americans, among them the young and the nonwhite.

■ ■ ■

Lena began the civil rights decade with a well-aimed missile to a bigot's head—*not* a nonviolent protest. Early in 1960 she and Lennie had a dinner date with Kay Thompson at Hollywood's Luau Restaurant. Kay was late. While Lennie went to call her, Lena overheard a waiter telling a boorish drunk that he would be with him in a minute, as soon as he'd finished "serving Lena Horne." But the drunk wanted instant service. "Where is Lena Horne, anyway?" the drunk wanted to know. "She's just another nigger," he added. At that point Lena stood up and said, "Here I am, you bastard! Here's the nigger you couldn't see," and proceeded to hurl a large glass ashtray at the man's head. Lennie returned from the telephone to find Lena steaming, the drunk bloodied, and the restaurant in an uproar. The bigoted drunk was hustled out before he knew what hit him, and Lena became a heroine in the popular press. Later that year she was featured on the cover of *Show* magazine, posed in the crack of a symbolically torn white curtain of prejudice. One half of her was visible. The rest was behind the curtain—like most of the rest of black America.

My job may have been "serious," but my social life was not. In 1960 I became a "girl of the year" when my picture—along with those of such other girls of the year as Countess Christina Paolozzi—appeared in *Esquire* magazine. The caption, headlined "Counselor Cutie":

> Gail Jones, counselor for National Scholarship Service and Fund for Negro Students. Daughter of Lena Horne. Home, New York. Diploma, Radcliffe. Acted off-B'way. Likes knitting. Loves parties.

As far as knitting was concerned, I had once made half a sweater for a Yalie TV director who took me sailing in Cape Cod Bay, where we saw whales.

Le Club was the place to go after dark, and I was there nearly every night. Although I was twenty-one years old, Lena and Lennie still waited up for me. It was clearly time to get my own Gramercy Square walk-up apartment. When I did, I continued to send my laundry home and kept the ice box empty of everything except orange juice and frozen spinach. If I didn't go out, and I was hungry, I just went home.

In 1962 I took a leave of absence from NSSFNS and returned to California for the first time in ten years. The place was still very seductive.

Lena and Lennie had a house in Palm Springs, with a guest house and a pool. I went down for weekends with my new friend Julie Payne, the daughter of John Payne and Anne Shirley. She was also the former step-daughter of Hollywood Ten member Adrian Scott. Now her stepfather was Charlie Lederer, Hollywood's beloved wit and rascal, the favorite nephew of Marion Davies. Julie and I lived the lazy Hollywood life to the hilt, spending our weekends in Palm Springs. In the midst of this carefree California scene, a telegram arrived, forwarded from New York. Apparently I had been invited to a White House state dinner, but had never replied because the invitation was unopened at West End Avenue. The dinner, in honor of André Malraux, was two nights away. I was in a panic until Charlie Lederer came to my rescue. He commandeered plane tickets, made hotel reservations, and arranged for a Washington limo. He then pressed hundred-dollar bills, and a handful of tiny yellow pills (he took them to "relax"), into my hands and told me to have fun. I arrived in Washington just in time to wrap my hair in a French twist, put on my short black lace dress, pop one of Charlie's yellow pills into my mouth, and get into my limo to go to the White House. I was the only woman there without an escort, and the only woman in a short dress. I was also "stoned" to the eyeballs—and no one, including myself, knew it. A silent, shorn, white-gloved marine walked me about. I saw the White House in a golden glow. Everything seemed to dance and gleam: faces, candles, the Marine Corps band. My silent marine escort directed me toward the receiving line, which was al-phabetical. I stood behind Senator Henry Jackson, who said "Hi! I'm Scoop Jackson!" and in front of my friend Chris's father, Elia Kazan. It seemed that every famous or great American artist was in the line. I remember Agnes de Mille, Martha Graham, Leonard Bernstein, Virgil Thomson, Thornton Wilder, and Tennessee Williams. We all passed through to greet the President, Mrs. Kennedy, and Malraux. Jackie Kennedy looked beau-tiful, and wide-eyed, in shocking pink. Malraux was saturnine, French, and heroic. But Kennedy was the one we really looked at. His blue eyes gave off sparks, and his coppery hair shone. He seemed to have a sort of inner spotlight—when he turned it on, it crackled. They called it "charisma."

■ ■ ■

In 1962 I took a job at *Life* magazine. It was the fulfillment of an earlier aspiration. On college applications I had always listed Edward R. Murrow and Dorothy Thompson as the public figures I most admired—two crusad-

Lena spoke out about civil rights in an article featured in <u>Show</u> magazine, 1960.

A souvenir of my short-lived theatrical career, 1960.

The photograph published in <u>Esquire</u> in 1960, when I was a "girl of the year"

ers for truth and justice. The Luce empire could hardly be called a champion of the underdog, but a lot of the world would not have seen the dogs and hoses of Birmingham, Alabama, without it.

I started at *Life* on the clip desk. As far as I was concerned, it was the most important job on the magazine. I was guardian of the Associated Press and United Press teletype machines, and I sat in solitary splendor, in a sort of central passageway, all day long—reading, clipping newspapers, and checking the wires every hour on the hour. I was, therefore, first with the news. Bulletin bells—an insistent multiple ring followed by a sputtering semi-silence—signaled that the machine was revving itself to transmit a Big Story. I would then rip the sheets off the machine and run around to the editors. In this case, the more dreadful the news, the warmer the messenger's welcome. If the story was heart-grabbingly superimportant I took the sheets upstairs to Andrew Heiskel and Henry Luce.

Although civil rights was the big story in 1962–63, there were others as well. *Life,* for example, was obsessed with the astronauts. The editors all seemed to have little-boy fascinations with outer space. Astronauts roamed the halls and came to all the *Life* parties. My favorite (and the funniest) was Alan Shepard. When fished out of the ocean, he said, "Take me to your leader!" Another big non–civil rights story was the *Thresher* disaster, in which a United States submarine sank, with all hands, off the New England coast. I had the news first—and saw *Life* spin into action. Planes, choppers, even other submarines were requisitioned for the story. *Life* had money, and everything else, to burn. Nothing was too much to get the story, and nothing was too good for the staff. The empire was generous even to its minions. My pay might be "girlishly" meager, but weekly closings were the scene of Lucullan feasts of food and drink. And the mere act of saying, "This is Gail Jones, from *Life* magazine," on the telephone was a gratifying open sesame.

In 1963 America celebrated the centennial of the Emancipation Proclamation. South Carolina—old Calhoun family seat, first state to secede from the Union, and last holdout—agreed to desegregate its public schools. And Attorney General Robert Kennedy, along with assistant Burke Marshall, met with a group of black "leaders" to discuss the newly burgeoning anger of younger blacks. The group had been brought together by James Baldwin and Harry Belafonte. It included Lorraine Hansberry, author of *Raisin in the Sun;* psychologist Dr. Kenneth Clark; and white Texas-born actor Rip Torn, who was a friend of Baldwin's. (Rip was a good white Southerner, but hardly the first person one thought of for such a discussion group. Yet

Rip made an impassioned plea for human understanding when he spoke of
his own conversion from small-town Texas bigotry.) Also present were Lena
and, most important, Jerome Smith, a young SNCC field worker. The
meeting, at first, seemed to consist of cross-purpose conversation. Kennedy
and Marshall stated, quite correctly, that the Kennedy Justice Department
had done more for black civil rights than any administration since Reconstruction. The assembled blacks then reasserted that, yes, it was all good
—but it was still not enough. After a while Jerome Smith, who had been
quiet through most of the meeting, got up to speak. No one, he said, who
did not live in the South could possibly understand the situation. Certainly
Mr. Belafonte, Dr. Clark, and Miss Horne—"fortunate Negroes"—who
had never seen the inside of a Southern jail, were incapable of understanding it. As was a Justice Department that sent prejudiced Southern white
FBI men to investigate civil rights violence. Indeed, a government that
continued to promote the economy of a region that treated blacks as non-
citizens could not be expected to understand. Jerome Smith then recalled
for the group how many beatings he had barely survived. (Smith was, in
fact, permanently disabled.) He ended by saying that he would never fight
for America in Vietnam as long as America tolerated the condition of black
people in Mississippi. Everyone, especially Kennedy, was shaken by the
depth of Smith's anger and bitterness. After the meeting Lena called the
NAACP and told them that she wanted to go South. Later that year they
sent her to Jackson, Mississippi.

In June 1963 everyone at *Life* gathered around newsroom TV sets to see
President Kennedy deliver his Emancipation Centennial speech.

> One hundred years of delay have passed since President Lincoln
> freed the slaves, yet their heirs, their grandsons, are not fully free.
> They are not yet freed from social and economic oppression. And
> this nation, for all its hopes and all its boasts, will not be fully free
> until all its citizens are free. . . . Are we going to say to the world
> —and much more importantly, to each other—that this is the land
> of the free, except for the Negroes; that we have no second-class
> citizens, except for Negroes; that we have no caste or class system,
> no ghettos, no master race, except with respect to Negroes.

And the following day Medgar Evers, NAACP field secretary in a state
that gave its White Citizens Council $160,000 in public funds, was mur-
dered in Jackson, Mississippi. Medgar was also *Life*'s Mississippi stringer.

In grief and outrage, *Life* zoomed in on the tragedy. Reporters and photographers were dispatched to Mississippi. And *Life* arranged for Medgar's Arlington burial. Lena had appeared with Medgar at a voter registration rally the night before he was killed—she sang "This Little Light of Mine" and presented him with a substantial NAACP check. On the day that Medgar Evers was buried, in Arlington National Cemetery, John Kennedy sent to Congress the boldest civil rights program ever sponsored by an American president.

Two months later 250,000 people, 60,000 of whom were white, marched to Washington to hear Martin Luther King say, "I have a dream . . ." on the steps of the Lincoln Memorial. Lena was there, wearing her NAACP cap. Cora Horne was probably there in spirit. The day before the march, Cora's old friend W. E. B. Du Bois died in Ghana, at the age of ninety-five. At ninety-three he had joined the Communist Party. At ninety-four he became a Ghanaian citizen. It had taken him almost a century to finally give up on America.

In October 1963 Lena organized an enormous Carnegie Hall benefit for SNCC. It was actually a two-evening co-benefit: Frank Sinatra agreed to costar if one evening's proceeds went to an international orphans' fund. The benefits were "beautiful people" sellouts. Lena opened each show, and Frank closed it. They were two glamorous New York nights, probably the real birth of radical chic. Betty Comden, Adolph Green, and Jule Styne wrote a new song for Lena called "Now!," a civil rights song to the tune of "Hava Nagila." "Now!" was considered so inflammatory that it was banned from some radio stations.

I had opted to miss the march on Washington. I wanted to stay in town with my fiancé. I was now planning to marry television and movie director Sidney Lumet, whom I began seeing early in my career at *Life*. We met in the summer of 1962 at the East Hampton house of Broadway producer Kermit Bloomgarden, for whom Sidney was directing a musical. Sidney was now in the process of separating from his second wife, Gloria Vanderbilt. He had just finished directing *Long Day's Journey into Night*, with Katharine Hepburn, Ralph Richardson, and Jason Robards, Jr. Now, throughout the summer of 1963, he was shooting *The Pawnbroker*, with Rod Steiger. Lena was not totally thrilled by the prospect of Sidney as a son-in-law. From a mother's point of view, her reasons were "reasonable." I was fourteen years younger than Sidney, and I would be his third wife. But the more Lena tried to dissuade me, the more I dug in my heels. Sidney was my idea of the perfect older man. He was forty years old (my favorite age), a World War

II veteran (therefore a hero), and "creative" (Radcliffe's favorite descriptive adjective). I was flattered to be joining his roster of wives; three was not necessarily an immodest amount. We planned to marry toward the end of November. Early in November Lena went to Washington for a White House photo session with President Kennedy—composer Richard Adler was rallying theatrical luminaries for a big re-election gala to be held in early 1964. In the general conversation, the President asked Lena how I was. When she told him that I was about to marry Sidney, he sent us his congratulations, but also asked a typically direct presidential question: "Do you approve of this marriage?"

The wedding itself was almost a nightmare. We were married on November 23, the day after the assassination. Half the guests did not come, and Lena canceled the music. It was a joyless occasion. We were astounded that photographers could ask us to smile. An Episcopal priest who was a wedding guest led the glum reception group in a prayer for the President.

I soon threw myself into marriage, motherhood, and Sidney's moviemaking. I was in New York, suffering morning sickness with my first child, when the Beatles were announced to be coming soon to Carnegie Hall. Since my morning sickness generally lasted all day, I plodded off for tickets. I was horrified to discover that hundreds of other people had the same idea; the "unknown" English group was not so unknown after all. I gave up the idea of getting Beatles tickets; the line was far too long for my queasy stomach. In a way, it was symbolic of the rest of the decade. We were now approaching the second half of the 1960s. Somewhere people were protesting a war. Somewhere they were smoking marijuana cigarettes and wearing micro-minis. But I was wrapped up in Liberty smocking, Beatrix Potter, and Dr. Spock.

Amy, the child who made me give up the Beatles, was born in London in November 1964. Her younger sister, Jenny, was born in New York in February 1967—one of the rare years we did our moviemaking at home. Although I spent a great deal of the mid-to-late 1960s in famously Swinging London, I missed out on the "swinging" part. I seemed always to be pregnant or lactating, so never got into drugs or Carnaby Street gear. I remember writing a plaintive letter to my friend Baby Jane Holzer, with whom I used to "twist" at the Peppermint Lounge in New York. Now I lay like a beached whale, while she (enviably nonpregnant), in Courrèges booties and yards of hair, was in all the magazines.

If 1964 had been a bad year to be away from home (we were all convinced that Goldwater would be the next President), then 1968 was disastrous. I was in a taxi in Rome, on the Via Veneto (Sidney was making a movie with Anouk Aimée and Omar Sharif), when I saw the headlines "King Assassinato." In a language mix-up, I thought at first that they referred to ex-King Umberto. Lena wrote to me in Europe about Martin Luther King's funeral: the mule-drawn farm wagon bearing the body, the denim-clad SNCC honor guard, and the person of Robert Kennedy. Lena was struck by the intensity of Kennedy's grief, and the intensity of black response to him. All the black people in the crowd seemed to want to touch him—as if to let him know that they knew his brother had died, partly, for them. With the paranoia born of homesickness, I wrote my mother that Bobby Kennedy would probably be next.

We were back in London, in fact, when Robert Kennedy was killed. I was in the bathtub when the Portuguese maid burst in with the news that Senator Kennedy had been shot. Desperately I called Betty Bacall, the one person in New York who might succinctly make sense of the nightmare. All Betty could say was "It's horrible."

> *See the wicked bracing their bows;*
> *they are fixing arrows on the string*
> *to shoot upright men in the dark.*
> *Foundations once destroyed,*
> *what can the Just do?*

Senator Edward Kennedy quoted these words from Isaiah at the funeral of his brother Bobby. By 1968 the movement was owned by its martyrs. After Martin Luther King was killed, the black ghettos erupted. After Robert Kennedy was killed, white youth erupted. Sidney, the girls, and I were in Stockholm during the horrors of the Democratic Convention. I remember asking four-year-old Amy which city she preferred, "London, Rome, or Stockholm?" Her wistful reply was "New York." It was time to go home.

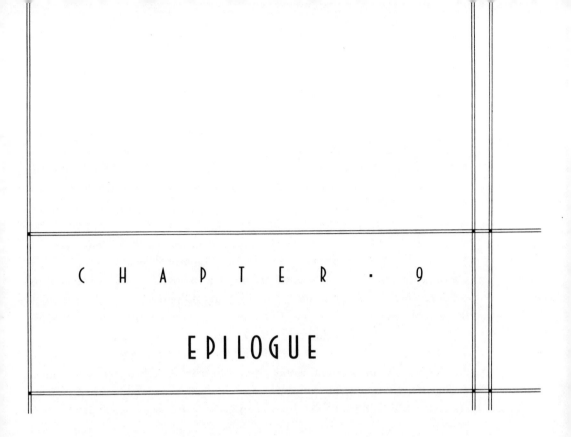

CHAPTER · 9

EPILOGUE

We came home to a brick and brownstone row house, on the corner of an Upper East Side avenue. The house was dark, wisteria-wrapped, and old-fashioned. It had a small garden with rambling roses and a tulip tree. We also had a pretty, old-fashioned house in East Hampton, Long Island.

Sidney was busy being an East Coast movie director. Amy and Jenny were busy being little children. I had the demanding roles of wife, mother, and hostess—with a live-in staff of three domestics. There was little for me to do except direct traffic—I had no idea what housewives actually *did.* But the domestics were well versed; mostly we did things *their* way. (We were "equal opportunity" employers: black, white, foreign, and native-born.) It was a "tough" life: breakfast in bed and a car to take me to Bergdorf's. My greatest activity, besides shopping, was needlepoint. I avoided utter atrophy only because I was a passionate dabbler. Ballet, yoga, tennis, jogging (I never got much beyond reading George Sheehan's *Running and Being*), Transcendental Meditation, and Mind Control. I received my Mind Control diploma, but that was the only course I ever completed. I was a classic 1970s case: a "pilgrim" without a "way." I had no idea then, of course, that I was looking for other than activity.

Because I had missed the "mind-expanding" aspects of the swinging 1960s by virtue of motherhood, I was still a hopeless prisoner of the boring 1950s. "Find the *Real* You!" 1950s fashion magazines constantly shrilled to their readers. Were you career girl, glamour girl, or girl next door? In the 1950s you created a persona to fit your life-style. It was only a matter of the right make-up and accessories. In the 1950s, as long as your lipstick and eye shadow did not clash with your dress, who was really at home was not an issue. For 1950s women, marriage was the *only* role. "Jobs" were merely holding patterns for the happy landing of a husband. It behooved me, as Sidney's third wife, to be successful. Having no real role model, as well as no idea of real life, I basically re-created my prize-winning college performance of Agnes, the child bride, in Molière's *School for Wives*.

"Director's Wife" was a dream part for a former teenage voyeur. Each cast and location brought wonderful new friends. Theatrical and movie endeavors, like political campaigns and combat, create climates of intense colleagueship. Lifetime friendships can be forged in a few short weeks with people as diverse and fascinating as James Mason, Simone Signoret, and William Holden. *Murder on the Orient Express,* made in the early 1970s, was the perfect combination of great stars and good old friends. Most of the cast had worked with Sidney before; and the movie's producer, John, Lord Brabourne, was married to my former London maternity hospital chum, Patricia, daughter of Earl Mountbatten of Burma. (My daughter Amy and Patricia's twin sons were born on the same November 1964 day at King's College Hospital. The nurses were thrilled because Patricia got flowers with a card signed "Lilibet" and I got flowers with a card signed "Sean." The Queen came to visit Patricia's boys, but when she toured the nursery it was Amy, an unusually pretty baby, who captured her attention. "That's the one *I* want," she is reported to have said.) The entire production was a constant round of fairly royal activities, among them a lunch party on the set with the Prince of Wales and the movie's cast: Albert Finney, Lauren Bacall, Richard Widmark, Sean Connery, Ingrid Bergman, Wendy Hiller, Rachel Roberts, Jean Pierre Cassell, Michael York, Jacqueline Bisset, and Anthony Perkins. Everyone was there except Vanessa Redgrave. Vanessa is a wonderful woman, but at that time she did not sit down with royalty. At the party after the film's gala opening, in the presence of Her Majesty the Queen, I sat next to "Dickie," Lord Mountbatten, the handsomest man in the world. I was agog at the ease with which he dropped the grandest of

names, like rare pearls, into my plate. "As I said to Franklin . . . Winston
. . . the King," he would say. And he turned to our table mate, eighty-year-
old Dame Agatha Christie, to ask, "Isn't it true, Agatha, that I gave you the
idea for *The Murder of Roger Ackroyd?*" "Quite so, Dickie," Dame Agatha
replied. Later, when Dickie and I got up to dance, he said, "Cole wrote this
tune for Edwina and me." I was sure that I had died and gone to "Director's
Wife's" Heaven.

In all honesty, though, my favorite role was "Mom." I felt most at home
with my children, feeling not unchildlike myself. I enjoyed *Squirrel Nutkin,*
Babar, and *Curious George* as much as they did. We could often be found
watching cartoons together. Our favorite was "Bugs Bunny." One day little
Jenny finally asked, "Who *is* this Greta Garbo, anyway?" Garbo was one of
Bugs' favorite "drag" impersonations. It was important to me that my children feel loved and secure. And it was important to me (lonely child of hotel
corridors) that they have "fun." Naturally I overdid it. Even *they* admit that
they were spoiled. I committed the sin of allowing my children to believe
that life was not only fair, but munificent.

I was not an *all*-bad parent, despite encouraging unreal expectations
and avid consumerism. But I was certainly not good enough. I was a "nervous" liberal. There is nothing worse than a nervous liberal mother. That
my daughters turned out to be wonderful young women is sheer grace. It
was also thanks to a great pediatrician, a *true* liberal, who took a more
holistic and generous view of life. "Don't worry, she won't wear diapers at
Radcliffe," he would say, or, "Don't worry, she won't suck her thumb going
down the aisle." Real liberals "don't sweat" the small things. Liberalism
belongs to the second half of life, to the older and wiser among us. Young
mothers, like conservatives, tend to be nitpickers. "You know more than
you think you do" was the opening line of Dr. Spock's baby book. If I had
to do it again I would be more relaxed and I would not try so hard to be
popular with my children. This was the time of Kid's Lib, the "me generation" for children. (We all sang along to "Free to Be You and Me.")

The 1970s were a period of great intra- and intergenerational stress,
among blacks as well as whites. The move from Martin Luther King's early
nonviolence to the later "Black Power" split the black world as violently as
Vietnam split the white. And, once again, I viewed events from a personal
ivory tower. As a sort of half-baked "celebrity," wife and daughter to
"stars," I was as isolated from the black mainstream as I was from the
white. I might not *live* as black, but I could certainly *learn* about blackness.
I took a personal course in black letters: from Phillis Wheatley to Langston

Hughes, from Ralph Ellison to Frantz Fanon, from Herbert Apthecker to Howard Zinn. I learned about *being* black, but I still did not know about *feeling* black. When a reporter from *The New York Times* asked me how often I wore red, green, and black (the African colors), I could only reply, "Never." Although I did meet a possible African distant cousin, the Honorable Winston Tubman, former Liberian ambassador to the United Nations (before the Sam Doe coup). It was at a party for Alex Haley, who calls all Africans "cousin." I told the ambassador about my great-great-great-grandmother's Liberian colonizer sibling, and he called me "cousin" and invited me to visit Monrovia. In the bloody aftermath of the Doe coup, Tubman lives were specifically spared. It said a lot for my "cousins."

What I did feel after reading about blackness in America was a new sense of anger. Black American history (like brown, yellow, and red American history) should be subtitled *Injustice*. As black history became known (there was a conspiracy of silence on the subject until the 1960s), more and more blacks began to feel this anger. My brother, Teddy, was a very angry young black man indeed. He was also smart, ironic, and full of charm. He had the Horne cheekbones, and his grandmother Edna's blue-green eyes. Like his grandfather namesake, he was incredibly attractive to women. In the early 1960s Teddy, a Nixonite young Republican (our father was one of the rare black stalwarts of California Republicanism), transferred from the University of California at Los Angeles to its northern campus at Berkeley. He became repoliticized. On trips to New York in the late 1960s his new heroes were H. Rap Brown, Herbert Marcuse, and Hermann Hesse. He wore wire spectacles, a faded safari jacket, and buttons reading "Free Angela and Huey." He was bearded and gaunt and looked to me like a brown Prince Mishkin. But I was not ready to give up Roy Wilkins for Rap Brown. And whenever Teddy smoked marijuana cigarettes, I ran around the house cluck-clucking and raising windows. These intragenerational gaps were not unknown among our Horne, Smith, and Scottron cousins. Siblings were often divided between the raised fist and middle-class business-as-usual.

Unfortunately, Teddy's gaunt left-wing look was partially nonpolitical. Bad medical treatment in Paris had given him hepatitis from which he never fully recovered. Teddy was on the sidelines of the political struggle against his will, more and more handicapped by chronic illness. Eventually he lost the use of his kidneys. Against doctor's orders, he continued to lead a semi-high-speed life. He refused to stop trying to enjoy his youth. Teddy was barely thirty when he died. He left four wonderful children.

The 1970s became a decade of funerals. It seemed as if most of the

Hornes and their loved ones were being struck down. There were funerals for Lennie, big Teddy, Edna, Frank, and Burke. (And there was Billy Strayhorn's funeral, where Ray Nance stood in the balcony of St. Peter's Church and played "Take the A Train" as a dirge for solo violin.) Lena was finally devastated. She retired to Santa Barbara, California, to plant cacti.

Standing in for Lena, I took Amy to Paul Robeson's funeral at the Mother Zion African Methodist Episcopal Church in Harlem. Mother Zion is the oldest black church in New York; Harriet Tubman and Frederick Douglass both belonged to its congregation. That day the beautiful old church spilled over with people of every age and race, from little old black ladies in flowered hats to bearded white youths standing in the back. The choir sang spirituals in the balcony ("We Are Climbing Jacob's Ladder" and "Ev'ry Time I Feel the Spirit") and Paul's own voice rolled out at the end, at the consignment of the body to the elements, with "Deep River."

Amy, of course, had no idea why we were there. But I wanted somehow for her to know Paul Robeson: not just for who he was to the world, but for who he was to her. He was a friend of her great-great-grandparents. Not only did Robeson represent a link to Cora and Edwin Horne, he also belonged to black American history. Robeson, like Frederick Douglass and Jackie Robinson, embodied the idea that blacks had to be "superior" just to be "equal" (note the proportion of the black Nobel Peace Prizes and Purple Hearts to the black population). The amazing thing about Paul's death was the almost instant historical revisionism that occurred. All the newspapers that had once called him traitor now editorialized him as a hero. It was as if America had been waiting for Paul to die in order to "forgive" him, in other words, to forgive itself.

■　■　■

In the 1970s, if you were neither authentically black nor authentically white, it was most important to be authentically yourself. But I was not all that sure about Gail Horne Jones Lumet. She seemed to be a little bit of too many things, nothing quite adding up: part "brown bourgeoise" (like the Jones, Horne, Smith, and Scottron cousins); part Hollywood brat (without the surfing-before-breakfast mentality); and part Ivy League. I was also a "celebrity" wife and "model" mother. It had become imperative to find out who Gail Horne Jones Lumet really was, to discover what lay beneath the mask of race, gender, and class.

One summer in East Hampton, toward the end of the first decade of marriage, I began to grow up. I awoke in the middle of the night and *knew*

My brother, Teddy, 1960

My daughters, Jenny and Amy Lumet, at home in New York, 1976

with total conviction that *God* loved me. I had gone through religious "phases" before. I was a pious child. The first book I remember reading was *A Child's Lives of the Saints.* And I had an inordinate love of lighting candles in church. In adolescence I attended Quaker meetings, and read and reread Thomas Merton's *Seven Storey Mountain* (right along with *The Catcher in the Rye*). Later, after my experience with the young Civil Rights Movement in the early 1960s, I had another round of churchgoing. This time it was high Episcopalian, thanks to a Harvard-friend priest. (I had no idea at the time that I was merely following in the footsteps of my Congregational, Catholic, Ethical Culturist, Bahai great-grandmother.) Then I took the job at *Life* and had no more "time." But now, in the summer of 1975, it was real. I have never had a greater sense of conviction about anything. The trouble with spontaneous religious conversions in middle-class twentieth-century people is feeling rather foolish. Unlike Saul on the road to Damascus, I was not prepared to give my life over to the great event. I was not ungrateful for the gift, but I was afraid of sounding like a Bible Belt bumper sticker: "Honk If You Love Jesus!" So I kept the good news pretty much under wraps. Although the "me generation" of the 1970s tended to look positively upon "life-enhancing transcendental experiences," it took both therapy and divorce for me to have the courage to examine my newfound conviction. When I did, I discovered that I had found myself.

■ ■ ■

The American life is said to have no "second acts." But the Calhouns and Hornes seem regularly to have disproved this theory. Lena's "second act," for example, was *spectacular.* Her Broadway show, *Lena Horne: The Lady and Her Music,* was the smash of the 1981–82 theatrical season. It began as a limited engagement (after nearly a decade of cactus planting) and ended as the longest-running one-person show in the history of the New York stage. Every performer or artist dreams of reviews he would write for himself; Lena's reviews were so good she could not have *dared* write them herself. Running out of superlatives, the critics variously compared her to Caruso, Pavlova, Nijinsky, Edwin Booth, George M. Cohan, Fred Astaire, Mary Martin, Maria Callas, Frank Sinatra, and Charlie Parker. Lena was rediscovered.

In 1943, when Lena was *first* "discovered," she was the symbol of successful tokenism. Forty years later she was the symbol of successful *personhood.* It took 1960s politics, and 1970s personal grief, for her to have the courage to present *herself* (Lena Mary Calhoun Horne Jones Hayton) to an audience. When she did, she enjoyed the greatest triumph of her career. And if there were prizes to be given, she won them. There were the Antoinette Perry Award, the Drama Desk Award, the Critics Circle Award, the Handel Medallion (New York City's highest cultural prize), the Actors Equity Paul Robeson Award, the Kennedy Center Honors, and the NAACP's Spingarn Medal, to name only a few.

Every award was special, some more special than others. In 1983 Lena was only the sixteenth artist to be honored in the long history of the NAACP's Spingarn awards. She had always considered the NAACP a *family* organization. Thanks to Cora, she had been a "lifetime" member since the age of *two*. And the 1945 Award to Paul Robeson had been one of the last photographed gatherings of Ted, Frank, and Burke Horne. In her Spingarn acceptance speech, Lena quoted the poem "Fundamental Difference" by Alice Walker:

> *The grace with which we embrace*
> *Life in spite of the pain, the*
> *Sorrow*
>
> *Is always a measure of what has*
> *Gone before.*

Lena was thinking of herself, and the Hornes, and she called it a *family* blessing. There were actually two families represented here. She could have been referring also to the larger tribe whose values, ideals, and struggles she had inherited along with the Horne family talent and good looks. The woman who appeared, to the world at large, to be the epitome of glittering "chanteuse" chic was not the real Lena Horne. Inside the creature in the Georgio Sant'Angelo gown there was always a former Junior Deb, ideally more suited to white gloves, flowered hats, and handbags on the arm. Lena's strongest identity had always been "Lena Horne of Brooklyn." She was indelibly influenced by Cora and the world into which she had been born. They had shaped her most vulnerable and receptive years. Of course, she had learned enough, since leaving, for two Brooklyn lifetimes. Her world had been enlarged. She had been economically, culturally, and socially assimilated. But she would always feel most at home in the bosom of the black bourgeoisie. The Spingarn was welcome recognition from the larger family circle.

The Kennedy Center Honors, like all *national* events, were fraught with

Lena, 1981

Lena and her grandchildren at the June 1982 closing night of <u>Lena Horne: The Lady and Her Music</u>. *Standing (left to right): Thomas Jones, William Jones, Lena, and Amy Lumet. Seated: Lena Jones and Jenny Lumet.*

glamour and history. The 1984 honorees (for lifetime achievements in the arts) were Lena, Danny Kaye, Gian Carlo Menotti, Arthur Miller, and Isaac Stern. A historical high spot of the Kennedy Center dinners was the sight of Lena and Lillian Gish embracing. The star of *The Birth of a Nation* and the NAACP's movie "secret weapon"—Walter White would have loved it. The Hornes, of course, would all have been delighted. Edwin, in particular, had longed for *national* recognition. He had badly wanted the job that President Benjamin Harrison dangled and withdrew in 1899. Washington is not only the nation's capital, it is black America's capital. Washington *is* black American history. The Great Emancipator broods in simple, awesome majesty over the Potomac (arguably the most beautiful public monument in the world); Frederick Douglass's house at Anacosta is a museum; and the Emancipation Proclamation, black cherubs and all, is on display in the Archives. Edwin would have been happy to see that the Horne family had found its niche in black American history. Here was his son Frank's photograph in the old Smithsonian (as part of FDR's New Deal "Black Cabinet"). And here was his granddaughter Lena, memorialized at Kennedy Center, and her picture hanging in the National Portrait Gallery.

■   ■   ■

Since Americans remain to some extent divided into ethnic tribes, people (often newly arrived immigrants) occasionally ask me "what" I am. Like Harry Truman, I disapprove of hyphenated Americanism. My response is always very firmly *American,* trying hard to sound like Paul Robeson on the "Ballad for Americans" record. (Robeson first sang John Latouche and Earl Robinson's "Ballad for Americans" on CBS radio in November 1939. It was an instant smash hit, acclaimed as *the* new patriotic song of brotherhood. The 1940 Republican convention adopted the ballad as its theme song. The lyrics defined an American as ". . . just an Irish, Negro, Jewish, Italian, French and English, Spanish, Russian . . .") Americans used to be taught that the best thing about our country is its amazing possibility for unity in diversity. Early writers often equated America with Utopia, but this rare capacity for brotherhood-at-large actually works. Compare American racial animosity with the inter-sect violence of Northern Ireland or India, and you realize that America is almost a functioning Family of Man.

My daughters, of course, are brotherhood-in-action simply because they are their parents' children. They represent the "united nations" of America, born into the liberated upper middle class. As privileged young people of the post-1960s they are natural racial mediators. Before 1960 the best of black-white relations were still paternalistic. Paternalism requires that one party be big and the other small. Little Black Brother was told that he was fine in his place (at sports, at war, or at simple fun), but he would never be big enough to play indoors with the tycoons and decision makers. The 1960s civil rights revolution changed all that. Racists are always there, but America no longer endorses racism. American society is now, in theory, open to anyone with the price of a ticket (an elite in itself). And the riches of the post-1960s lucky black few go far beyond anything dreamed of by their elders. There was real money to be made (for a fortunate handful) in the racially affirmative 1970s, and in ways formerly closed to blacks. It seems that benevolent capitalism is probably the only realistic hope for peace and racial harmony. Uncle Sam was born a capitalist, "baptized" with a meat merchant's packing barrel trademark; he knows (in the world since OPEC) that green power is more important than black or white power. The new black middle class includes both aggressive newcomers and old names with new investment potential. They were the first black boardroom faces and black entrepreneurs. Today, because the whole world is so sharply divided between rich and poor, color is less important than the fact that they are "haves" in a "have-not" world. They have six-figure cooperative apartments, summer homes on the Cape, and children at Choate and Harvard. And many of them, by birth or by interest, enjoy the old bourgeois tribal rites: from Jack and Jill, for the small fry, to the annual Comus Ball. But the 1980s, like the 1880s, revealed the black middle class to be still only a fortunate few. The Census Bureau in 1985 reported that the number of black-owned businesses grew by 47 percent between 1977 and 1982. But according to the survey, while 1,129 black companies had receipts of $1 million or more, half of the firms had gross receipts of less than $5,000.

Despite the demise of Jim Crow, the question of *race* remains confusing. When one of my daughters was very small she wondered, if she ever went to Africa, whether her "ancestors" would "recognize" her. How we "recognize" our ancestry is another way to put the question. It took me a very long time to "recognize" either my blackness or my *American*-ness. Writing this book gave me the gift of both. I was never able to find those parts of myself until I opened my grandfather's trunk and uncovered those family artifacts. What I uncovered went far beyond race and nationality, of course. I found amazing affinities of human attitudes and aspirations. I felt that I was part of a recurring biological theme—a sort of Horne family song. It was a happy inheritance.

I see the same affinities in my children and my niece and nephews. We are all irredeemably linked, generations slipping by as subtly varied as a rosary. In terms of racial attitude, my daughters are the generation of Richard Pryor, Eddie Murphy, and "Archie Bunker." Black Pride is here to stay. So is "Kiss me, I'm Italian." My daughters refuse on principle to take race seriously in America. They have no illusions about it, but they refuse not to laugh. America is not *seriously* racist. South Africa is *seriously* racist. My children are as irreverent about race as they are about religion. "Hi, Mom, how's God?" is my usual greeting. They are young New Yorkers. To be black and Jewish (or Asian and Hispanic) is to be part of the street scene. It is like being street-smart. ("To avoid being mugged, dress like a mugger.") For New Yorkers, good race relations mean a black high school band playing a song from *Fiddler on the Roof* in the St. Patrick's Day Parade. Like most of their generation, my daughters seem to ponder the past more in terms of how people dressed than how they thought. They refuse to dwell, therefore, on past injustices. But far more than all their ancestors before them, they have the luxury of knowing that their *characters* are more important in the eyes of the world than their race. They refuse to take that seriously, too. But being variations of the family theme, they will soon enough.

For most of the "old" Hornes, racism seemed the only bad fairy at the family party. One could imagine that if it were not for race, Moses might have been a tycoon; Edwin might have been President of the United States, or at least a Republican senator from Indiana; and Lena might have been a *real* movie star. (They were still editing out her scenes in the South through most of the 1950s.) Each of the "old" Hornes ultimately discovered what every other black shut out of the American Dream has had to learn: that the greatest victory can only be in the struggle. Now that the Dream is open to my children and their children, I hope they all will be permitted to learn that same color-free and universal truth.

ILLUSTRATION CREDITS

PAGE 31: Atlanta University—Robert W. Woodruff Library, Atlanta University. PAGES 50, 52, 53: Indiana State Library, Indianapolis, Indiana. PAGE 76: Red Cross unit —Collection of William Miles. PAGE 123: Collection of Duncan P. Schiedt. PAGE 130: Black Cabinet—Bethune Museum and Archives, Washington, D.C. PAGE 146: Estate of Carl Van Vechten; Joseph Solomon, Executor. PAGE 171: *Life* magazine. PAGES 175, 176: Collection of Eduoard E. Plummer. PAGE 179: Top—Schomburg Center for Research in Black Culture, The New York Public Library. PAGE 192: Top—Collection of Eduoard E. Plummer. PAGE 193: Bottom—Bethune Museum and Archives, Washington, D.C. PAGE 211: Lena Horne with Walter White—Collection of Eduoard E. Plummer. PAGE 216: Top right—*Life* magazine. PAGE 244: Courtesy of China Machado. PAGE 245: Bottom—Courtesy of Robert Benton. PAGE 259: Top—Christian Steiner. Bottom—Robin Platzer.

A NOTE ABOUT THE AUTHOR

Gail Lumet Buckley was born in 1937 in Pittsburgh,
Pennsylvania, and was educated at Radcliffe College. She
lives now with her husband, Kevin Buckley, in New
York City.

A NOTE ON THE TYPE

This book was set in a digitized version of Fairfield, a type face designed by the distinguished American artist and engraver Rudolph Ruzicka (1883–1978). This type displays the sober and sane qualities of a master craftsman whose talent has long been dedicated to clarity. Rudolph Ruzicka was born in Bohemia and came to America in 1894. He designed and illustrated many books and was the creator of a considerable list of individual prints in a variety of techniques.

Composed by Dix Type Inc.
Syracuse, New York

Printed and bound by The Murray Printing Company
Westford, Massachusetts

Designed by Cecily Dunham